APPALACHIA ON THE TABLE

Appalachia on the Table

Representing Mountain Food and People

Erica Abrams Locklear

The University of Georgia Press
Athens

This publication is made possible in part through a grant
from the Bradley Hale Fund for Southern Studies.

© 2023 by the University of Georgia Press
Athens, Georgia 30602
www.ugapress.org
All rights reserved
Set in Garamond Premier Pro by Copperline Book Services

Most University of Georgia Press titles are
available from popular e-book vendors.

Printed digitally

Library of Congress Cataloging-in-Publication Data
Names: Locklear, Erica Abrams, author.
Title: Appalachia on the table : representing mountain food and
people / Erica Abrams Locklear.
Description: Athens : The University of Georgia Press, [2023] |
Includes bibliographical references and index.
Identifiers: LCCN 2022032452 | ISBN 9780820363400 (hardback) |
ISBN 9780820363394 (paperback) | ISBN 9780820363370 (epub) |
ISBN 9780820363387 (pdf)
Subjects: LCSH: Cooking, American—Southern style. | Cooking—
Appalachian Region, Southern. | LCGFT: Cookbooks.
Classification: LCC TX715.2.S68 L67 2023 |
DDC 641.5975—dc23/eng/20220803
LC record available at https://lccn.loc.gov/2022032452

For Faith

CONTENTS

ACKNOWLEDGMENTS

So many people have offered their support, knowledge, and talents to make this book possible. I am grateful beyond words.

Without Elizabeth Engelhardt, this project would not have happened. Thank you, Elizabeth, for being a kind mentor and friend who has offered generous support at every step of this long and sometimes difficult process. Sandra Ballard deserves an equally heartfelt thank you: she has been a steady mentor and friend whose valuable advice I treasure. Likewise, Ronni Lundy, a woman whose knowledge about Appalachian food and history knows no bounds, consistently offered her time and expertise when I asked for her advice. I am indebted to my writing partner, Carrie Helms Tippen, whose smart critiques helped me reorganize and make sense out of chapter 3, to Katie Algeo, who generously shared her research with me, and to Tom Lee, who also shared his work with me. I am equally indebted to Kevin O'Donnell: without his and Helen Hollingsworth's *Seekers of Scenery*, it would have been impossible to conceptualize chapter 1. Moreover, Kevin offered his expertise by reading and commenting on that chapter and kindly supplied me with a choice image from James Lane Allen's "Through Cumberland Gap on Horseback." I owe a huge debt to Nathaniel Holly at University of Georgia Press, who has been patient, kind, and supportive, consistently offering helpful feedback every step of the way. A big thank-you to David Whisnant, who sent me useful information every time he came across it in his own research. I am grateful to many members of the foodways community of scholars, writers, and chefs, including April McGregor, who helped me figure out mystery ingredients from old cookbooks; Elizabeth Sims and Marcie Cohen Ferris, who welcomed me to the study of foodways and offered constant support and encouragement; Megan Elias, who offered incredibly helpful feedback early in the process; David Shields, who tirelessly answered my tedious questions, often directing me to invaluable sources; and David Davis and Tara Powell, whose invitation to contribute to their collection, *Writing in the Kitchen: Essays on Southern Literature and Foodways*, catalyzed my interest in literary food depictions. I am tremendously grateful to Robert Gipe and Crystal Wilkinson, both of whom have supported this project in important ways. I am especially grateful for the insights Crystal and Ronni Lundy shared with me during an Appalachian Studies Association panel: they enriched my discussion of Wilkinson's work in profound ways.

This project also would not have been possible without the help of a fleet of knowledgeable librarians and archivists. A huge thank you to Gene Hyde, Ashley McGhee Whittle, and Amanda Glenn-Bradley at UNC Asheville; Sharyn Mitchell and Rachel Vagts (who was then) at Berea College; Tim Hodgdon, Alison Barnett, and Jason Tomberlin at UNC Chapel Hill; Kira Dietz at Virginia Tech; Todd Kosmerick, Cathy Dorin-Black, and Clara Wilson at NC State University; Jenny McPherson at Western Carolina University; and Dean Williams, who has now retired from Appalachian State University (ASU). Dean deserves special thanks: over the course of many months, Dean and I emailed one another about resources available at ASU; without Dean, I would never have discovered Thomas Dawley, whose work is a primary focus in chapter 2, nor would I have found the many helpful sources he sent me on springs and spas in late nineteenth- and early twentieth-century Appalachia.

I am indebted to Joseph Urgo, then provost at UNC Asheville, for granting me a semester of professional development leave in the spring semester of 2017. That time away from teaching allowed me to conceptualize the project in ways I had not yet been able to do. Likewise, funds from the University Research Council supported essential archival research in multiple libraries, while funds from the Mills Faculty Research Development Award made indexing this book possible. A huge thank you to my wonderful indexer, Victoria Baker. My colleagues in the English and History Departments also deserve heartfelt thanks: Kirk Boyle, Lori Horvitz, Rick Chess, and Merritt Moseley were all supportive chairs as I worked on this project; I also extend a huge thanks to Gary Ettari, Evan Gurney, Will Revere, Dan Pierce, Ellen Pearson, and everyone else in those departments, all of whom offered constant encouragement. Thank you, too, to Karin Peterson, who believed in this project.

I am especially grateful for family and friends who have listened to me talk about this project for years. That must have grown old, but they kept asking about my progress and kept offering support. A big thank you to Wayne Caldwell, who has supplied me with a stack of fascinating Appalachian community cookbooks and whose friendship I treasure. Thank you to my friends Melissa Johnson and Melanie Clayton, who are unfailingly supportive. Thank you to my dear friend of almost twenty years, Kirstin Squint, without whom I would be lost. Thank you to my parents, Bert and Darlene Abrams, who believed in me from day one. I hope this book makes you both proud. Thank you to my husband, Mark Locklear, who for years has helped me find time in our busy lives for my scholarship. Thank you to our sweet daughter, Faith, who knows how many hours her mama has spent on this book. Lastly, thank you to our lovable dog, Max, who has proven himself an excellent writing buddy in these final stages of revision.

Introduction

MY MATERNAL GRANDMOTHER KEPT EVERYTHING. FROM disposable pie pans repurposed as cat food bowls to balls of yellowed aluminum foil that cracked apart in your hand to a dusty seashell knickknack on permanent display from a beach trip long since taken, she was not one to throw things away. She even kept her wood cook stove after purchasing an electric one: both still occupy her kitchen in an appliance standoff of old versus new. This inclination makes sense: born in 1915, she was a teenager during the Great Depression. Though her family fared well overall, during those years and for many after, she learned to save things that might later prove useful. When she passed away in 1996, she left behind a house full of treasures mixed with all the things she "might need some day."

Rather than cleaning out the house then, my bachelor uncle continued to occupy it and his other home just down the road. When he passed away in 2014, my mother and her sister finally started the long, arduous process of sorting through the things that had been accumulating since 1946, when my grandparents moved into the house. Going through all of my grandmother's things is a job that will probably never be completed, but my mother keeps trying. By the summer of 2016 I had started working on this project, and after one of her exhausting cleaning sprees, my mother called to tell me that she had found something I might be interested in seeing. As she often does, she began by listing all the reasons I might not really want to see the mystery object: it was old; it was dirty; it was in poor condition; it must have been stored in the smokehouse for a number of years because mice had nibbled its pages; and surely I would not be interested in such a bedraggled thing. After a long list of why-nots, she finally told me that she had found a cookbook my grandmother made.

My initial reaction is the reason I believe *Appalachia on the Table* and many more books like it need to be written: I was surprised.

My grandmother, Bernice Ramsey Robinson, was an avid reader her entire adult life until macular degeneration rendered her favorite pastime impossible, and she was one of the most intellectually curious people I have ever known. She was also creative, sewing beautiful, colorful quilts that she passed on to various family members; she kept her French textbooks from college and could still recite poetry she had memorized decades earlier. So I was not surprised that she made her own cookbook with a photograph album cut to size for the cover and black string to hold it together. Nor was I surprised that the cookbook adhered to genre conventions: it even has a section for home remedies and health tips in the back, complete with advice about how to "relax properly" by stretching. My favorite clipping offers advice for mailing fruitcakes, recommending that bakers line a box with waxed paper and bury a "gaily wrapped cake" in freshly popped corn, which adds a "festive touch" to the gift and cushions it for mailing. Even a quick flip through the cookbook reveals that my grandmother subscribed to a number of different publications, was interested in many varied approaches to cooking, and was well versed in how to organize a cookbook to resemble one that had been published by a press.

What surprised me were the recipes.

Of course, I had heard about my grandmother's cooking from my mother, though I never experienced her homemade meals. By the time I came along she was crooked over with osteoporosis and relied on convenience foods like frozen Banquet "fried" chicken with canned biscuits and vegetables to feed us when we helped her set tobacco every spring. But I had heard about the fresh fried chicken, vegetables from the garden, and chocolate gravy drizzled on biscuits for dessert that appeared on the table during my mother's childhood. Maybe that's why I had written my own culinary script for my grandmother that turned out to be naïve, close minded, and downright wrong.

I make my living reading, writing, and teaching about Appalachia and its people. As a seventh-generation Western North Carolinian, I am keenly aware of the hurtful and lasting impact stereotypes about mountain people have. So why was I so surprised to learn that my grandmother had not one but two identical recipes for devil's food cake with coconut icing? Did I expect to see only recipes for "traditional" mountain desserts like apple stack cake, apple leather, and pie made with sulfured apples? I must have. While

Fig. 1. My maternal grandmother's cookbook. Photo © Tim Barnwell.

the cookbook contains some recipes that I apparently expected to find in the Southern mountains—apple dumplings, biscuits, and chow chow—it also has a plethora of recipes I did not expect to see, from royal fruit dressing to date nut fondant to streusel. It also contains recipes for some creations that seem downright bizarre to imagine on South Turkey Creek, where my grandmother spent the last fifty years of her life: a handwritten recipe for grape catsup "to be eaten with fried eggs, meat, or lima beans," and my favorite, fig pickles.

It seems as though she started the cookbook in 1936, the same year she married my grandfather. She saved a *Dental Snuff* advertising booklet with 1936 and 1937 calendars in the back and empty pages that she filled with recipes. In those pages, my grandmother wrote a recipe for tomato catsup that instructs the reader to use a food chopper. I lingered over this detail for a long time: my grandmother, who later struggled to make ends meet while raising tobacco and three children, had a food chopper? I was also surprised to see so many recipes that featured product ingredients, from Bisquick to Swans Down flour to Calumet baking powder. The one that really got (and still gets) my attention is the recipe for Blossom-Time Cake that instructs, "Now, while your orchard is all abloom, is just the time to entertain your club, give a shower—or just have a party for no other reason than that beautiful drift of pink or white. . . . Bring spring indoors by decorating a big marble cake with sugared blossoms . . . a centerpiece that's lovely to behold, luscious to eat" with "real blossoms on top sugar-dipped for sparkle."

It's not that these recipes are unusual in the mid-twentieth century South. And it may be that the cookbook was more of a wish book than a guide to everyday cooking for my grandmother. As foodways scholar Megan J. Elias points out, "Cookbooks are aspirational texts" that represent desirable "life-style[s] and values."[1] But I cannot stop thinking about the fact that despite my immersion in the interdisciplinary field of Appalachian studies and bur-geoning field of foodways, until finding this cookbook I never imagined that my grandmother—whom I had always thought of as distinctly mountain in terms of cultural identity—would have saved recipes between 1936 and 1952 (the last dated entry in the book) for pecan loaves, cheese twists, Baby Ruth cookies, Jiffy featherweight biscuits, or Kellogg's Krispies Marshmal-low Squares. Why is that? Had I imagined my own romanticized version of cured ham, leather britches, pickled watermelon, and apple stack cake only to find that my grandmother's culinary tastes were far more varied? Had I expected her to use ingredients procured on the farm, not from the store? Moreover, how had such a powerful script come to dominate the way I imag-ined my grandmother's cooking without me even knowing it existed until I confronted its antithesis? What implicit judgments had I made about my grandmother based on the foods I imagined she would have been interested in cooking? Where did my Appalachian food script come from, and how have mountain residents responded to those scripts? These are the questions this book begins to answer.

It's About the Food . . . and It's Not

Appalachian food is having a moment. From *Washington Post* articles pre-dicting mountain fare will be "the next big thing in American regional cook-ing" to Ronni Lundy's showing at the 2017 James Beard Foundation awards ceremony—*Victuals*, her cookbook featuring mountain recipes, won best in American Cooking and the highly coveted Book of the Year Award—Appalachian food has arrived on the foodie scene.[2] These accolades venerate a cuisine and people that have long been derided. Yet despite these efforts, that derision lingers, often in places where I don't expect to find it.

In the fall of 2016, *The Bitter Southerner* featured a piece by Kelly Bembry Midura called "A Story About a Mountain" in their Folklore Project series. Midura writes about a childhood trip to visit her mother's friend, a woman named Peggy Jo, on Clinch Mountain in eastern Tennessee. To be sure that readers understand a trip to the mountains is not at all like a trip "Down South," Midura first explains visits to relatives in flatlands western Tennessee. She writes that among these people, whom she describes as "solidly blue collar workers" and "diligently respectable middle class," "Sunday dinners were hearty—if a little heavy on the desserts—but loaded with healthy vegetables from the gardens. Corn beans and squash were just a start. . . . There was always a dish of green peppers and tomatoes on the table."[3] According to Midura, there's no mistaking that these flatland Southerners are people to admire, even if a high school diploma "was all they needed" in terms of education: they worked hard, they went to church, and they grew their own food.

Conversely, Bobby Jo on Clinch Mountain, whose "ramshackle house" was "up a winding gravel road" in a hollow, did not inspire admiration. She writes, "We stayed the night there, in our sleeping bags on ancient couches. Supper was creamy Skippy peanut butter or store-brand hot dogs on white Wonder Bread with Lay's potato chips and liters of Coke on the side. No vegetables to be seen," later commenting that Peggy Jo took Midura and her brother to the nearby Sonic for lunch, "since breakfast had consisted of more white bread and potato chips." She then writes about returning home to her "excellent school" and "fancy college education," explaining: "I have just turned 50, and have begun to reflect on my life, as one does. I realize that weekend trip was actually my first visit to a foreign country: a place like nothing I had ever seen before, with people I could barely understand." Midura ends the essay by noting how friendly and hospitable the mountain people were, closing with "Thanks for the Wonder Bread and Coke, you'uns."

In examples like this one, food takes on meaning far beyond its nutritional value or culinary history, meanings in which food and all of its cultural baggage come to represent those who consume it. Despite the fact that Midura's essay was published in 2016, if we take away the processed foods she writes about and replace them with food once deemed "coarse," including poke sallet, creasy greens, leather britches, cornbread, and pork—notably all foods that are finally garnering praise—then her essay could be from the late 1800s or early 1900s instead, give or take a few stylistic revisions. In other words, since the conception of Appalachia as a distinctly different region from the rest of the South and United States, the foods associated with the region and its people have often been used to socially categorize and stigmatize mountain people. When Local Color writers and travel writers from the turn of the twentieth century wrote about mountain food as virtually inedible, those descriptions fueled a national perception that was just then gaining traction: mountain people are different. They are Other. The trend quite obviously continues today, though the menu has rotated to feature processed foods. This focus consequently ridicules those who may not have access to fresh food for a number of reasons. What writers from the turn of the twentieth century and Midura have in common is that often, neither consider the circumstances that result in the culinary choices that mountain people made and make. Even so, some late nineteenth-century and early twentieth-century writers, such as Rebecca Harding Davis, complicate this trend in fascinating ways.

Midura only tangentially mentions "Pappy," Peggy Jo's husband, who she describes as "a tough, leathery, former coal miner" who "had a nasty cough due to 'the black lung.'" This is Midura's only mention of extractive industry, though it may have a lot, or everything, to do with the food that she consumed on her visit, not to mention the fact that Pappy's black lung may have rendered him unable to garden. Moreover, Midura's essay makes broad claims about the diets of all mountain people, suggesting that everyone in the mountains must subsist on Skippy and Coca Cola. Likewise, writers from the late 1800s and early 1900s used a similar approach, even when the story was much more complicated.

In a similar example in which foods deemed inferior implies inferior people, Chris Offutt, a writer who grew up in eastern Kentucky, published an essay about "trash food" in the spring 2015 issue of *Oxford American*. In it, he writes about a phenomenon known as "'white trash parties' where partygoers are urged to bring Cheetos, pork rinds, Vienna sausages, Jell-O with marshmallows, fried baloney, corndogs, RC cola, Slim Jims, Fritos, Twinkies, and cottage cheese with jelly. In short—the food [Offutt] ate as a kid in the hills."[4] Though Offutt's article considers the South broadly, the connection he makes to Appalachia—and the ways in which these parties denigrate people from there—is clear. As Midura's essay emphasizes, consumption of high-fat, high-sugar, processed foods implies poverty-stricken consumers making poor choices, an implication that does not consider the circumstances under which those choices are made. Offutt concludes, "The term 'trash food' is not about food, it's coded language for social class. It's about poor people and what they can afford to eat."[5] As this project explores, this trend is not new: descriptions of "coarse food" from the late nineteenth and early twentieth centuries and "trash food" from the present day are remarkably similar.

That is not to say, however, that such descriptions silence those depicted. In Dorothy Allison's *Trash,* she offers no apology for her food preferences: "Poor white trash I am for sure. I eat shit food and am not worthy." She writes sarcastically, poking fun at the idea that worth may be judged by the food someone eats. She laments the fact that her stomach can no longer tolerate the dishes of her childhood, insisting that her "dreams will always be flooded with salt and grease, crisp fried stuff that sweetens [her] mouth and feeds [her] soul." For Allison, food functions as a powerful reminder of cultural identity. She remembers the difficulty she had digesting cafeteria food her first semester away at college, so her mother sent her back with a batch of biscuits "stuffed . . . with cheese and fatback." Allison remembers, "On the bus going back to school I'd hug them to my belly, using their bulk to remind me who I was."[6] In this instance and in many more discussed in this project, food functions as a way to categorize, judge, and denigrate mountain people; but it also serves as hearty sustenance that signals a connection to home, one that has just as much potential to inspire celebration as it does shame.

Thinking about these examples helps frame the larger trends this project begins to unpack. Rather than the actual foods consumed, of interest here are the *representations* of foods consumed, implied moral judgments associated with those foods, and how those judgments shape reader perceptions of those depicted. Scholars have written extensively about where and how ideas about Appalachians became so firmly entrenched in our cultural landscape, exploring the role that Local Color literature played, as well as travel writing, fundraising efforts, and media depictions, but little has been written about the role that food played—and still plays—in forming ideas about mountain people.[7] As foodways scholar Catarina Passidomo explains, "food studies in general . . . need not be about the food itself, but rather about what the food and its related processes can teach us about what people care about, what they fear, and how they construct meanings about places, people, and events."[8]

Consuming food is so much more than chewing, swallowing, and processing energy to fuel our bodies; food and literary scholars David Davis and Tara Powell remind us that "Eating is a means of performing identity."[9] In the spring of 2017 my husband and I dined at Rhubarb, a farm-to-table restaurant in Asheville, North Carolina, run by acclaimed chef John Fleer. While reading that night's menu, I had to grin when I saw "ramps in a bag" listed as an eight-dollar appetizer. Thinking that the "bag" must be some kind of edible encasement—maybe a pastry puff?—I was surprised to learn that the bag was literally a paper bag. Our server explained that the pungent wild onions were minimally seasoned with olive oil, salt, and pepper, put in a paper bag, and placed in a convection oven. Though I did not order them, I am sure they were delicious.

What struck me about that menu item is that in the mid-twentieth century, eating ramps out of a paper bag would have been seen as something only a poor mountain person might do, someone who did not have access to other fresh greens in the early spring. The scent of ramps stays with its consumers, often for days, a kind of olfactory marking that in 1950 signaled lower-class hillbilly status but in 2021 translates to a foodie insider appreciation for a distinctive regional ingredient. As food scholar Katharina Vester contends, "How food and identity interact is determined by cultural narratives and the specific historical moment. . . . Food is given significance by how it is narratively framed, and by the significance we digest along with the calories." As Vester goes on to explain, "food discourses aid in producing the subject."[10]

For a region like Appalachia, the discourse that began forming around mountain food in the late 1800s has had a lasting impact on the way we have come to see the Mountain South. References to undesirable food associated with mountain people undoubtedly predate the 1880s and were applied throughout much of the South, but using that approximate time frame as a starting point helps illuminate the simultaneous development of the concept of "Appalachia" and the foods associated with it in the American consciousness.

The Food

Attempting to define a specific list of foods that qualify as "mountain" is an impossible task. Those in search of such an authoritative list in the pages of this book will be disappointed. Although there are plenty of foods commonly associated with the region, from leather britches to ramps to pickled watermelon to apple stack cake, there are plenty of others (like fried chicken, biscuits, and casseroles) that are just as frequently associated with the South more generally. As food scholar Marcie Cohen Ferris explains, there is little point in claiming culinary exceptionalism for specific regions or people. No one group or area "owns" any particular food or recipe: cultural exchange is the hallmark of ever-evolving food habits.[11]

Moreover, long-held ideas about Appalachia and whiteness have had—and continue to have—a tremendous impact on what people have come to think of as "mountain food." Perhaps the most obvious example is cornbread, a dietary staple that appeared—and still appears—on many mountain tables, often several times a day. Writers from the late 1800s to the present day comment on this fact, but those writers typically do not mention where settlers got corn from in the first place, nor its cultural significance to many American Indians. Selu, the Cherokee corn mother, is as "mountain" as any granny woman drying apples, but readers seldom encounter descriptions of her in accounts of mountain food.

Similarly, cuisine known as "immigrant food" is often overlooked in discussions of mountain fare.[12] West Virginia's pepperoni roll gives us just one example of how a food that is decidedly Appalachian has only recently begun to receive recognition as such, presumably because neither the inventor nor the food itself fit stereotypical notions of Scotch-Irish mountaineers or their preferred foods. Invented in the 1920s by Giuseppe Argiro, an Italian man living in West Virginia, pepperoni rolls provided a transportable lunch that miners could take with them underground.[13] As West Virginia–born food writer Courtney Balestier explains, they are the official West Virginia state food and an important marker of cultural heritage.

Likewise, mainstream perceptions of race in Appalachia frequently fail to include African-American people or food traditions associated with those communities. For those looking to distance themselves from the history of enslavement associated with Southern food, the false—but commonly accepted—mythos of a mountainous region free from such oppression can feel liberating. In general, the foods that currently draw positive—though historically negative—attention (leather britches, soup beans, cornbread, ramps, apple stack cake, and so on) are inextricably connected to "pure Anglo-Saxon stock" of Scotch-Irish descent in the popular imagination, a concept perpetuated by Local Color writers, missionaries, and anthropologists in the late nineteenth and early twentieth centuries.[14] But reality tells a much more diverse story.

One fascinating example involves Malinda Russell, a free woman of color born and raised in eastern Tennessee who "wrote what is known to be the first complete African American cookbook, published in Michigan in 1866."[15] Foodways scholars including Doris Witt and Toni Tipton-Martin have played a crucial role in recognizing Russell's talents, and in February of 2021, Eater.com featured a story about Russell.[16] I first learned about her at the 2016 Appalachian Food Summit held at Berea College, where Ronni Lundy and Toni Tipton-Martin gave a joint keynote address about Russell's *Domestic Cook Book*.[17] Their conversation emphasized the fact that not only was Russell the first African-American—of any gender—to publish a cookbook, but that she was also an Appalachian African-American. Even a cursory glance at *A Domestic Cook Book* reveals a seasoned and confident author; Russell includes "An Experienced Cook" under her name on the cover page. Her recipes offer insight into her depth and knowledge as a cook, not to mention an obvious familiarity with a variety of ingredients, yet her name is seldom associated with mountain foodways.

Likewise, Ronni Lundy explains that the tradition of preserving green beans by drying them and then rehydrating and cooking them when needed (known as leather britches or shuck beans) may have begun with southeastern American Indians including the Cherokee, or "the practice may have originated in Germany and been brought to the mountains by early settlers from the Palatinate. . . . *Getrocknete Bohen* is the term used in Germany to refer to any number of dried beans, including whole green beans strung on thread and dried."[18] Likewise, ramps are an important part of Cherokee culture, which makes present-day dig restrictions all the more problematic.[19] As Lundy also explains, the iconic mountain dessert of apple stack cake "appears to be a cake based on the Eastern European tradition of tortes with many thin layers glued together by a sweetened filling" that "likely came to the region with the earliest immigrants from Germany."[20] The need to briefly review the varied origins of a few foods that seem quintessentially "mountain" feels unnecessary at best and ridiculous at worst, yet pervasive ideas about ethnic homogeneity in the mountains persist. This project examines where and how these assumptions originated.

Descriptions of mountain food, whatever food that may be, follow a strikingly discernable pattern. In the early depictions that chapters 1 and 2 explore, writers repeatedly used the word "coarse" to describe the food mountain people were eating. As Vester contends, "Food discourses . . . are authoritative, normalizing, and disciplining."[21] For readers of *Harper's New Monthly Magazine*, *Lippincott's*, Local Color novels, and popular travel narratives, the authoritative message about Appalachia, its food, and its people was one of coarseness. Despite some notable exceptions to these types of portrayals, if you are what you eat, then the syllogistic reasoning followed that mountain people were just as rough as the food they consumed. The word "coarse" also suggests uncouthness, an unseemly trait apt to cause indigestion or problems in general; considered in this way, coarseness takes on new meaning within the context of Progressive Era uplift discussed in chapter 2.

Social reformers wrote much about impoverished conditions they found in the mountains, offering approaches to improve standards of living. But because the rhetorical purpose of much of their writing was to raise awareness about these problems and the funds to address them, they did not pay nearly as much attention to those who fared well. Even food scholars writing in the 1980s, like Harvey Levenstein, seemed to accept such narratives, commenting on the "impoverished land" of Appalachia.[22] Levenstein makes no mention of coal or timber industries, which had significant impacts on the productivity of the land, nor of middle- to upper-class residents, nor of the popular resorts found in parts of the region.

Specific stories of individuals in the area provide valuable counterevidence to the dominant narrative of culinary depravity in the mountains. North Carolinian Caroline Nichols McEwen, for example, kept a scrapbook following her marriage to Wooster Baird (W. B.) McEwen. Although W. B. was from New Haven, Connecticut, his interest in the timber industry brought him to Western North Carolina, where he was president of McEwen-Gibson Lumber Company and also where he met Caroline Nichols. The couple married on July 18, 1904, in present-day Barnardsville, North Carolina, and after an extended honeymoon in surrounding areas, they lived in Asheville until moving to High Point sometime around 1923. Following their marriage they honeymooned at the Toxaway Inn, roughly fifty miles southwest of Asheville. Caroline saved a hotel menu from July 19, 1904, that lists a variety of foods from which guests could choose, from cream of cauliflower soup to beef braised with spaghetti to pineapple sherbet.[23] Caroline also saved a breakfast menu from The Wheeler in Hendersonville, North Carolina, that lists a variety of foods to start the day, from bananas and codfish cakes to broiled veal chops and graham muffins.[24] Although such resorts typically attracted tourists from different parts of the country, as Caroline's scrapbook reveals, local people like her also frequented them for various reasons. Moreover, some locals would have had contact with such foods working in hotel kitchens preparing and serving meals. Those struggling to feed themselves were not

Fig. 2. Postcard of the Toxaway Inn, a luxury hotel for travelers. From the Collection of Hunter Library, Western Carolina University. Stone and Barringer Company, Copy and Reuse Restrictions Apply, Inventory number HL_RP_1536.

likely to visit these resorts, but the very existence of menus offering a selection of items—complete with a rather extensive wine list in the case of Toxaway Inn—complicate long-held generalizations about homogenous, limited offerings in the mountains.[25]

Asheville, North Carolina, had long been a popular tourist destination, so it might seem that such variety was an anomaly limited to tourists visiting Western North Carolina. But one need look no further than the Greenbrier Hotel in White Sulphur Springs, West Virginia, to prove otherwise. The hotel first opened in 1778, when travelers visited the sulphur springs for their healing properties. With the exception of a few notable closures during wartime, since its opening it has operated as a luxury resort offering fine accommodations to presidents, diplomats, and high-society travelers. As one might expect, food served at the Greenbrier was often impressive in its quality and variety. As historian William Olcott explains, the 1869 menu in particular signaled the "year of good food and drink." It featured ribs of beef from a $500 steer,[26] "chicken livers en brochette, bœuf à la mode, saddles of venison and lamb, and—for southern traditionalists—middling and greens."[27] Likewise, a menu from August 13, 1885, offers lobster salad, Cincinnati ham with

Fig. 3. Postcard of the Grove Park Inn, Asheville, North Carolina, circa 1913. From the Collection of Hunter Library, Western Carolina University, Copy and Reuse Restrictions Apply, Inventory number HL_RP_1033_A.

Madeira sauce, and Crabes a Coquille tender, while a menu from August 14, 1889, displays several multiethnic influences, including Indian chutney and Hungarian goulash with noodles; both menus offered page-long wine selections.[28] Likewise, the Homestead Hotel in nearby Virginia offered dinners of spaghetti with oysters on December 12, 1899, and fricassee of veal on December 16, 1899.[29] By 1919, the Grove Park Inn in Asheville was serving "Genuine Little Neck Clams" and "Boiled Sea Bass Anchovy Sauce (Received by Express from Beaufort, N.C., Boiled with Fish Broth and Served with Sauce made of Creamery Butter, Anchovies and Pure Lemon Juice)," with a variety of beverages ranging from imported teas to Horlick's Malted Milk to "Richelieu Vacuum Coffee, free from Toxic Properties."[30]

Hotels in the region were not the only places in the mountains offering a variety of foods. Evidence from private homes also reveals that for some families, food was plentiful and recipes were diverse. The Litchfield family ledger from Abingdon, Virginia, provides one such example: although curators are not entirely certain, a woman named Elizabeth Pannill Peirce Litchfield probably created an extensive household ledger from about 1870 until roughly 1890.[31] In the years following the Civil War, it is notable—particularly in a pro-Confederacy state—to find recipes for Siberian crabs and oil mangoes that call for imported ingredients like ginger.[32] The recipe for tea cakes calls for lemon, while the coconut cake recipe instructs bakers to "grate two cocoa-nuts."[33] Similarly, in 1883 Bettie D. Cramer of Wheeling, West Virginia, made a cookbook with recipes for lobster farci, "Smith College fudge," and "coconut candy."[34] Certainly imported items such as coconuts, lemons, and lobster would have been expensive, unlikely ingredients for many people's daily cooking routines, but as these documents reveal, some people in the area were using them in their recipes. Even so, they rarely make an appearance when discussing Appalachia and its food. This project examines how and why that's the case: How did the dominant culinary narrative of the region come into existence and what consequences has that narrative had for people in the mountains?

Chapter Descriptions

The book's first chapter, "Fiction Made Real: Mountain Food in Local Color and Travel Writing" discusses the ways in which writers encouraged reading audiences to imagine mountain fare, and by extension, mountain people. If the food that residents ate was consistently described as coarse, then by extension, so too were the people. The chapter builds on but also complicates Henry Shapiro's assertion that in the late nineteenth and early twentieth centuries, travel writing about Appalachia functioned much like Local Color fiction: both genres relied on exaggerated regional eccentricities for audience appeal, consequently giving readers a rather skewed perception of life in the mountains. Because these accounts were "real," their effect had the potential to significantly shape the way audiences viewed the Mountain South. Many of these depictions were negative with long-lasting consequences, yet when we take a closer look, we see that at the same time some writers cast mountain regional cuisine as hopelessly coarse, others wrote enthusiastically about resorts and their healing waters, not to mention the food served at these establishments. Writers like Rebecca Harding Davis in turn criticize tourists who frequent such locales, advocating instead for social justice issues through her portrayals of food. Ultimately, chapter one makes the case that depictions of mountain fare in Local Color fiction and travel writing had a profound effect on the way readers came to think about food in the mountains and those who prepared it, just not always in the ways we might expect.

The second chapter, "Competing Culinary Discourses: Writing Food in

Early Twentieth-Century Appalachia" uses three case studies to examine the rhetoric Progressive Era reformers employed when discussing food in the mountains. Through careful analysis of both public and private documents written by William Goodell and Eleanor Marsh Frost; John C., Olive Dame, and Grace Buckingham Campbell; and Thomas Robinson Dawley, the chapter argues that the more public these documents became, the less nuance they revealed about mountain cuisine. The chapter contends that these blunted portrayals of food in the mountains had a lasting effect on public perceptions. Thus considering these century-old documents prompts a present-day re-examination of mountain people, their culinary habits, and the inherent complexities of Appalachian food.

Chapter three, "Writers Respond: Critiquing the Live at Home Program," interrogates how fiction writers responded to government programs that grew out of the same Progressive Era ideology that motivated reformers discussed in chapter two. Brief analysis of Marie Van Vorst's 1904 novel, *Amanda of the Mill*, helps us see how some writers imagined the food-related tension between subsistence-based farming and work in textile mills. Moving forward roughly three decades, chapter 3 argues that two novels published in 1932 about the 1929 Loray Mill Strike in Gastonia, North Carolina—Grace Lumpkin's *To Make My Bread* and Olive Tilford Dargan's (penname Fielding Burke) *Call Home the Heart*—may be read as powerful critiques of North Carolina's "Live at Home" program, even when authors do not explicitly refer to it as such. "Live at Home" was a government initiative during the late 1920s and early 1930s designed to encourage farmers to produce enough food for their families instead of relying too heavily on income from cash crops at the expense of their own sustenance. Drawing from cooperative extension archival materials available at North Carolina State University, I contend that Lumpkin's and Dargan's portrayals function as important correctives. Their novels make clear that the primary problem farmers faced was one of capital, a problem not easily solved through educational programming. Chapter three also explores how Julia Franks, a twenty-first century writer, imagines local responses to cooperative extension agents in *Over the Plain Houses*. Considered together, these fictional novels give voice and agency to the real people government programming efforts targeted.

Chapter four, "'Feeling Poor and Ashamed': Food Stigmas in Appalachia," analyzes Appalachian memoir and fiction to examine how the long history of food shaming discussed in chapters one and two manifests in mountain writing from the mid-twentieth century to present-day. Using French theorist Pierre Bourdieu's notion of cultural capital, the chapter investigates how Cratis Williams and James Still portray the complicated, ever-evolving schema of which foods elevate a person's social standing and which further entrench one's perceived inferiority.[35] Aspirational eating, a term most used in folklore studies to describe the act of eating as a means of aspiring to a higher social standing, factors into these discussions of regional identity, food choices, and shame.[36] Williams's memoir, *Tales from Sacred Wind: Coming of Age in Appalachia*, also portrays the problematic ways in which food shaming may be connected to bodily dominance, a thread that connects his portrayal to Crystal Wilkinson's 2016 novel, *The Birds of Opulence*. Careful analysis of food in Wilkinson's novel reveals that for the Goode women, land, fertility, food, assault, and shame are inextricably tied together.

Chapter five, "'The Main Best Eating in the World': Responding to Past and Current Food Narratives," considers the counter to food shaming: that is, the chapter explores how writers from the mid-twentieth century to the present-day have celebrated mountain food in Appalachian literature, long before it was trendy to do so. Mid-twentieth century writers Harriette Simpson Arnow, Jean Ritchie, and Wilma Dykeman write lovingly about the foods associated with Appalachia, while late-twentieth and twenty-first century writers Denise Giardina, Crystal Wilkinson, and Michael McFee continue that trend in ways that offer essential commentary on the racial and ethnic diversity of Appalachian people and cuisine. The chapter concludes with a discussion of Robert Gipe's fiction, where food figures prominently in his novels (*Trampoline, Weedeater, and Pop*) but most overtly in *Pop*. Ultimately, Gipe's postmodern depiction of recent national interest in mountain food urges readers to examine whether they are fetishizing mountain foodways and if so, the effect that fetishization may have for mountain people who were preparing and consuming heritage foods before doing so was popular. Most importantly, *Pop* highlights the ways in which mountain characters can re-claim their culinary narratives by claiming ownership of their own food traditions and using them how they see fit.

Finally, the book's conclusion, "From Coarse to Haute: A Gentle Reminder," constructively critiques the contemporary celebration of mountain food, making clear that such veneration is welcome and long overdue. But this section also cautions that we should be mindful of a number of things in order to avoid the fetishizing Gipe depicts.

CHAPTER I

Fiction Made Real

Mountain Food in Local Color and Travel Writing

FICTION IS POWERFUL. WHEN WE READ STORIES OR NOVELS SET in locales different from our own, we are transported there. Mentally escaping to another reality is sometimes the point of reading fiction in the first place. As part of the process, readers learn about the geography of the place where the fiction is set, the culture of the people living there, and often, about the food that they consume. Travel writing can serve the same purpose for readers by providing vivid descriptions of places and people that may be unfamiliar, sometimes rendering them curious and exotic. While theoretically "true," the genre of travel writing allows for exaggeration and omission to suit the writer's rhetorical goals. For Appalachia, thinking through the impact that American Local Color fiction and travel writing published before and during the Gilded Age had in shaping ideas of mountain people is crucial. Henry Shapiro's seminal 1978 book, *Appalachia on Our Mind: The Southern Mountains and Mountaineers in the American Consciousness, 1870–1920*, argues that Local Color fiction and travel writing, often published side-by-side in syndicated monthlies during the Gilded Age, had an enormous impact on the way the rest of the country came to view the region. Scholars generally agree that the idea of Appalachia as a separate place began to take root in the American consciousness following the Civil War. Several factors influenced the creation of the idea of Appalachia following Reconstruction, including efforts by the American Missionary Association to minister to "mountain whites," a problematic definition that omitted the very real presence of indigenous peoples, African Americans, and European immigrants. A generation later, Progressive Era initiatives were also part of the equation, including fundraising efforts by people like Berea College president William Goodell

Frost and settlement school women like Katherine Pettit and May Stone. But this chapter is primarily concerned with Shapiro's claim that "it was through literature that the otherness of the southern mountain region was introduced as a fact in the American consciousness."[1] For Shapiro, both Local Color fiction and travel writing were inextricably linked to the way the reading public came to view the mountains. As this chapter explores, descriptions of food permeate these narratives as characters and travelers venture into the mountains, encountering new dishes, preparation methods, and culinary customs. Although numerous examples support Shapiro's claims about the power of such descriptions to solidify Appalachia's otherness in the national mindset, this chapter also explores counterexamples that usefully complicate the story.

Shapiro cites Will Wallace Harney's 1873 essay, "A Strange Land and a Peculiar People," as the beginning of publications that described Appalachia as a land apart. The piece appeared in *Lippincott's Magazine*, a national publication with a large readership. Shapiro goes on to explain that "[b]y 1890 the sense of wonder which characterized the local colorists' sketches of Appalachia as terra incognita had begun to disappear," replaced instead by what Shapiro calls "uplift" literature that highlighted the so-called distressing differences between life in mainstream America and Appalachia (5). Shapiro explains that Local Color writing about the mountains was "enormously popular" and that "the vision of reality thus offered had consequences beyond the pages of the magazine in which a sketch or story appeared, to the degree that it became the basis for private or public action" (8, 18). Scholars have written extensively about the long-lasting effects such portrayals have had on the way past and contemporary Americans view the Mountain South and its inhabitants. Such analysis considers the formation and effects of stereotypes, representations in film and television, and much more.[2]

But what catches my attention in these descriptions of Appalachian life—whether in fictional or travel writing form—are the ways in which writers depict the culinary landscape of the Mountain South. These descriptions offer rich and varied clues about perceived social class, cultural capital, education, nutritional knowledge, and cooking know-how. If we take Shapiro's largely agreed-upon assertion that writing about Appalachia from roughly 1870 to 1920 shaped the nation's ideas about the region and its inhabitants, then how do food descriptions factor in? While some culinary depictions undoubtedly support Shapiro's claims, we also discover that careful analysis of culinary descriptions offer a more nuanced portrayal of the region. If we expand

Shapiro's timeline to consider the years leading up to the Civil War, then we encounter writers like David Hunter Strother ("Porte Crayon"), who wrote positively about mountain food and people. In the 1870s we find writers like Rebecca Harding Davis, who offer tongue-in-cheek critiques of vapid tourists in search of authentic wilderness experiences for their summer vacations. Perhaps most fascinating, careful analysis of culinary descriptions reveals writers like Frederick Law Olmsted and again, Rebecca Harding Davis, who were deeply concerned with social justice issues. In other words, although plenty of troubling descriptions equate mountain food with the inferiority of its consumers, a surprising body of literature exists that portrays a far more complicated view of the mountain culinary scene.

Even so, not all foodways scholars recommend using literary depictions of food to draw conclusions. Robert Dirks, for example, writes, "[n]arratives often tell of feasts and dishes consumed on special occasions. Authors usually have little or nothing to say about normal, everyday fare. Literary accounts, in general, are apt to address foods haphazardly. On top of that, distinguishing the figurative from the literal can be difficult."[3] Dirks goes on to make a distinction between nutrition history and food history, contending that food history has two branches: culinary history, which "covers food preparation, food service, tastes and styles, manners of eating, and how people used to think about foods. The goal of culinary history is to find meanings and develop understandings about the food habits of a bygone era," while the other branch is sociocultural studies, which "looks for relationships between food habits and other aspects of society."[4] Certainly this project falls into the sociocultural line of inquiry, but it also argues that literary representations of food—at least in the examples discussed here—do not function in the way Dirks claims. While special dishes are described, so is everyday fare, sometimes in ways that re-inscribe harmful stereotypes and sometimes in ways that combat them. Moreover, focused analysis of how authors in the late 1800s and early 1900s were writing about food in Appalachia reveals the construction of a narrative that has persisted for well over a hundred years, one that as this chapter explores, is more complicated than it first appears.

Inferior Foods Mean Inferior People

When I began researching how Local Color and travel writers portrayed food in Appalachia, I had a clear sense of what I expected to find. I anticipated reading derogatory descriptions about mountain people and the food that they prepared and consumed. Despite the examples to the contrary discussed later in this chapter, plenty of these depictions exist in literature about Appalachia from post–Civil War years to the early 1900s. When considering such descriptions, American studies scholar Katharina Vester's assertion that "narratives in which food figures prominently generate knowledge in which power relations are inscribed and produced" becomes paramount.[5] As she explains, "Food choices disclose an individual's station in society, making and marking his or her subject position. As food helps to nourish the individual, food discourses aid in producing the subject."[6] Although her points are about contemporary life, I argue that they apply just as much when thinking about the late 1800s and early 1900s. In a time when America was just beginning to conceive of Appalachia as its own discrete region, the foods described in the stories and travel narratives had the potential to shape reader perceptions of their consumers. In many cases, those descriptions were not favorable.

Southwestern humorist George Washington Harris offers one example in his 1867 story, "Trapping a Sheriff (a vile conspiracy)," which appears in *Sut Lovingood. Yarns Spun by a "Nat'ral Born Durn'd Fool." Warped and Wove for Public Wear.* Although Harris's story takes place two years after the conclusion of the Civil War, the Southwestern humor movement began much earlier. As literary scholar John Grammer explains, fiction categorized as such was "composed mainly during the 1830s, 1840s, and 1850s, [and was] set somewhere near the frontier line of the South as it moved from the Appalachian mountains to the Mississippi River and beyond."[7] In the *Sut Lovingood* collection, a narrator named George introduces each of the stories, but protagonist Sut Lovingood quickly and routinely takes over, immersing the reader in a "moral and grammatical wilderness" from which they find no reprieve.[8] Harris casts Lovingood as an eastern Tennessee farmer, and his Appalachian speech patterns are nearly indecipherable unless read aloud. Even then, they present interpretive challenges. Scholars, including Grammer and Lloyd Pratt, agree that the genre was written primarily for a middle-class, white, male audience. Pratt also points out that "at the height of Southwestern humor's popularity, aspiring and middle-class white men found themselves standing on unstable social ground."[9] In the case of Sut Lovingood, reading dialect-heavy depictions of a "nat'ral born durn'd fool" from the mountains of Tennessee could provide not only comic relief for readers but also a counterpoint from which they could measure their own social standing post–Civil War. Sut's otherness as a mountain man compounded with his speech patterns, which Harris presumably intended as humorous if difficult to translate, presented a potential antidote to anxieties about fallen social class. In other words, however dire the situation may be for the reader in real life, surely things were worse for Sut. Sut's humorous antics were also entertaining for readers, meaning that one could feel good about themselves while laughing at Sut's shenanigans.

When we focus our attention on the ways in which Sut discusses food, Harris presents a situation in which food can be—but is not always—abundant. Yet Sut's reactions to it present him as a buffoon who does not regularly have access to such fare. In a complicated ruse to catch another character, a woman described only as "Wirt's wife" cooks an elaborate meal, which Sut narrates in great detail: "Thar wer chickens cut up, an' fried in butter, brown, white, flakey, light, hot biskit, made wif cream, scrambil'd aigs, yeller butter, fried ham, in slices es big es yure hen, pickil'd beets, an' cowcumbers, roas'in ears, shaved down an' fried, sweet taters, baked, a stack ove buckwheat cakes, as full ove holes es a sifter, an' a bowl ove strained honey, tu fill the holes." Sut especially relishes the buckwheat cakes, explaining: "I likes tu sock a fork intu the aidge of one of them spongy things 'bout es big es a hat crown, put a spoonful ove honey onder hit, an' a spoonful ove honey atop ove hit, an' roll hit up ontu the fork like a big segar, an' start hit down my froat aind fus', an' then jis' sen' nine more after hit, tu hole hit down."[10] The humor of the passage is manifold: Harris encourages readers to imagine Lovingood rolling up buckwheat cakes like cigars and shoving ten of them down his throat, all narrated in heavy dialect. Later in the story, Sut makes clear that he greatly admires Wirt's wife's cooking, explaining that he gets "dorg hungry" (dog hungry) every time he sees her (262). But Sut's apparent compliment also reveals thinly veiled misogyny, which denies Wirt's wife a name in the story and one that equates her value with her labor, not her personhood. His comment could also be read as a sexualized one, suggesting the consumption not only of the food she prepares, but also her body.

Feminist interpretations aside, taken within the context of the larger collection, it becomes more difficult to see the humor in Sut's situation. While it could be that he is just a mountain man narrating a scene about a good meal, readers know from the first story in the collection, "Sut Lovingood's Daddy, Acting Horse," that his family was so large and impoverished that when their only horse starved to death, Sut's father strapped a plow to his own body in a desperate attempt to plow the fields so they could plant crops. On the surface, the story is humorous because his father literally acts like a horse, neighing and snorting while working in the field. At one point he is chased into the creek by a swarm of bees, plow and all. But a more careful reading of the story reveals crushing poverty and a scarcity that makes starvation seem an imminent threat. Read within this context, we come to see Sut's description of the bountiful table in "Trapping a Sheriff (a vile conspiracy)" not as a lighthearted description of a buckwheat cake–loving man but rather as a feast that he presumably rarely—if ever—enjoyed as a child in eastern Tennessee. Thus the humor of the story becomes dark and entirely dependent on deprivation in the mountains.

Fifteen years later, in 1882, an unsigned piece called "Poor White Trash" appeared in the July issue of *Eclectic Magazine of Foreign Literature, Science, and Art*. In it, the author describes spending two months in the mountains of Kentucky, where he[11] "was so shut off from the nineteenth century that it was like a dream to think that out beyond the mountain-barrier, existed a contemporaneous world, full of ideas, projects, motion."[12] As in Harris's story, a bountiful table fails to elevate the social standing of its consumers. For Sut Lovingood, his reactions to the fare suggest the rarity of such abundance, while in "Poor White Trash" the unnamed author makes a similar statement but one that he also racializes. The article's title suggests that the people described within it are an exception to "normal" whiteness in that these people are poor and trash-like. The implication is that anyone not white is already understood to be poor and synonymous with the word "trash."[13] Yet the "poor white trash" described in the article eat very well. The author describes a valley "rich in corn" and "every mile or so a little log-cabin sits in a varied growth of beans, potatoes, maize, and tobacco" with "groves of young pawpaws" (129–130). After a church service the author explains that the preacher, who "belonged to rather the better class of poor whites," invited him home for dinner (131). The author writes, "We had everything that the land and the season could produce—chicken, bacon, green maize, beans, sweet and Irish potatoes, honey and baked apples, biscuit, 'cookies,' cake, and a jovial apple pudding" (132). Yet rather than marvel at the variety of foods served or remark upon their quality, he writes that "they raise an easy living of maize and bacon," as though the land produces food on its own, without laborious tending and farming know-how (129).

He also uses food to make implicit comparisons between these "poor white trash" and Southern African-Americans. While the author waits with members of the church for Sunday dinner at the preacher's home, he comments, "A dozen water-melons had already been eaten; but the Kentuckian never counts water-melons" (132). Though subtle, the racialized implication here is that like Southern African-Americans, these white mountain people in Kentucky have a predilection for watermelons and eat so many of them that they don't even count them as food. Earlier in the piece, the author calls them "a prime resource of Kentucky hospitality" (130).

Historian William Black explains that before the Civil War, "Americans were just as likely to associate the watermelon with white Kentucky hillbillies or New Hampshire yokels as with black South Carolina slaves," but in the postwar years, for whites invested in maintaining legacies of racially dominated power, watermelons became a reviled symbol of African-American freedom since many formerly enslaved people grew and sold them.[14] Black explains that white Southerners who felt threatened by such economic acuity symbolically recast the fruit to instead represent uncleanliness, laziness, childishness, and an unwanted public presence: "Uncleanliness, because eating watermelon is so messy. Laziness, because growing watermelons is so easy, and it's hard to eat watermelon and keep working—it's a fruit you have to sit down and eat. Childishness, because watermelons are sweet, colorful, and devoid of much nutritional value. And unwanted public presence, because it's hard to eat a watermelon by yourself." As historian James Klotter points out, in the fifty or so years following Reconstruction, popular descriptions of Southern African-Americans and mountain whites shared striking similarities.

According to Klotter, such depictions "would eventually result in the formation of an image that allowed many late-nineteenth-century reformers to turn their backs on the ex-slaves, as they told themselves that Appalachia needed aid as well."[15] The 1882 publication date of "Poor White Trash" places it precisely within the time frame Klotter references. Moreover, when speculating about mountain people, the author observes they are so "ancient in their type," concluding that "in former times, they had no money with which to buy slaves, machinery, and land, and so could not compete as farmers" (132). Historians including John Inscoe have explained that slavery did occur in the Mountain South, but inaccuracies of the author's speculations aside, taken within the larger context of the article, the suggestion is that without the practice of slavery to distinguish owner from enslaved, distinctions between civility and barbarity became blurred.[16] Likewise, historian Angela Jill Cooley points out that nutrition reformers in the early twentieth century saw

"African American cooking as slapdash and unsophisticated," a perception also applied to cooking associated with "mountain whites."[17] What initially appears as a preference for watermelon becomes instead a marker of inferiority, a symbol that we see again in discussions of Progressive Era initiatives in the Mountain South.

Portrayals of fruits not native to Appalachia seem to hold particular significance in narratives about mountain people. In the watermelon example, consumption signals implicit racist undertones. In other instances—like with bananas—the fascination characters display upon encountering the fruit suggests humorous and simultaneously hopeless backwardness, as well as the implication that characters are fundamentally Other. One key example occurs in Local Color writer's James Lane Allen's 1886 "Through the Cumberland Gap on Horseback," which appeared in *Harper's New Monthly Magazine*. Although Allen set most of his fiction in the Bluegrass region of Kentucky—he only published two pieces about the mountains including this one and "Mountain Passes of the Cumberland"—critic Kevin O'Donnell explains that Allen's "New York editors were interested in the mountains," even though Lexington-born Allen "was never comfortable writing about them."[18] O'Donnell contends that for Allen, "the difference between the Bluegrass and the mountains is the difference between the civilized world and the savage" (29). Although Allen was from Kentucky, his Bluegrass background was vastly different from the landscape and people he encountered in the mountains and his portrayal of food delineates those differences.

It matters that "Through the Cumberland Gap on Horseback" was a commissioned piece of travel writing that was intended to be read as "real." Early in the piece Allen emphasizes his entrance into Burnside, Kentucky, referencing "two entirely distinct elements of population" in Kentucky.[19] After positioning his hotel as a kind of liminal space that bridges "the civilization [he] had left behind and the primitive society [he was] to enter," he references the introduction of the railroad to the area and the new foods it brought with it: "When the railway was first opened through this region a young man established a fruit store at one of the stations, and as part of his stock laid in a bunch of bananas. One day a native mountaineer entered. Arrangements generally struck him with surprise, but everything else was soon forgotten in an adhesive contemplation of the mighty aggregation of the fruit. Finally he turned away with this note: 'Blame me if them ain't the darnedest beans *I* ever seen!'" (52). As seen in figure 4, an illustration of a tall, barefoot mountain

"BLAME ME IF THEM AIN'T THE DARNEDEST BEANS!"

Fig. 4. "Blame Me If Them Ain't the Darnedest Beans *I* Ever Seen!"
James Lane Allen, "Through Cumberland Gap on Horseback."
Harper's New Monthly Magazine, June 1886.

man looking suspiciously at a bunch of bananas accompanies the description. As with George Washington Harris's portrayal of Sut's reaction to a plentiful meal, Allen's depiction of this mountain man's reaction to bananas is meant to be humorous. Presumably readers of *Harper's New Monthly Magazine* would have been familiar with bananas even if they did not have regular access to them and would have scoffed at the shoeless mountain man who confuses them with beans.

Yet considering the history of bananas in the United States lends a different reading to this scene. As historians Linda Gross and Theresa Snyder explain, bananas were featured at Philadelphia's Centennial Exhibition in 1876, just ten years before "Through the Cumberland Gap on Horseback" was published.[20] Moreover, as Virginia Scott Jenkins explains, the relatively short shelf life of the fruit made it difficult to transport before spoilage occurred. She explains that in the mid-1880s, "bananas were expensive and remained a luxury item for some time," but by the beginning of the twentieth century they became more accessible even though they were often "too expensive to be generally used by most families living in and near . . . small towns."[21] By the early 1900s, United Fruit Company accomplished a year-round national supply of bananas using a "refrigerated distribution network comparable to that of meatpackers" (42). Considered within this historical framework, the mountain man's reaction to the bananas seems understandable: if the fruit had only been exhibited ten years prior, it makes sense that a nonnative tropical fruit would be mostly unknown to rural people in eastern Kentucky. Perhaps more importantly, what Allen seems to miss is the fact that bananas were, in fact, for sale in eastern Kentucky when they were still largely inaccessible to Americans who did not live on the East Coast or in large cities. At a time when they were still difficult to procure, their presence in Appalachian Kentucky signals a kind of modernity and connection with the larger world that Allen seemed unable or unwilling to acknowledge. Moreover, as food writer Ronni Lundy pointed out to me in conversation about this scene, the joke may have been on the store owner, not the other way around. That is, the mountain man may have been intentionally playing into the ignorant hillbilly stereotype, thus rendering the fruit stand owner the fool for not knowing the difference.

Although Allen's piece is problematic in a variety of ways, he is at times complimentary when discussing certain foods. One aspect of hospitality that impresses him is the willingness of mountain people to share their gritted bread. Allen explains, "In the late summer and early autumn, while the grain is too hard for eating as roasting ears, and too soft to be ground in a mill . . . [they tack] a piece of tin through which holes have been punched through the under side, and over this tin the ears are rubbed, producing a coarse meal, of which 'gritted bread' is made" (59). Allen writes that the bread is "a sweet and wholesome bit for a hungry man" (60). Yet even though he compliments some aspects of their diet, he criticizes their farming practices, and his point that mountain people prefer wild meat indicates a certain kind of savagery.

Massachusetts-born attorney, editor, publisher, and writer Charles Dudley Warner relied on similar tactics when writing about food in the mountains. Warner was part of an elite circle of New England writers: he cowrote *The Gilded Age* with Mark Twain, and his neighbors in the Nook Farm community were Twain and Harriet Beecher Stowe. He was an avid traveler and often published accounts of his adventures. In the summer of 1884, Warner traveled with his friend and Yale University English professor, Thomas Raynesford Lounsbury, through the Southern mountains (O'Donnell and Hollingsworth, 194). The pair began their trip in Abingdon, Virginia, and "rode southeast to the vicinity of Boone, North Carolina, then up and over Roan Mountain through Bakersville to Burnsville. . . . From Burnsville they rode across Mount Mitchell to Asheville. From there they traveled down the French Broad, over the Bald Mountains to Watauga and upper Holston Valleys in Tennessee, and back to Abingdon" (194). Warner's account of their journey appeared as four separate issues in *Atlantic Monthly* from July through October 1885, and was republished as part of a larger book by Houghton, Mifflin, and Company that included "Notes of Travel in Mexico and California" in 1888.

Like Allen, Warner gives culinary credit where credit is due, but his criticisms of mountain food are at times quite harsh. Early in their trip he and his traveling partner enjoy a fine meal at Ramsey's Boarding House, but the farther the pair travels away from Abingdon, the more unsavory the food becomes.[22] Near the Tennessee–North Carolina border, Warner reflects, "The simple truth is that the traveler in this region must be content to feed on natural beauties. And it is an unfortunate truth in natural history that the appetite for this sort of diet fails after a time, if the inner man is not supplied with other sort of food. There is no landscape in the world that is agreeable after two days of rusty bacon and slack biscuit"; Warner's companion even remarks, "How lovely this would be . . . if it had a background of beefsteak and coffee!" (31). Certainly food is a requirement when traveling on horse-back, but Warner seems reluctant to acknowledge the food that is offered to the pair, especially when it does not meet their expectations. He is quite crit-ical of the food offered in Burnsville, North Carolina, remarking, "It should be said that before the country can attract and retain travelers, its inhabi-tants must learn something about the preparation of food" (77). Conversely, Warner expresses great relief upon reaching Asheville, North Carolina, where he finds "ice-water, barbers, waiters, civilization" (110). Warner sets Asheville apart as an oasis of hospitality.[23] Moreover, his national standing lends cre-dence to his judgments, as does the fact that his travel account appeared not only in the *Atlantic Monthly* but also as its own separate volume.[24]

Yet we should also keep in mind that descriptions like Warner's were not uncommon in previous years. Food historian Sam Bowers Hilliard points out that "before 1835 or 1840," over half a century before Warner's work appears, "many travelers reported an almost total lack of luxury items in the interior and often complained about the coarse food."[25] Hilliard quotes an 1830s de-scription by Thomas Hamilton of food served in Alabama: "We were now beyond the region of bread, and our fare consisted of eggs, broiled venison, and cakes of Indian corn fried in some kind of oleaginous matter" (38). Like-wise, a traveler named James Creecy reported "rusty salt pork" and "musty corn-meal dodgers" in Berrien, Georgia, in 1837 (39). Thus Warner continues an already established trend of writing about the perceived inadequacies of foods available in rural Southern locales.

Lesser-known author Mary Nelson Carter provides an even less flattering portrayal of culinary know-how and food storage in a piece entitled "Now is the Winter of Our Discontent." The selection appears in a collection called *North Carolina Sketches: Phases of Life Where the Galax Grows* published in 1900 that blends oral history, fiction, and first-person accounts of her time in Western North Carolina. At the time of publication, Carter had been living in Blowing Rock, North Carolina, since the 1880s, though she moved there from Philadelphia and spent her childhood years in New York and Connecti-cut. The selection describes the apparent inability of many mountain resi-dents to plan ahead for winter, as well as the utter destitution of the Dent family. From the beginning Carter makes clear that she and her husband were good planners: "It was a time to look well to the winter's supply of food and fuel. We, with the prudence born of experience, had done so, but many of our neighbors were trusting to luck to save them from the inevitable."[26] Notably, a local woman named Mrs. Hansley shares Carter's disdain for an inability or refusal to properly prepare for winter. When Mrs. Hansley visits Carter, the community has just experienced its first hard freeze, and Mrs. Hansley comments that every year, some people fail to plan ahead. Early in the piece Carter explains that the houses there do not have cellars, so some foods must be buried before winter to preserve them. After criticizing those who did not bury their cabbages, potatoes, and apples to protect them against frost, Mrs. Hansley remarks, "Folks is so unthoughted."[27] She goes on to explain that as a last-minute effort to save the food, some people in the community would take their cabbages, potatoes, and apples to market in an attempt to sell them. But she also comments that many would not insulate them well enough in their wagons and thus allow them to freeze, rendering them both unsalable and inedible. Both Carter and Mrs. Hansley deem this kind of unnecessary waste abhorrent. The piece continues with a description of the impoverished Dent family, people who repeatedly make poor decisions and can never seem to get ahead. Mrs. Hansley hopes that the family's problems are ameliorated when they move off the mountain to work as tenant farmers for a wealthy man named Mr. Nye. In both instances, Carter makes clear that the land is perfectly able to produce enough food for its inhabitants, but in some cases the flawed inhabitants are the problem.

Harvard-educated Kentucky author John Fox Junior makes a similar assertion in his 1908 *New York Times* best-selling novel, *The Trail of the Lonesome Pine*. Scholars, including Emily Satterwhite, have done extensive work investigating the impact that work like Fox's had for reading audiences. Satterwhite uses reader response theory to group Fox's audience into three main categories: nationally identified readers who did not live in Appalachia or identify with the region; locally identified readers who associated their identity with the mountains; and transitional readers who were from the mountains but saw themselves as transitioning away from a "traditional" lifestyle. Satterwhite asserts that for the nationally identified readers, Fox's novel functioned "as an antimodernist tonic that celebrated mountain quaintness, rationalized industrial interventions, and affirmed readers' nationalism, racism, and imperialism," while many locally identified readers were outraged at their portrayals as "stereotypical buffoons." Conversely, Satterwhite contends that the novel resonated with some transitional readers, "whose pursuit of schooling, professional work, or—in the case of regional elites—advantageous matrimonial matches compelled their social and geographical movement away

from the people and places of their childhood."[28] Appalachian studies scholar
Katie Algeo also explores the effect the novel had on national perceptions
of people in Appalachia by investigating a fascinating—and upsetting—
incident in which details from the novel, which is set in Kentucky and Virginia, were used verbatim to describe people and living conditions in Madison County, North Carolina. Algeo concludes that even though Western
North Carolina residents spoke out against their inaccurate representations,
"If Appalachian protests over Appalachian stereotypes were not better heard
it was because the rest of the country was not listening."[29]

In terms of food representations, Fox continues the trend of culinary degradation that was already well established. If we apply Satterwhite's approach
to those representations, their effect for a nationally identified audience becomes clear: heathen foods equal heathen people. The novel depicts protagonist June Tolliver's journey away from her mountain heritage and the resulting identity conflicts that ensue. When she returns home after receiving
a boarding school education, June is critical not only of the food that her
family consumes but also the ways in which they consume it. The narrator
explains: "The table was covered with an oil-cloth spotted with drippings
from a candle. The plates and cups were thick and the spoons were of pewter.
The bread was soggy and the bacon was thick and floating in grease.... They
gobbled their food like wolves, and when they drank their coffee, the noise
they made was painful to June's ears. There were no napkins and when her father pushed his chair back, he wiped his dripping mouth with the back of his
sleeve.... Poor June quivered with a vague newborn disgust."[30] In the same
way that Mrs. Hansley criticizes members of her own community in Carter's
collection, here June is repulsed by her family's eating practices. This narrative approach sends a clear message that once enlightened, anyone—even a
mountain girl—could see that the family's eating habits are distasteful. From
using serving ware deemed inappropriate to eating soggy bread and greasy
bacon, the people portrayed in this passage appear barbaric and uncouth,
perfect targets for civilization efforts like the one June undergoes in the novel.
Moreover, Fox imposes dominant, mainstream value systems about food and
proper table manners onto the characters through June, and in that way she
becomes a reluctant yet nevertheless critical tourist in her own home.

Algeo explains how the novel affected representations of mountain people
in Western North Carolina, and a two-part piece called "In Search of Local
Color" published in *Harper's Magazine* in 1922 provides another example of

the impact Fox's work had. At the age of twenty-two, the author, Laura Spencer Portor, traveled to the Kentucky mountains in search of a more realistic version of mountain people, explaining, "I believed that John Fox had written of these people too romantically; what was needed, I opined, was greater realism."[31] Yet on the same page she admits that she was "definitely seeking local color," and she finds it. In part two she visits Breathitt County, "the roughest of all Kentucky mountain counties, among a different and less gentle type of mountaineers."[32] Portor's description of her supper at a hotel reads much like June's description of her family's eating habits once she returns home from the Gap: "My companions, already seated, were five men of the typical mountain type. They all ate wolfishly, bending low over their plates, and balancing huge knives between outspread fingers and thumbs, using their forks only for stabbing purposes when anything was to be held down on their plates, preparatory to cutting."[33] Portor's word choice of "wolfish" echoes June's description of her family, and Portor's heavy focus on violence also suggests a kind of dangerous savagery present at the dinner table.

Portor is aware that her dinner companions would not approve of her observational purpose in eating with them. She reflects: "Perhaps one of the best bits of local color then available was just that—the absolute necessity of hiding that I came in search of it."[34] In the same way that residents of Madison County, North Carolina, were denied the agency to speak out on a national platform about their misrepresentation, the men Portor represents here were not made aware of her intent to watch and write about them. In denying them consent, she takes ownership of their representations and depicts them as hungry, savage animals in a national publication with a large readership.

Alabama writer Martha Gielow continues a similar trend in *Old Andy the Moonshiner* (1909) and *Uncle Sam* (1913). Like in the 1882 article, "Poor White Trash," Gielow's work capitalizes on so-called similarities between Southern African-Americans and mountain people. These limiting categories also suggest that one cannot be both African-American and Appalachian, a racist inaccuracy rooted in depictions of "pure Anglo-Saxon stock" from this era. Before she began writing about Appalachia, she wrote sketches about the antebellum South that glorified Lost Cause mythology popularized by writers including Thomas Nelson Page. With titles like *Mammy's Reminiscences and Other Sketches* (1898) and *Old Plantation Days* (1902), her allegiance to the South and its history of inequality is clear. Despite her admiration of a way of life built on the enslavement of others, she considered herself a philanthropist. Like many Progressive Era workers who became disillusioned with uplift efforts aimed at African-Americans in the Deep South, Gielow turned her attention to Appalachia. In 1905 she established the Southern Industrial Educational Association, an organization designed to promote industrial education to impoverished and ill-educated people in Appalachia. In a pamphlet written about Gielow and published by the association in 1914, the author explains that Appalachia "is peopled with the only unadulterated Americans we have," implying that the rest of the country owes it to these theoretically racially "pure" mountain residents to "save" them.[35] This philanthropic approach was not an uncommon one for organizations to use: William Goodell Frost, president of Berea College from 1892 until 1920, used similar logic to make a well-known case for the work Berea College was doing in his 1899 *Atlantic Monthly* article, "Our Contemporary Ancestors in the Southern Mountains."[36] But Gielow did not find a ready supply of donors, and as Lillian Messenger explains in her pamphlet about Gielow, "It was soon found out that the vernacular of the mountains could be as *compelling as the dialect of the plantation*, and her stories of the children of the hills as thrilling as her monologues of the old mammies of the Southern nursery." As such, Gielow's portrayals of mountain people cast them as dim buffoons who not only denigrate their own food but are hopelessly out of touch with contemporary life.

Gielow's 1909 novella, *Old Andy the Moonshiner*, was written as a "gift to the Association to use as campaign literature," and it raised more than $2,000, including a $500 gift from philanthropist Olivia Sage.[37] In it, an old moonshiner named Andy and his wife Priscilla are desperate to send their granddaughter, Sal, to school. Andy has been to town to see the school in person and knows from speaking with the teacher that they must raise $50 to procure Sal's spot. Gielow presents the couple as earnest and hardworking, especially in their willingness to make approximately 200 jugs of moonshine to generate school funds. The family is willing to do without "shortsweet'ning" (granulated sugar) and instead rely on sorghum syrup, "lay off . . . 'baccy," and "eat 'taters to lighten up on the bread."[38] Early in the story readers understand that the couple's rationing serves a dual purpose: Sal will be able to attend school, and while there, she will learn culinary habits that her grandparents see as an improvement over the foods they eat. When trying to persuade Sal that she will like school, Andy tells her that she can "larn to cook cake" and "lan' sakes erlive, [he] haint never tasted no stuff liken hit."[39] What's notable about this passage is not that Andy admires the fact that Sal will presumably learn baking skills but rather that Gielow casts Andy as critical of his own pantry and presumably his wife's skill set. As John Fox Junior does with his portrayal of June Tolliver's disgust with her family's eating habits, Gielow relies on a mountain character to convey the inferiority of his own foodways. In other words, Andy may not be educated in a formal sense, but he knows enough to understand that he and his kind need help, especially in the kitchen. Such paternalistic, offensive tactics were at least partially effective in raising money for the organization as well as furthering national misunderstandings about culinary deprivation in the mountains.

Gielow depicts even more uneducated, gullible characters in her 1913 story, *Uncle Sam*. In it, a government worker named William Vincent visits an isolated section of Appalachia that is never clearly identified by state. While there, he meets Jo Douglas, who goes by Uncle Jonah, and his wife, Aunt Cindy. Gielow portrays the couple as remarkably backward. When Vincent asks them whether they have considered growing apples on their land, Uncle Jonah answers that they have not, though he is unable to explain why. Vincent recommends that Uncle Jonah apply to Uncle Sam, who would send Jonah apple slips. Jonah has never heard the expression "Uncle Sam," nor does he understand the basic structure of American government. Vincent tries to hide his amusement at Jonah's ignorance, and the narrator comments, "That there could be a corner of the nation so shut in as to not know the meaning of Uncle Sam seemed unbelievable."[40] Yet rather than explain a few fundamental principles of government to Jonah, Vincent allows Jonah and Cindy to believe that they have a distant relative named "Uncle Sam" who lives in a faraway place called Washington, DC. Vincent requests that a number of slips and seeds be sent to the couple, all of which they put to good use: apple trees grow, corn flourishes, and Cindy plants decorative flowers, finally comprehending their purpose of beautification. The couple is so pleased with their orchard and garden that they decide to visit their long-lost Uncle Sam and to bring him corn and other goods so he can see their bountiful harvest firsthand. Upon arriving in Washington, DC, the couple meets the president of the United States, who treats them kindly if condescendingly, and his daughter sweetly explains the identity of Uncle Sam and his role. Upon returning to their mountain home, Jonah and Cindy praise their "uncle," the American government, and the Department of Agriculture: "All we hez ter do air ter jes' go ter thet Department uv Agy'culchy an' ax fer jes' what seeding we-uns wants."[41] When they explain the wonders of this system to their twin sons, Tim and Jim, "the twins become a power of strength in [the community], leading the boy brigade of embryo soldiers preparing to give their services, as their ancestors did, to fight, bleed and die for Uncle Sam."[42]

In many ways, the story functions as a snapshot of Progressive Era rhetoric, one that suggested people like Jonah and Cindy must be educated, reformed, and saved by the American government, so in turn they could become will-ing soldiers willing to defend that government. The 1913 publication date is also significant since it falls just one year before the Smith-Lever Act of 1914, a federal law that established cooperative extension services focused in part on improving agricultural and domestic practices in rural areas. As dis-cussed more thoroughly in chapter 3, in various states cooperative extension work was already happening before 1914. Additionally, Appalachian historian Tom Lee has pointed out that in some cases, railroad companies were also in-vested in encouraging mountain people to establish successful orchards, espe-cially in Western North Carolina. According to Lee, in 1910, "North Carolina state horticulturalist W.N. Hutt bemoaned the methods of North Carolina farmers . . . [and] expressed a belief that the apple growing regions of West-ern North Carolina held great promise."[43] Hutt was in correspondence with Richard F. Brewer, an industrial agent who worked for the Carolina, Clinch-field and Ohio Railway. Lee's research demonstrates that Hutt and Brewer were attempting to work together to teach mountain people how to establish and better tend their orchards using the latest scientific recommendations for pesticide spraying, pruning, and transporting the fruit to market.

One of Hutt's comments in a letter to Brewer reads like something Vin-cent from Gielow's story could have written about Uncle Jonah and Aunt Cindy: "I have been working with your people for some years but my experi-ence has been similar to your own, that they do not take very readily for up-to-date methods. These people have been so far back in the mountains that they are not much in touch with markets and for that reason it is hard to in-struct them in proper methods."[44] If we trust Brewer's and Hutt's assessment of mountain isolation, then it is not improbable that a couple like Jonah and Cindy may well have existed. Yet in Gielow's story, Jonah and Cindy are ea-ger learners, while the people Brewer and Hutt tried to work with were ap-parently resistant to their efforts. Thus applying Lee's work about initiatives to cultivate orchards in Western North Carolina to Gielow's fictional story provides two insights: first, Lee's work shores up the contextual legitimacy of her tale, and second, it allows us to read Gielow's story as a corrective to the difficulty people like Brewer and Hutt encountered when trying to introduce new farming practices to mountain communities.

Yet what remains so damaging about Gielow's portrayal of Jonah and Cindy is that they are made the laughingstock of the story, both for characters and readers. Gielow casts the American government as the couple's savior, whereas in Lee's example extractive industry assumes that role. As he points out, after railways had been built to haul away timber, railroad companies were often eager to promote other ways to make the land profitable, especially if those efforts could be interpreted as benevolent. Even though Gielow's story casts Jonah's and Cindy's willingness to change as a positive trait, her portrayal of them functions in the same problematic way as other authors discussed in this section.

In the same year that Gielow published *Uncle Sam* (1913), Horace Kephart published *Our Southern Highlanders*, a 450-page-plus book detailing his time spent living in the mountains of Western North Carolina, the majority of which was on Hazel Creek in Swain County, though he traveled frequently and lived for a time in Bryson City. In some ways, the text reads like a sociological study with a "reported from the frontlines" tone, one that narrates the customs and culture of the people he lived among. But in other ways, as Kephart scholar George Ellison contends, the text "is at once historical, sociological, and autobiographical," comparing it to Marjorie Kinnan Rawlings's 1942 depiction of Florida in *Cross Creek*.[45] Ellison also calls *Our Southern Highlanders* a "direct descendant of the humorous-descriptive-realistic accounts of life in the rural settlements and backwoods of the Old South and Southwest" (xlii). In other words, stylistically speaking, Kephart borrows heavily from writers like George Washington Harris, and like many of his literary antecedents discussed thus far in this chapter, Kephart was very interested in food. As the Western Carolina University digital Kephart exhibit on Cooking and Food Preparation asserts, "all varieties of cooking and food preparation particularly interested Kephart."[46]

Born in Pennsylvania and raised in Iowa, Kephart worked as a librarian in St. Louis for thirteen years until discord in his family life, a drinking problem, and his increasing preference for solitude in the wilderness culminated in his leaving his wife and six children in 1904. He relocated to a remote section of Western North Carolina, where he hoped living a simple life in nature would be curative. Kephart was already well equipped for living in the wilderness.

He had long been interested in camping and even published *The Book of Camping and Woodcraft* in 1906, *Camp Cookery* in 1910, and subsequent expanded and revised editions thereafter. In *Camp Cookery*, Kephart includes extensive advice to campers, making specific recommendations about how to plan for cooking outdoors, which kinds of equipment to pack, and how to prepare meals. In the "Provisions" section, for example, he instructs, "Go prepared to lend variety to your menu. Food that palls is bad food—worse in camp than anywhere else, for you can't escape to a restaurant."[47] Throughout the text he makes specific recommendations about which utensils yield the best results and advises campers to pack well and carry lightly. In other words, the text reveals Kephart as a man of particular food preferences, preparation techniques, and opinions.

Though not a cookbook, *Our Southern Highlanders* also emphasizes food. Like many of the authors considered in this section, Kephart's negative opinions about food and agriculture in the mountains are clear. Like the real-life examples of Brewer and Hutt and the fictional example of Gielow's *Uncle Sam*, Kephart confirms that "The Carolina mountains are, by nature, one of the best fruit regions in eastern America. Apples, grapes, and berries, especially, thrive exceeding [*sic*] well. But our mountaineer is no horticulturist. He lets his fruit trees take care of themselves, and so, everywhere except on select farms near towns, we see old apple and peach trees that never were pruned, bristling with shoots, and often bearing wizened fruit, dry and bitter, or half rotted on the stem."[48]

He is similarly critical of gardens and beef cattle, lamenting that "The butchering was done with an axe and a jackknife. The meat was either sliced thin and fried to a crackling, or cut in chunks and boiled furiously just long enough to fit it for boot-heels. What the butcher mangled, the cook damned" (43–44). At this point in the text, Kephart directs his criticisms at food and preparation techniques, but later he extends his less-than-flattering comments to mountain people themselves: "The backwoodsmen through ruthless weeding-out of the normally sensitive have acquired a wonderful tolerance of swimming grease, doughy bread and half-fried cabbage; but, even so, they are gnawed by dyspepsia. This accounts in great measure for the 'glunch o' sour disdain' that mars so many countenances. A neighbor said to me of another: 'He has a gredge agin all creation, and glories in human misery.' So would anyone else who ate at the same table. Many a homicide in the mountains can be traced directly to bad food and the raw whiskey taken to appease a soured stomach" (222). Here Kephart portrays mountain residents as tough people whose stomachs have mostly—though not completely—adapted to coarse, difficult-to-digest foods. But in pointing out the upset stomachs many apparently experience, he sets up a causal relationship between "bad food," "raw whiskey," and homicide in the mountains, effectively conflating several problematic stereotypes: inferior food, inferior people, and a tendency toward violence. But Kephart also acknowledges food scarcity in the mountains, as when he chronicles names of settlements that indicate poverty, including Needmore, Poor Fork, Long Hungry, No Pone, and No Fat (252).

Yet at the same time that Kephart draws reader attention to poor food or lack thereof, he seems equally enamored with mountain food preferences. He writes, "Once, as an experiment, [he] took a backwoodsman from the Smokies to Knoxville, and put him up at a good hotel. Was he self-conscious, bashful? Not a bit of it. When the waiter brought him a juicy tenderloin he snapped: 'I don't eat my meat raw!' It was hard to find anything on the menu that he would eat" (254). Kephart does not linger over the man's refusal to consume rare meat, but the man's resistance is noteworthy. Rather than Kephart criticizing meat so tough it could be used to sole boots, here readers glimpse that culinary critique goes both ways: the man Kephart quotes knows what he likes, and it apparently does not appear on the Knoxville hotel menu.

Kephart also seems fascinated by the culinary practices of those around him. At some parts in the text he explains food customs that might be unfamiliar to nonmountain readers, similar to James Lane Allen's description for gritted bread, which Kephart also discusses. Kephart explains: "When one dines in a cabin back in the hills he will taste some strange dishes that go by still stranger names" (292). Kephart provides a brief list of items for readers: leather britches (dried beans that are reconstituted and cooked), poor-do (scrapple), lath-open (bread made from biscuit dough with soda and buttermilk and shortening worked in at the end of the process), and sass (apple sauce). Kephart also warns that "the word love is commonly used here in the sense of like or relish" (293). In instances like these, *Our Southern Highlanders* functions as more of a guidebook rather than a compilation of all that is inferior about Appalachian people and their tables. Even so, Kephart's criticisms are clear and no doubt contributed to national perceptions of mountain people that were less than flattering. By 1967, "Macmillan [Company of New York] had reprinted the book eight times" and it was considered a key text for understanding the region.[49]

Situating Mountain Food Narratives within
National Culinary Trends

These descriptions that suggested a connection between inferior mountain food and inferior people provided non-Appalachian readers with an imagined vision of rustic pioneers, people who were able to survive on unsavory fare. When contextualized within national food trends happening during the same time, portrayals of Appalachia may be read as a counterpoint—and in some cases a corrective, though at times a problematic one—to dominant fads. Foodways scholars Harvey Levenstein, Helen Zoe Veit, Robert Dirks, S. Margot Finn, and more have explored nutrition and health trends during the late nineteenth and early twentieth centuries. From obsessions with European food, purity, health, thinness, and at times, very limiting diets, middle- and upper-class people were interested in a multitude of culinary landscapes that were decidedly not Appalachian.[50] Yet as Appalachian studies scholars like Henry Shapiro, Emily Satterwhite, and others have pointed out, it was during this very same time that America's reading public became interested in fiction set in the mountains. Stories and sketches published in *Harper's New Monthly Magazine* and the *Atlantic Monthly* provided reading audiences with vivid descriptions of beautiful mountain landscapes and simple people. Even stories that cast mountain people as violent, feuding degenerates could function as an antidote to reader anxieties about living a "modern" life. The popularity of imagined simplicity was also not limited to literature. As Jane Becker explains, by the late 1800s and early 1900s, the Arts and Crafts movement was flourishing, and "a ready market for [handmade domestic] products existed, particularly among northern urbanites."[51]

It is not a stretch to speculate that a non-Appalachian reader could have been fascinated by unfamiliar mountain foods and preparation methods: descriptions of leather britches, creasy greens, sass, gritted bread, and more encouraged audiences to imagine a foreign place, people, and culinary landscape. The coarse, greasy foods blamed by some authors as the cause of frequent mountain dyspepsia would have been a notable departure from foods recommended by various nutrition gurus of the day. In other words, readers could have sated their curiosity if nothing else by reading about the foods they would not have consumed in their everyday lives.

In her book-length study of how food trends are related to class anxiety, Margo Finn draws parallels between contemporary obsessions over thinness, health, and similar obsessions that occurred during the Gilded Age and Progressive Era. Moreover, Finn argues that "the dominant social classes have disproportionate influence over the process of cultural legitimation, meaning they have more of a say over what counts as good taste. . . . They tend to win more of the battles over the narratives people create to give their preferences social meaning."[52] For people in these dominant social classes, some of whom were also reading publications about the mountains, imagining Appalachian food and people as inferior made sense: mountain food was almost certainly what health-conscious readers avoided.

Yet a surprising number of popular authors do not fit this paradigm, perhaps suggesting that readers were more willing to imagine a different view of Appalachia than we often give them credit for. If we allow pre–Civil War writers to inform our understanding of the mountains—that is, if we consider writing set in Appalachia before the rest of the nation conceived of Appalachia as such—then we find some positive depictions of the region and its food. Both before and after the Civil War, we encounter writers who overtly criticize derogatory descriptions of mountain people and their tables. We even find writers who use fiction set in the mountains to mock health and tourism trends popular in their day and to make important commentary on a globally connected Appalachia.

Complicating the Culinary Script: *David Hunter Strother, Rebecca Harding Davis, and More*

David Hunter Strother was born in 1816 in what is now West Virginia but was then part of Virginia. Kevin O'Donnell and Helen Hollingsworth explain that as a painter and illustrator, Strother "became one of America's most financially successful writers in the 1850s" (99). O'Donnell also points out that "aside from George Washington Harris, of Knoxville, Tennessee, Strother was the only southern Appalachian writer to gain a national audience before the Civil War" (18). Like Harris, Strother wrote about food in the mountains, but Strother's depictions were quite different from the fare Sut Lovingood was accustomed to eating. While Harris's depictions of Lovingood indicate impoverished, ill-educated mountaineers, Strother's depictions were far more positive. The popularity of Strother's writing and illustrations indicates a willingness by the reading public to accept positive portrayals of Appalachia, at least in the years leading up to the Civil War, before the concept of

Appalachia was cemented in the American consciousness. O'Donnell points out that soon after *Harper's* began publishing Strother's work, the magazine's circulation more than doubled, and at one point Strother was *Harper's New Monthly Magazine*'s highest paid contributor with a standing commission.[53]

Strother published several series for *Harper's*, many of which began in Berkeley Springs, West Virginia (then Virginia), a town that refers to itself as "The Country's First Spa" on their town website. One such piece, "A Winter in the South," was published in seven installments from September 1857 to December 1858, and as historian David Hsiung notes, the story is based on a trip Strother took with his wife and daughter in 1857.[54] The story features a few central characters and pokes fun at all of them. If there is a protagonist, it would be Squire Broadacre, a plump man whose name indicates his bodily form. When the story opens, he is so upset by the political unrest of his time that he suffers from dyspepsia. He seeks rest and restoration at "Berkeley Springs, a jolly old bathing-place."[55] Located in Morgan County, West Virginia, the spa is still in operation and as their website explains, it was "First noted as Medicine Springs in 1747 on a map drawn by Thomas Jefferson's father.... George Washington first visited in 1748 and made the area his favorite getaway through the 1760s." Squire Broadacre's century-later visit to the spa indicates not only his high social standing but also his awareness of current health trends.

But his experience there does not heal him, and Strother's depiction of the spa's remedies, especially where diet is concerned, openly criticize these seemingly superior nutritional regimens. For example, the narrator tells us,

> Here, with a childlike simplicity not uncommon among persons who have never been used to sickness, [the Squire] asked and followed every body's advice in regard to his ailments. . . . He tried crackers and black tea one morning at breakfast, but it seemed rather to set him back. He took pepsin one day, and then an old fat lady recommended to him to chew dried gizzards, which she assured him had nearly cured her of indigestion. He had about a peck prepared, and chewed perseveringly for two days, when one morning he threw up his breakfast. This unusual event so alarmed him that he immediately consulted a physician. The medical gentleman . . . told him that, unless he had a mind to eat half a pint of sand or gravel every morning to assist the gizzards, they would not benefit him, and had better be discontinued.[56]

Fig. 5. This modern-day photograph features Berkeley Springs Resort,
"a jolly old bathing-place" according to the narrator in "A Winter in the South."
West Virginia Collection within the Carol M. Highsmith Archive, Library
of Congress, Prints and Photographs Division.

This passage's humor indicates the absurdity of bizarre dietary treatments
people were apparently eager to spend money trying. Squire Broadacre gives
up on the spa and decides to take a trip instead. His trip through the Southern mountains cures his ailments, and by the end of the series readers understand that time spent in the mountains—eating mountain food—is far more
restorative than time at a spa where odd, restrictive diets are part of the daily
routine.

The first indication readers receive of this finding occurs in the second installment. The group—the squire is traveling with his wife, two daughters, a
cousin, his sketch artist nephew, and a body servant—is leaving Bristol and
his daughter, Betty, becomes hungry, so they stop at a cottage and ask for re-
freshments. "A pretty, smiling, country-woman responded to the requisition
with a load of cold spare-ribs, biscuits, and sugar-cakes, stoutly refused all re-
muneration therefor, and lamenting at the same time, that she had nothing
better to send."[57] The narrator explains that the food afforded a "good lunch"
to many in the party, but Squire Broadacre refuses to eat the food not because

of its quality but rather because he wants to wait "until [they] get one of these substantial juicy suppers that [he has] sometimes seen in the mountains."[58] This exchange is a significant departure from later representations that would likely portray the woman as toothless, poor, and utterly lacking in culinary knowhow. Instead, here we have a "pretty, smiling" woman whose biscuits are described as white and her ribs juicy, food the squire no doubt finds enticing.

Equally remarkable considering derogatory depictions that begin appearing in the 1880s, the squire references prior positive experiences eating mountain food and hopes to find another such meal. After fording the Clinch River, his hopes are granted when the party arrives at Neil's Tavern, "where the Squire got a supper that fully justified his philosophic self-denial and glowing faith in the cuisine of the mountains."[59] The phrase "glowing faith in the cuisine of the mountains" stands in stark contrast to the vast majority of references to mountain food in the 1800s, especially after the Civil War. As discussed later in this study, these negative portrayals only became positive on a somewhat larger scale in the mid-twentieth century in fiction by mountain writers and on a large, nationwide scale in the last fifteen or so years by cookbook writers like Sheri Castle, Ronni Lundy, and Sean Brock and fiction authors like Robert Gipe.

Other complimentary descriptions of food and those offering it appear throughout the remaining installments of "A Winter in the South." In Jonesborough, Tennessee, "they . . . par[take] of a hearty old-fashioned supper of steaks, sausages, preserves, batter-cakes, and biscuits, and very soon after [go] to sleep" at the Eutaw House.[60] As seen in figure 6, an illustration of Jonesborough suggests a bustling town, not an isolated landscape of deprivation.

Likewise, near Roan Mountain they are "received after the fashion of the country [and] got a hearty supper."[61] At one point the party travels with Tom Wilson, a well-known hunter and mountain guide who found geology professor Elisha Mitchell's body after he fell from the mountain that was later named in his honor. Wilson's wife provides a substantial meal for the travelers that was apparently commonplace according to the narrator's description: "Having already described one meal at length, we will not dwell upon the supper at the cabin, nor tell what buckwheat cakes and biscuits, what pork and fried chicken, what stewed pumpkins and cabbage, disappeared from the groaning board, nor enumerate the cups of milk, coffee, and persimmon beer that were swallowed during the meal."[62] Hsiung references this particular scene, noting that "The story describes not only the mountaineers' hospitality and

JONESBOROUGH

Fig. 6. A drawing of Jonesborough. The narrator describes Jonesborough as having "an old-fashioned, substantial air" with "adjacent hills . . . crowned with neat private residences, and several academies of some architectural pretension." David Hunter Strother, "A Winter in the South: Second Paper." *Harper's New Monthly Magazine*, October 1857.

openness to strangers but also the abundance of food."[63] Such descriptions suggest a culinary bounty unknown to the likes of Sut Lovingood.

But perhaps the more important point is that in the same way Strother pokes fun at spa cuisine and in turn lauds mountain food as superior in both quality and health benefits for Squire Broadacre, the narrative also boldly critiques mainstream notions about civility, education, and sophistication that readers of *Harper's New Monthly Magazine* in 1857 and 1858 likely shared. After summiting Mount Mitchell with the help of Tom Wilson, the men of the party rejoin the women and travel through Burnsville in Yancey County, North Carolina, staying with local families along the way. The first cabin they visit can only offer corn and pumpkins, which are still in need of cooking. They travel on and are warmly received; like the smiling, pretty woman they encountered earlier, the women of this family are quite attractive, and Robert the sketch artist says to his uncle, "I can not help thinking what a superb figure that child might make one day, if, perchance, she were taken and educated in all the graces of civilization." The uncle retorts, "Civilization! Robert. What do you mean by that? Hoops, the polka, and point lace?" Robert responds, "They are merely incidental, Sir. But I mean a general cultivation of the tastes, sentiments, and intellectual faculties."[64] Then, in a move that defends mountain people and their customs, Squire Broadacre responds at length:

> That sounds very well for a flourish, Robert, but is not sufficiently specific for an argument. Now let me talk awhile. Have you observed our good hostess here, how she hurries to and fro, bringing out her stores of dried pumpkin shavings, prepared corn, maple sugar, and sweetmeats—how she bakes, boils, and stews—striving, with all grace and cheerfulness, to do honor to her husband's guests? Have you marked how tidy she keeps her handsome brood. . . ? Or the elder daughter, diligent and meek, how smilingly she skips to do her mother's bidding—to fetch dried apples from the loft—to keep the coffee-pot from boiling over—to help with the big kettle?"[65]

While this passage is ripe for analysis through a feminist lens, within the argumentative context that this chapter establishes, it is noteworthy that not only are the women of this family described as attractive and well versed in the ways of hosting guests, but their table is also plentiful. They are not poverty stricken, nor do they lack the skills or know-how for cultivating and preparing a bountiful meal. While many of their ingredients—pumpkins, corn, and apples, for example—are local, the women know how to preserve those foods to last through the year and know how to prepare them in a pleasing way for visitors. The family is also financially able to purchase coffee, an imported good that signals the family's socioeconomic standing as relatively comfortable. As seen in figure 7, an illustration titled "An Interior" appears at the beginning of the story. Presumably the image is meant to represent a typical eastern Tennessee dwelling; notably, the room is spacious and clean, the space boasts furniture and a clock, and dried food—perhaps beans, peppers, or apples—hangs from the ceiling. It looks like a comfortable place to rest and eat while traveling.

The fifth installment of the story goes even further: "East Tennessee is one of the most delightful countries in the world. Possessing a genial climate, a fertile soil, abounding in all those natural resources whose development and

AN INTERIOR.

Fig. 7 A drawing of an interior representative of the kind of home where Squire Broadacre and his travel companions dine. David Hunter Strother, "A Winter in the South: Fourth Paper." *Harper's New Monthly Magazine*, January 1858.

use constitute the true wealth of a state, her virgin forests, lovely rivers, and majestic mountains, offer, at the same time, a rich and varied feast to the romantic tourist."[66] In this passage the narrator could be setting a precedent for later Local Color portrayals in which beautiful landscapes juxtapose the ignorant, unsavory inhabitants of that scenery, but this does not seem to be the case here. Hsiung makes the point that "Such generalities about the physical environment and its natural resources could easily be found in published works by the mid-nineteenth century."[67] But he seems to miss the significance of the narrator's next comments that the traveler "meets every where the luxury and polish of modern refinement. There are colleges, railroads . . . electric telegraphs, and fancy stores. Old folks have already begun to shake their heads at these things, but old folks are always shaking their heads at something."[68] The story even includes an illustration of East Tennessee University (present-day University of Tennessee in Knoxville), as seen in figure 8.

Although favorable descriptions of Appalachian scenery were common, extending those compliments to the region's civility and culinary prowess was

EAST TENNESSEE UNIVERSITY.

Fig. 8. A drawing of East Tennessee University. The narrator calls the
university (present-day University of Tennessee in Knoxville) a "great centre
of commerce, learning, and the arts." David Hunter Strother, "A Winter in the
South: Fifth Paper." *Harper's New Monthly Magazine*, May 1858.

rare. Equally significant is the fact that "A Winter in the South" was based
on Strother's own trip through the mountains, suggesting that these lauda-
tory depictions, though technically fictitious, were also true to life. In many
ways Strother seems prescient, overturning portrayals of the mountains that
will begin thirty or so years in the future. In the sixth installment the narrator theorizes, "As a man grows old he naturally takes to grumbling and fault-
finding. . . . The green soda-biscuit and patent-yeast rolls of the present are
compared with the crisp Johnny-cake of forty years ago."[69] Here the narrator

draws reader attention to the tendency for culinary nostalgia, but the passage also privileges the "crisp Johnny-cake," a departure from the bread hierarchy discussed later in this project, one that routinely places corn-based breads at the bottom.

Strother's positive portrayals of food in the mountains should also be placed within their antebellum context. In the years leading up to the Civil War, those who were not enslaved had greater access to food than during or immediately following the war. Historians John Inscoe and Gordon McKinney describe the hardships families in Western North Carolina experienced: crops were not grown at the same rates, government provisions were not provided equally, and "the disruption of the market economy on which the broader mountain community was so dependent" had long-lasting food consequences.[70] In part, this may explain Strother's 1850s depictions of refined, plentiful society in the mountains while writers like those discussed at the beginning of the chapter portrayed dramatically different circumstances postwar. Other earlier positive portrayals also imply abundance in the mountains while critiquing nutrition fads. In an 1840 newspaper article published in the Christmas Day issue of the *Carolina Planter*, the author writes, "Almost all dyspeptics are trying the prescription of this or that friend who has been similarly affected. They are moping about, eating what is indigestible and consulting every one for some remedy, while the most powerful tonic qualities of air and exercise are usually not noticed."[71] The author goes on to recommend that invalids spend time in Buncombe County, North Carolina, where travelers will find that "the substantial fare of the country [is] good enough for even captious stomachs" and "we really think injustice is done to worthy people by unreflecting visitors who expect too much and are soured by disappointment." In other words, the script that Local Color and travel writers develop in the years following the Civil War is flipped in this example from 1840: it is the travelers with high expectations who are the problem, not mountain people or their foods.

Rebecca Harding Davis continues these criticisms roughly thirty years later. Davis was born in 1831 in Wheeling, West Virginia (then Virginia), and is best known for her first publication, "Life in the Iron Mills," which appeared in the *Atlantic Monthly* in 1861. Davis biographer Sharon Harris explains that the *Atlantic Monthly* was the "premier literary periodical of [Davis's] day," and most American literary scholars cite it as some of Davis's best writing, frequently calling it an example of "pioneering realism."[72] The story depicts the heart-wrenching tale of two Welsh immigrants, Deb and Hugh, who are barely able to survive despite their strong work ethic. Davis's story makes clear that the American formula of working hard to earn financial security does not hold true for these characters. The story indicates that even from the beginning, Davis was a socially conscious writer whose work carried a political message for readers. That her fiction should read in this way is not surprising, given that she first worked as a newspaper reporter, often covering controversial topics, especially as tensions leading to the Civil War increased. Harris calls her "one of America's early and notable women journalists" (1). The body of work that Davis produced in her lifetime is indeed astounding. Bibliographer Jane Atteridge Rose states that Davis published over 500 pieces, including "novels, serialized fiction of all lengths, essays, and juvenile fiction," all set in various locales.[73]

In addition to "Life in the Iron Mills," several of Davis's pieces are set in Appalachia. Seemingly all of them issue a social critique—either about the way mountain people are portrayed in popular media or about the neglect Cherokee people endured in the years following removal—and descriptions of food play an integral role in the lessons Davis conveys to her readers. Davis's upbringing in Wheeling and subsequent time spent at the Female Seminary in Washington, Pennsylvania, help explain her interest in depicting West Virginia and parts of Pennsylvania, but Davis was also especially interested in Western North Carolina. Harris explains that "in August [of 1874] Rebecca . . . traveled to North Carolina [and] part of her trip involved lengthy travel on mules into the high mountain country" (168). The following year, she published two pieces based on what she learned during her travels.

The first one, "The Yares of Black Mountains," appeared in the July 1875 issue of *Lippincott's Magazine*, while the second story, "Qualla," appeared in the same publication in November. As literary critics Kevin O'Donnell and Helen Hollingsworth explain, "The story is of special interest to students of 'local color' fiction, since it may well be the first such story, featuring southern mountaineers, to appear in a national magazine" (173). At its core, the story justifies why some people in Appalachia, and Western North Carolina in particular, refused to fight for the Confederacy. But the story also offers a nuanced critique of tourism, cultural understandings of the mountains, and the role that food can play in those ideas. Like some of Davis's later work, the story satirizes tourists who travel to the mountains in search of beautiful scenery only to be shocked by the "primitive" conditions they encounter.

The story opens in Old Fort, North Carolina, where a group of tourists disembarks and a man named Nesbitt declares, "Civilization stops here, it appears."[74] The travelers, including a young widow with a baby, visit a restaurant and bar near the train station. Upon entering the restaurant, one of the patrons directs the widow to a separate room where the air will be less smoky for the baby. After a few moments Nesbitt checks on her, exclaiming, "There is a bare wooden table set in a shed out yonder, and a stove alongside where the cooking goes on. You would not have wanted to taste food for a month if you had seen the fat pork and cornbread which they are shoveling down with iron forks" (36). Nesbitt deems the entire situation unacceptable and declares that he's going to try a trip to Texas instead. Another woman from the train, Miss Cook, remarks, "It's absurd, the row American men make about their eating away from home. They want Delmonico's table set at every railway station" (36). Miss Cook's comment suggests that the substandard fare offered at the train station is more indicative of food one encounters when traveling rather than mountain food overall. Davis demonstrates this point when the widow and Miss Cook begin their journey and stop at a "large log hut" for food. Although the narrator describes the house as dirty and bare, the chicken, rice, honey and "delicious" butter they receive are a welcome contrast to the train station options.

Yet Davis also offers a clear critique of Miss Cook, a woman whom readers soon understand is a biased journalist given to ridiculing mountain residents for their "queer mistakes in accent" (39). When the widow realizes that Miss Cook is traveling to learn about mountain people, the widow remarks that Miss Cook will need all summer to gather those facts. Miss Cook responds, "Why child, I have them all now—got them this morning. . . . I have the faculty of generalizing you see. . . . I've done the mountains and mountaineers. . . . I should not learn that fact any better if I stayed a week" (40). Miss Cook soon leaves, presumably to write thinly researched reports of mountain people, while the widow continues her journey and is rewarded with hospitality from the Yare family.

Five years later, in the summer of 1880, Davis returned to Western North Carolina. In midsummer of that same year, she published "By-Paths in the Mountains" in three installments in *Harper's New Monthly Magazine*. Biographer Helen Sheaffer categorizes "By-Paths" as a "story-essay" while Harris calls it a "blended-genre story," but both biographers agree that it blends nonfiction and fiction.[75] Like "The Yares of the Black Mountains," "By-Paths" satirizes the tourism industry in Appalachia and continues the culinary themes Davis established in previous mountain stories. The story opens with a generalization about the "typical" hardworking American with a modest income who still wants a nice summer vacation. The narrator pokes fun at this desire, explaining that he "carries the luxury [of a holiday] uneasily; it discomforts him; he does not know how to use it."[76] But, "there are certain essentials, to be sure, which he must have when he leaves home for enjoyment: sublime scenery, pure air, no mosquitoes, plenty of game, milk, fruit, and eggs, congenial society, spring mattresses, [and] well-cooked meals."[77]

In the first installment, the travelers—Dr. Mulock, his wife, a single woman named Sarah, and two men who function as her suitors, Mr. Morley and Judge Hixley—visit Virginia, and in the second part they venture into Pennsylvania and later North Carolina. In Pennsylvania they encounter beautiful landscapes and prosperous farms. The narrator describes a Pennsylvania farmer's wife as in constant motion, picking peas in the garden, making soap, or "drawing great loaves of flaky bread from an oven in the yard, while innumerable pans of gingerbread or cherry pies waited their turn. There was the sluggish calm of physical luxury, of rude plenty, everywhere. The air was full of the odor of pig-pens and drying meat, mixed with new-mown haw and honeysuckles."[78] The narrative tone here is one of condescension with phrases like "rude plenty," but the overall depiction is still one of nutritional bounty. The narrator remarks that the white mountaineers are "uncouth but decent people," a recurring trend when meals—even very good ones—are described.

Davis also highlights characters whose culinary situations are not nourishing, as is the case with a young woman named Victoria who has yellow skin, black teeth, and a "steady diet of pork and strong coffee." Even so, the narrator is quick to point out that "Pork and coffee had tainted her no deeper than the skin. At heart she was a pure, modest little woman."[79] As the narrator explains, some of the characters become "possessed with a missionary spirit," and when Mrs. Mulock is in Highlands, North Carolina, she and Sarah visit women on mountain farms. Mrs. Mulock remarks to Sarah, "It makes my blood run cold to see them frying this delicious mountain mutton in lard—yes, actually in hog's lard."[80] The narrator follows her statement by explaining, "Her seeds of knowledge usually fell on stony ground," indicating the unwillingness of mountain women to learn new cooking techniques.

Yet in the same story in which Davis depicts stubborn mountain women determined to fry cuts of meat in pork fat, she also defends mountain tables and people. When the travelers are just outside of Asheville, Dr. Mulock criticizes mountain people for not profiting more from the beautiful scenery around them. He complains that rates on Southern railways and in hotels are exorbitant, and as a result, keep away Northern tourists. He exclaims, "We paid as much for a surfeit of greasy fried chicken and pork, vilely serviced, at Salisbury, as for a meal at the best hotel in New York. They drive away the goose before it has time to lay a golden egg." But Judge Hixley responds, "The mountaineers will not overcharge you. . . . If we should stop at one of these huts without windows, and bring the bahr-footed woman in from her ploughing [to] cook us a dinner, she would give us the inevitable chicken, delicious corn-bread, milk, plenty of vegetables and honey, and either make no charge at all, or be satisfied with ten cents."[81] The food listed here would have come from the woman's farm, and though she is barefoot and must work in the field, her offerings are described as "delicious." Davis also takes special care in pointing out that "there are always one or two families of educated, well-bred people [who] buy no new books, but they have read the old ones until they are like friends."[82] Even so, such defenses are always qualified: though a farm may be bountiful, it is a "rude plenty"; though a hardworking woman may offer travelers dinner, she is barefoot and the fare is not elaborate; though families may cherish books, including classics like Shakespeare, they are not current on the latest trends in fiction. Such a persistent trend of "not as terrible as you might think, but still substandard" is most apparent in the story's conclusion. The travelers arrive in Wallhalla, South Carolina, finding "the thrift, cleanliness, and homely beauty thus suddenly opened to their eyes a violent contrast to all the grandeur, the dirt, and appalling laziness which they had left behind them in the mountains."[83] In "By-Paths in the Mountains" and "The Yares of Black Mountains," Davis satirizes vapid tourists and critiques overly harsh portrayals of mountain people, but she also participates in them to a degree, at least until her next story set in the mountains.

Five years later, Davis published "The Mountain Hut" in the *Youth's Companion*, a magazine that Harris calls "the leading young adult and family magazine of the era" (147). The story provides a fascinating defense of mountain food, while also making the case that Appalachia—even in 1885—was part of a globally connected food market. Even so, the story has received scant critical attention: Jane Atteridge Rose does not include it in her bibliography of Davis' work, nor does Sharon Harris discuss it in her almost 500-page biography of Davis. Whereas Davis's earlier mountain stories vacillate between a defense and a critique of mountain people and their culinary practices, "The Mountain Hut" offers a clear defense of the region.

The story opens with a character named David who travels "far into the Balsam Mountains of North Carolina" with his uncle and sister.[84] The travelers are caught in a storm, and the uncle remembers a hut on the bank of a stream and suggests that they stop there. David remarks, "But it is more like a piggery than a dwelling for human beings, like most of the houses of these mountaineers." In the same way that Judge Hixley corrects Dr. Morley's misunderstandings in "By-Paths in the Mountains," David's uncle does the same here. Like most of Davis's mountain characters, the woman living in the "hut" welcomes them in, offering them corn and pork fat. David seems convinced that the woman is entirely isolated, but his uncle responds:

> It is impossible for any living beings to shut themselves off from their kind. If you look a little farther, you will be surprised to find how widely connected this poor lame creature is with the rest of the world. This coffee, which is making such a comfortable smell just now, came to her from the far-off Brazils; black-bearded mulattoes picked it for her on the shores of the Amazon; other slaves in the West Indies grew her the pepper which she is sifting on the meat; English mill-hands in Manchester wove her Sunday calico-gown; mild-eyed Chinamen gave her tea; even this hen clucking at my feet came from eggs from Poland. (271)

He continues to comment on sugar from Louisiana and rice from Georgia.

At first glance, the scenario just described seems to fit the status quo of the era. The mountain woman is a "poor lame creature" and David's uncle relies on problematic, stereotypical descriptions of a variety of people of color. Davis biographer Sharon Harris writes openly about Davis's racist tendencies and those are on display here if we read the narrator as a reflection of Davis's views. But it also seems as though Davis is up to something more complicated. Although the uncle stereotypes the woman, even in his defense of her, other elements of the story suggest that the woman has agency, especially when she speaks for herself.

First, she exerts agency by preparing delicious food for her visitors. Despite their arriving unannounced, she offers them a bounty of food. When it's ready, she tells them, "Fall to, young folks; there's plenty of it, sech as it is." The narrator describes "great chunks of hot Johnnycake ... and delicious yellow butter." Notably, David and his sister Polly "'fell to' with good will," making clear that his criticisms of her dwelling and isolation do not prevent him for enjoying the food she prepares.

The story also reveals the woman to be savvy in matters of business. When the uncle asks about the contents of various bags in her "hut," she reveals that she collects roots and other natural goods to sell. She explains that her ginseng will eventually go to China, where "them poor heathen will pay its weight in gold." While offensive, the comment demonstrates that she views herself above people in China in the same way that David sees himself as above her. In other words, she participates in the same problematic hierarchies as David and is not solely a victim but also a perpetrator.

She is also well aware of the value of the mountains around her. When Polly learns that people sometimes find sapphires or rubies nearby, she responds incredulously: "Do you mean that rubies are to be found here—*here?*" The mountain woman wryly comments, "I suppose the folks that live in towns couldn't get along very well without us North Carlinyans. . . . We send 'em lumber and iron and gold and medicine, and even rings for their fingers." By the story's end, the travelers are revealed as the condescending fools and the mountain woman as the talented cook who knows the value of her wares and her home. David finally admits at the story's close, "Instead of being in solitude, she is quite in the centre of things." It seems that in 1885 Davis makes the same points that historians including Ron Eller and David Hsiung make over a century later. That Davis argues for a globally connected Appalachia well aware of its position in a global economy—and how best to capitalize on that position, including by positioning oneself above others—is remarkable, especially since the story's 1885 publication date places it at the beginning of national understandings of Appalachia as a place apart, largely shaped by Local Color literature like Davis's and many who followed her.

Two years before Davis published "The Mountain Hut," lesser-known author Louise Coffin Jones published "In the Highlands of North Carolina" in *Lippincott's Magazine.* As Kevin O'Donnell explains, not much is known about Jones's background except that she taught school for six months in Western North Carolina in the 1870s (234). "In the Highlands of North Carolina" is presumably a travel narrative based on a real trip, one that describes a summer Jones spent in the mountains of North Carolina with two friends. In it, she praises the "*not* luxurious surroundings," writing, "We fancy, however, that the fireplace-cooking tastes the best: certainly nothing in the way of modern conveniences would improve the salt-raised bread, chicken pot-pies, and huge peach-pies."[85] Notably, the women are doing their own cooking and enjoying the experience of "roughing it," but Jones also indicates awareness of their outsider status. She critiques both that status and their stay in the community, echoing Davis's commentary on tourism in the mountains. Jones writes:

> But I am afraid that our lives do not harmonize with our surroundings. With such an environment we ought to be busy from morning till night, hacking or combing flax, carding or spinning wool, or attending to the other duties incipient upon a simple, patriarchal mode of existence. But we lie in our hammocks a good deal, we ramble in the woods or climb mountains, with not even the excuse of going to pick huckleberries, and we take frequent horseback-rides to every point of the compass. We raise nothing, we manufacture nothing, we have nothing to barter: we simply pay cash for all our supplies. (379)

She goes on to explain that "grizzled men" bring the women fish, "barefooted boys" bring berries, and mountain women bring them fruits and vegetables. In descriptions like these, Jones compliments mountain people and their ability to supply the women with fresh food.

But she also points out perceived deficiencies. Near the end of the narrative, she explains that some mountain residents use washbasins as serving bowls at the dinner table. Instead of commending a family's ingenuity to use one item for several purposes, Jones encourages readers to overlook such missteps since the people are "so hospitable and warm-hearted" (385). She ends the essay with an overview of why the highlands serve not only as a fitting vacation spot but also as a suitable place for permanent residence, even though "there are discomforts to be endured" (386). Overall, Jones's discussion of available food in the mountains and of mountain people is far more complimentary than most examples discussed at the beginning of this chapter. Like Davis, she also recognizes her privileged position. In her 1879 piece, "In the Backwoods of Carolina," for example, she describes a woman named Aunt Betsy who must prepare a meal in a "comfortless kitchen." Jones casts Aunt Betsy's daily routine as far less romantic than the cooking Jones and her companions do on their trip: "[Aunt Betsy] made a johnny-cake of Indian meal and baked it on a board in front of the fire, and boiled coffee in a coffee-pot set on the coals. As she bent over the fire, her face red with heat, giving the coffee-pot a spiral twirl or beating a final pat upon the johnny-cake with her broad hand, I thought I could see why she was short-waisted and round-shouldered. Fifty years' cooking by a fireplace, stooping over the hearth an hour or two three times a day, was enough to warp any form."[86]

Even less is known about Elizabeth Wysor Klingberg: she was born in Appalachian Virginia, in Pulaski County. She studied history at Yale University, worked as a teacher in New Haven, and in 1914 married Frank J. Klingberg, a history professor at the University of California at Los Angeles. In 1915 she published "Glimpses of Life in the Appalachian Highlands" in the *Southern Atlantic Quarterly*, a piece that offers a complex, nuanced portrayal of mountain people and their foods. Initially she writes about mountain poverty and inadequate foods: "The food served in [the] home was usually poor and coarse and in the winter months there was no variety, black coffee, bread, molasses and bacon being the staples."[87] But she follows this description with a firm statement about socioeconomic diversity in the mountains: "The term mountain people brings to most minds a picture of more or less level state of society, but it is a great mistake to generalize and to believe that all are either wretchedly poor or comfortably independent. There is as much difference in their flocks and herds, their material wealth and general progress, as in the various strata of a city population. They are alike only in certain peculiarities of outlook and development" (375–376). She devotes several paragraphs to describing living conditions in the "better homes in several states," including a discussion of African-American servants. At one point she observes that young people in these homes may prefer modern furniture, but "the kitchen seems to hold its own and makes an old-time picture, with its heavy iron pots and kettles—some very formidable in size" (376). Klingberg's emphasis on durable, expensive equipment, which has apparently been in the household for a long time, contrasts sharply with Jones's caution not to mock mountain residents for using a washbasin as a serving dish. Even so, Klingberg writes that "mountain civilization is a retarded civilization" and ultimately concludes that they bear "the touch of the primitive" (378).

Food and Social Justice

While David Hunter Strother, Rebecca Harding Davis, and Louise Coffin Jones used depictions of mountain food to both highlight and critique tourism in the mountains from pre–Civil War to post-Reconstruction, and historians like Klingberg emphasized the range of socioeconomic classes in the

mountains, other writers—namely, Frederick Law Olmsted and again, Rebecca Harding Davis—combined culinary descriptions with literary activ-
ism. In both cases, considering how these writers portray food in the mountains reveals advocacy for social justice in different contexts.

Frederick Law Olmsted is best known for his landscape architecture, including his codesign with Calvery Vaux of Central Park in New York City,
and in Appalachia, the grounds for the Biltmore Estate in Asheville, North
Carolina. But Olmsted was also a traveler and a journalist. In 1852 he accepted a position as a travel correspondent with the *New York Daily Times*
(now the *New York Times*) and traveled through the South to observe how
slavery affected Southern agriculture and economics. As literary critic John
Cox explains, Olmsted "assured his editor that [although he would investigate slavery,] he would not argue from a deeply partisan position."[88] Instead,
the three travel narratives that resulted from his trips in the South—*A Journey in the Seaboard Slave States*, *A Journey through Texas*, and *A Journey in the
Back Country*—explain in great detail how "the South was being ruined by
the institution of slavery."[89] His critiques of slavery focused not on the moral
wrongs of the practice but instead on its inefficiency.

A Journey in the Back Country, published in 1860, includes a chapter called
"The Highlanders" that includes detailed descriptions of mountain food.
Like his contemporary David Hunter Strother, Olmsted's portrayals of that
cuisine are more complimentary than one might expect given mountain food
descriptions that appear postwar, though he does complain about the fact
that "every thing was greasy."[90] But Olmsted also makes the case that travelers
like himself find the worst conditions—including foods served—in slave-
owning homes. Unlike pro-South literature depicting delicious foods prepared by enslaved people, in "The Highlanders" readers encounter depraved
people who seem utterly unable to provide a proper meal, whereas the non-
slaveholders supply much more acceptable fare.

He describes his visit to northeastern Tennessee, where he spent one night
with a wealthy slaveholding man and another night with a nonslaveholding
farmer. Olmsted explains, "The slaveholder was much the wealthier of the two...
but he lived in much less comfort than the other" and "the food at the table [was] badly cooked" (269). Conversely, "The house of the farmer without
slaves, though not in good repair, was much neater, and every thing within
was well-ordered and unusually comfortable" (269). He emphasizes the absence of a servant and remarks that "the table was abundantly supplied with

the most wholesome food—I might almost say the first wholesome food—I have had set before me since I was at the hotel at Natchez—loaf bread for the first time, chickens, stewed instead of fried, potatoes without fat, two sorts of simple preserved fruit, and whortleberry and blackberry pies. (The first time I have had any of these articles at a private house since I was in Western Texas)" (269–270). Instead of treating his experiences as isolated events, he draws general conclusions from them, explaining to readers, "It is a common saying with the drovers and wagoners of this country, that if you wish to be well taken care of, you must not stop at houses where they have slaves" (270). There are several things to note about Olmsted's rhetoric in passages like this one: he does not equate food choices with morality. Instead, according to Olmsted's logic, the yeoman farmer is better able to provide wholesome food because he runs a more efficient farm. Second, when compared with David Hunter Strother's positive depictions of the culinary scene in Appalachian Tennessee in the 1850s—notably the same area Olmsted writes about in the above passage and roughly during the same time—Olmsted is concerned not with depicting high civilization but rather with making a comparative case. But both Strother and Olmsted comment upon the abundance of food in the mountains and serve as important contrasts to the depictions that follow postwar, when the rest of the country begins to conceive of Appalachia as a distinct region.

Social justice also informs Rebecca Harding Davis's work. The same trip to Western North Carolina that inspired her to write "The Yares of the Black Mountains" also provided research material for a story called "Qualla." Sharon Harris contends that the story is "one of her most important works of the period," as it "combined her interests in Native Americans and North Carolina. It also . . . signaled a change in her attitudes, informed by firsthand exposure to Native American life and by the tensions between the Cheyenne and the US government that would develop in the next year into the Great Sioux War" (173). Distraught by the lack of attention given to Cherokee people during this time, Davis makes her agenda clear near the conclusion of the story: "I honestly acknowledge that my motive in writing this paper has been to ask the question, What can be done in the North for [Cherokee] people? I have tried to describe Qualla and the neighboring white population precisely as I saw them last summer, with the hope that I could make clear the difficulties that hedge these poor Indians, and convey to others the pathetic appeal which they made to me."[91]

In turn, Davis uses pathos to elevate Cherokee people above their white mountain neighbors, encouraging reading audiences to support her Cherokee advocacy. In part she does so by arguing that they are a superior people, and in part she does so by way of the kitchen. Although Davis and her traveling party encounter appealing fare at various points during their journey to Qualla from Asheville, especially at the Smathers Inn in Waynesville, she also highlights unsavory mountain food. Historian Bruce Stewart reads Davis's descriptions of white mountaineers in the story as complimentary, arguing that Davis praises "highlanders for their primitive lifestyle," but if they are complimentary, her descriptions are also condescendingly judgmental.[92] She describes their "unlighted log huts, split into half by an open passage-way, and swarming with children, who lived on hominy and corn-bread, with a chance opossum now and then as a relish," and she notes their lack of knives, forks, or dishes, ultimately describing them as "contented and good-natured . . . honest folk" (577). Yet these white mountaineers are not the people Davis highlights as worthy of social assistance. Instead, she describes similar conditions Cherokee people endure, making clear that they are a more appropriate focus for uplift.

Upon visiting a "miserable" hut where a Cherokee woman named Llan-zi lives, Davis highlights her lack of proper cooking and eating utensils by describing her "sole household property, the pot in which she had mixed the corn and beans early in the morning, leaving them to simmer: when they were cooked the whole family would squat around the pot, eating with wooden ladles." Davis explains that she visited many similar huts, but "the faces of these people, [she] is bound to confess, were of a far higher type than those of the same class of whites, American, English or Irish, would have been in a like condition" (583). She goes on to describe visits that she and her travel companions also made to more wealthy Cherokee homes: "The iron pot and wooden spoons were still the table furniture, but a little shelf on the wall with half a dozen cups and saucers of white stoneware, kept for show in beautiful glistening condition, hinted at a latent aesthetic taste" (584). According to Davis's domestic descriptions in "Qualla," Cherokee people are thus most deserving of aid, especially considering their treatment before and after Removal. Unlike her defense of the mountain woman in "The Mountain Hut," here Davis uses food and kitchen equipment descriptions to signal superiority.

Fertile Fields and Good Water

When writers weren't equating inferior foods with inferior people, or writing positively about mountain food to critique tourism, or commenting on

culinary scenes to make a larger social point, some of them—like James Lane
Allen—were writing about the virtues of agriculture to emphasize the region's suitability for extractive industry. Others wrote splendid reviews of the
pure, clean water in Appalachia to lure tourists to expensive spas and hotels,
where they could experience the healing waters.

As discussed earlier, in 1886 Kentucky writer James Lane Allen wrote about
a mountain man who mistook a bunch of bananas for large green beans. Just
four years later, his writing about conditions in the mountains indicate a
shift away from offensively humorous depictions to a more capitalistic focus, especially when describing agriculture, soil fertility, and available foods.
In "Mountain Passes of the Cumberland" (1890), he writes about his travels
through the Cumberland and marvels at the tremendous agricultural wealth
in the area: "water abundant, clear, and cold; fields heavy with corn and
oats.... The further you go, the more rich and prosperous the land, the kinder
the soil to grains and gardens and orchards; bearing its burden of timbers—
walnut, chestnut, oak, and mighty beeches; lifting to the eye in the near distance cultivated hill-sides and fat meadows. . . . Remember well this valley,
lying along the base of the mountain wall. It has long been known as the gra-
nary of southwest Virginia and east Tennessee; but in time, in the development of civilization throughout the Appalachian region, it is destined to become the seat of a dense pastoral population, supplying the dense industrial
population of new mining and manufacturing towns with milk, butter, eggs,
and fruit and vegetables."[93] As O'Donnell points out, this piece was Allen's
last publication about Appalachia. But in it he makes clear that although
some of the food served to him in the mountains was not acceptable—at
one point he describes a "dinner of corn-bread that would have made a fine
building stone"—he sees the potential profitability of the region's resources
and the land's ability to provide food for workers.[94]

Areas in Appalachia that boasted luxurious hotels, mineral waters, and
warm springs were also quite profitable. As historian Richard Starnes explains, in the early 1800s elite planter families from South Carolina, Georgia, and eastern North Carolina sought refuge from heat and diseases in the
mountains of Western North Carolina, and for those who were not wealthy
enough to purchase a second home, hotels in the area were plentiful.[95] Hot
Springs (then Warm Springs), North Carolina, was a popular destination, as
was White Sulphur Springs in Greenbrier County, West Virginia. As early
as 1835, Phillip Holbrook Nicklin wrote *Letters Descriptive of the Virginia*

Springs, the Roads Leading Thereto, and the Doings Thereat, a text that chronicles Nicklin's six- to seven-week tour in the mountains of Virginia. Nicklin describes the waters at White Sulphur as "very beautiful and tempting,"
due in part to their ability to cure a number of diseases and disorders, from
jaundice to hypocrisy to dyspepsia to diabetes to die-of-any-thing.[96] Likewise,
"Sawney's Deer Lick," a story published in *Scribner's Magazine* in 1895, depicts the value of spring-fed land owned by a mountain man: he is reluctant
to sell it, but with the help of the narrator, he procures a good price for it.[97]

In addition to praising the waters of such resorts, the food was also report-
edly good. In 1859 Henry Colton published a text to promote tourism in Western North Carolina in which he claims that "The products of the vales and
hillsides, when the appetite is taken into consideration, are, too, of a character
such as would make the veriest epicures smile with delight. The butter, milk,
honey, beef, and mutton of the mountains, are unsurpassed."[98] Likewise, in 1877
George Dimmock visited Western North Carolina and stayed at the Warm
Springs Hotel in Madison County, "where, as is usual at hotels in that part of
the South, good meals are served."[99] And in 1911 an article published in *Good
Housekeeping* recommended Skyland, Virginia, for wholesome food.[100]

Culinary Conclusions

As the texts discussed in this chapter reveal, depictions of food in literature
about Appalachia do much more than describe culinary experiences. They
may indicate inferiority or superiority; poke fun at tourists insistent on expe-
riencing "real" mountain life; make commentary on important social issues
including slavery and the lived realities of Cherokee people post-Removal; or
function as selling points for hotels and spas eager to attract wealthy visitors.
Although many culinary descriptions were negative and supported Shapiro's
larger claims about the power of literature to define a region, as this chapter
demonstrates the story is more complicated. What matters in these descriptions is not what people in Appalachia ate in the mid-1800s and early 1900s,
or how appetizing those foods may have been, but rather how descriptions of
that fare served various rhetorical purposes.

CHAPTER 2

Competing Culinary Discourses

Writing Food in Early Twentieth-Century Appalachia

I F DRAMATIC FICTIONAL ACCOUNTS AND EMBELLISHED TRAVEL
writing depictions influenced how the reading public came to view the
eating habits of mountain people—and by extension, the people themselves—then the discussions that Progressive Era reformers had about the
reality of food in the mountains added even more to a growing conversation
about "the mountain problem." Certainly many people in the region, and in
the South more generally, needed help addressing diseases caused by poor
nutrition, sanitation, or both. As historians and American studies scholars
have explored, in the early part of the twentieth century, pellagra presented a
significant health crisis in the South. Caused by a niacin deficiency, the disease causes dermatitis, diarrhea, dementia, and death.[1] At a time when vita-
mins were not well understood, the disease proved vexing to those struggling
to find a cure. Other problems like rickets, caused by a prolonged vitamin D
deficiency; hookworm, an intestinal parasite; and typhoid fever, a dangerous bacterial infection spread through contaminated food or water, were also
common in the South and Appalachia in particular.

As with all large-scale social problems, various groups responded in different ways. For some, like William Goodell Frost and Eleanor Marsh Frost, the
answer began with educating mountain residents. For others, like John C.
Campbell and Olive Dame Campbell, part of their solution also included
documenting and understanding the population to whom they were devoted.
And for still others, like Thomas Robinson Dawley, an immersion in mill life
removed from rural environments was the only remedy for those seeking better nutrition, health, and living standards.

These are only a few examples of a much larger trend at work during the early part of the twentieth century.[2] The American Missionary Association played an important role in identifying the region as one in need of moral, economic, and civic uplift. Churches and schools opened, and out of them flowed farming advice, hygiene classes, and cooking lessons. My goal here is not to chronicle most of those attempts but instead to highlight three varying culinary portraits of Appalachia written by the Frosts, Campbells, and Dawley. Considering these depictions does not reveal a monolithic narrative about pork and cornbread in mountain cabins but instead nuanced accounts of complex culinary worlds that varied widely from one ridge to the next. Emphasizing such complexity did not always work in favor of those seeking to raise funds for mountain mission work or even those in favor of a shift away from the mountains and into the mills; but in each case, the more public the accounts of food in the mountains became, the less nuance they revealed.

All of the examples considered in this chapter are written by nonnative residents, so opportunities to travel through mountain communities comprised an integral part of their research. The details of those trips are discussed in their respective sections below, but the fact that the Frosts, Campbells, and Dawley all spent time documenting their travels through parts of Appalachia links their impressions in important ways. In all three cases, authors describe foods encountered, as well as preparation methods, dining etiquette, and quality of food served. In some cases, such reflections appear only in private diary entries, whereas in other cases they provide draft material for more formal documents, from presentations written for Berea College administrators to fund managers at the Russell Sage Foundation to Bureau of Labor officials in Washington, DC. Studying such documents tells us much about the perceived living conditions of mountain people at the time and about implied authorial motivations. Some of those reports were published to a larger audience, while others have occupied library and foundation shelves in the intervening years, assumed by many to be matter-of-fact accounts. Meanwhile, private diaries, letters, and early report drafts are typically only accessible to those able and willing to spend time in archives, whether digitally or in person.

Though the perspectives offered by these workers are perhaps not the best medium through which to find the unfiltered voices of mountain people, in their pages hide rich, evocative descriptions of how Progressive Era workers viewed mountain people and their surroundings. Reading those accounts allows us glimpses of authorial motivations and traveler impressions, perspectives that over the last century have come to be understood as fact rather than one way of seeing Appalachia and its people. In other words, exploring which aspects of mountain life were highlighted and which were downplayed—especially while considering how a document's purpose shifts with different intended audiences—reveals an unstable narrative about Appalachia, its people, and its culinary history.

William Goodell Frost and Eleanor Marsh Frost

The concept of Appalachia as a "strange land and a peculiar people," one markedly different from the rest of the South and nation, was forming decades before William Goodell Frost became president of Berea College in 1892.[3] But Frost played a pivotal role in furthering the otherness of "our contemporary ancestors"; had he not been so invested in raising funds for Berea College for twenty-eight years, it is hard to imagine how national perceptions of mountain people might be different today.[4]

When Frost took over the presidency of Berea College, the institution was in serious financial trouble. John Gregg Fee had founded the college in 1855, a remarkable feat since it was the first in Kentucky to serve both black and white students, as well as women and men. In 1859, strong proslavery forces drove Fee, his family, and other abolitionists out of the state and Berea College closed until the Civil War was over, when Fee was able to return to Kentucky. By the time Frost assumed his role at the college, tensions were growing about the feasibility of an integrated college in a Southern state. In 1904 Kentucky passed the Day Law, which prohibited integrated education, but even before the law passed Frost had already redirected much of the school's mission to focus on the betterment of "mountain whites."[5]

As early as 1895, nine years before Berea was forced to stop teaching African-American students, Frost was already touting his "discovery" of the mountains to one group in Cincinnati: "I am here to announce to you the discovery of a new world, or at least a grand new division. We are familiar with North America and South America—have you ever heard of Appalachian America? Just as our Western frontier has been lost in the Pacific Ocean we have discovered a new pioneer region in the mountains of the central South."[6] In numerous publications and speeches, Frost lauded the hardy pioneer stock of people who fought at King's Mountain, classifying them as "our kindred of the Boone and Lincoln type."[7]

His best-known publication, "Our Contemporary Ancestors in the Southern Mountains," was published in the *Atlantic Monthly* in 1899. In it, he describes mountain people as caught in a "Rip Van Winkle sleep," insisting that
they have been "beleaguered by nature."[8] Yet at the same time, Frost admon-
ishes his readers that "the mountain folk should inspire more than an an-
tiquarian interest," especially since they belong "to the category of 'native
born.'"[9] In this and many other publications, he casts mountain people as
pure Anglo-Saxon stock worthy of redemption, boldly calling Appalachian
America "a ward of the nation," exclaiming to readers that it is "a ward as we
have never had before."[10] Likewise, in a memorial pamphlet designed to persuade those in charge of the estate of an apparently wealthy Horace Smith,
Frost insists that "these [mountain] people are patriotic, Protestant Americans, ready for Northern leadership. They are God's reserve forces."[11] As in
many accounts written about mountain people in the early twentieth century, Frost paints a simultaneously complimentary and derogatory portrait of
mountain residents. He counters most negative comments with paternalisti-
cally positive ones, suggesting that readers should admire the hardy pioneer
determination of mountain people at the same time they pity their ignorance,
concluding that "the aim should be to make them intelligent without making
them sophisticated."[12]

Frost's fundraising efforts had a profound effect on the way many elites
in America came to view Appalachia. From readers of the *Atlantic Monthly*,
to those interested in financially contributing to mission work in the mountains, to wealthy Northern industrialists to whom Frost appealed for funds,
his depictions of the mountains had far-reaching consequences. On a more
personal level, he was well connected socially and politically, speaking alongside Theodore Roosevelt, corresponding with Booker T. Washington, maintaining a friendship with Southern writer George Washington Cable, and
inviting the likes of Local Colorist John Fox Jr. to visit Berea.

When constructing the image of Appalachia that served his fundraising
goals, Frost also referenced food, though it was not the main focus of his efforts as it was for other progressives like Katherine Pettit, who founded the
Hindman Settlement School with May Stone in 1902. In some instances,
his description of mountain fare supported the image of self-sustaining pioneers, as when he writes about one family that was "supplied from their
own 'boundary' with abundance of corn-meal, string-beans, dried fruit,
'long sweetening' (syrup) and hog meat."[13] It is notable that Frost does not

criticize this list of foods but rather uses words like "abundance" to describe the family's rations.

But in other instances, Frost publicly criticizes mountain diets, as in an interview he gives describing the college, its goals, and why he accepted his role as president. In signature Frost fashion, he touts the toughness of mountain people, at which point the reporter comments, "They must have fine physiques." Frost replies, "In the Civil War they were the finest specimens of manhood in the Union army. In the Spanish-American War this was not true." When the reporter muses, "I wonder why," Frost responds: "I lay it to the wheat biscuits! They do not make bread. When they made their cakes out of corn, they had a wholesome food, but now that they eat hot biscuits three times a day, they don't develop so well. We are trying to show a better way in our Berea kitchens."[14]

For anyone unfamiliar with the beaten biscuit crusade led by reformers Katherine Pettit and May Stone, Frost's comment seems bizarre. But read within that context, it appears that Frost criticizes the culinary reform Pettit and Stone were promoting. As Elizabeth Engelhardt has explored, mountain women took cooking lessons at the Hindman Settlement School (roughly 115 miles from Berea) where they were taught that labor-intensive beaten biscuits were superior to cornbread. Beaten biscuits—made using imported ingredients (wheat) and expensive equipment (ovens and marble slabs)—were considered the food of the civilized, whereas cornbread—made using local ingredients (corn) and requiring little equipment other than a skillet and a fire—was considered the bread of uncivilized mountain folk.[15] Given Frost's insistence that Appalachia harbored "our contemporary ancestors," it seems surprising that in this instance, he defends their consumption of corn and even promotes it at Berea. But as foodways scholar Katharina Vester explains, during the early years of the American republic, corn came to represent American democracy and a pull away from Britain and its pretentious reliance on wheat or rye, which were considered superior grains.[16] Given Frost's insistence that mountain people represented the essence of American patriotism, his defense of corn makes sense.

It is also possible that instead of critiquing the efforts of Pettit and Stone, Frost may have been most interested in promoting what he believed was the route to good health for mountain residents. Frost helped write an undated booklet called "The Two Secrets of Health" that proclaims the "secrets of health and long life" are to "Keep the bowels open and the feet warm."[17] In order to keep the bowels open, the booklet advises readers to "Drink a great deal of pure water. . . . Eat little meat. Graham bread and corn bread are better than white bread. Raw cabbage is better than cooked cabbage, turnips are better than potatoes, sorghum molasses or honey are better than sugar. Hot wheat biscuits which ball up in the stomach are especially bad." Like much nutritional advice of the time, the recommendations made here are most concerned with proper digestion.

Regardless of his motivation behind the comments against wheat biscuits, neither publication—the newspaper article nor the booklet—reached a wide audience. So, whether Frost "sided" with mountain reliance on cornmeal or simply wanted residents to avoid biscuit-induced constipation, the impact of his comments was likely minimal. But the reading public was receiving messages from more public outlets about mountain people's food access and preferences. In 1896, an article by J. Cleveland Cady called "A Summer Outing in Kentucky" appeared in the *Outlook* magazine. Fundraisers at Berea College excerpted selections from the article and published them in a booklet called "Berea Commencement," stating at the top, "We hope [this booklet] may bring us other visitors at commencement time."[18] This particular publication detail matters, because it signals not only an acceptance of the article's content by Berea officials but also a promotion of it. This promotion is telling given its negative portrayal of mountain people.

Early in the article, Cady wryly comments that over five thousand people were present and "perhaps one's first thought would be that an interest in education had drawn together these pilgrims. Observation, however, soon dispels that idea, and it is seen to be a grand social function." Cady goes on to list the various reasons one might attend the event, from meeting old friends to swapping horses, also mentioning "the most abandoned indulgence in bananas, watermelon, lemonade, and peanuts."[19] Here Cady implies that the foods listed are not items mountain people would have consumed on a regular basis. As discussed in the last chapter, bananas were imported and not likely to appear in many rural areas; watermelons grew in the region but were only available seasonally; and lemons and peanuts did not grow locally.

But the list that Cady uses deserves closer examination. Bananas often appear in writing about Appalachia as a symbol of imported, exotic fruit accessible only to those with the most financial and cultural capital. Cady's article was published in 1896, only ten years after James Lane Allen's "Through the Cumberland Gap on Horseback," in which a mountain man mistakes bananas for beans. As discussed later in this chapter, Dawley, for example, uses the appearance of bananas in the mountains as a kind of litmus test for civility. As discussed in chapter 4, Appalachian Cratis Williams writes about feeling "poor and ashamed" on a train trip from Kentucky to Ohio as he and his family eat the food his mother packed for the journey.[20] Williams's father realizes that his family feels embarrassed and buys them bananas (or "banannies"), the first that Williams ever sees or eats.

The watermelon reference proves less straightforward. As David Shields explains in response to my questions about watermelons in late nineteenth-century Kentucky, "C. S. Brent's Seeds in Lexington [roughly forty miles north of Berea] operated from 1874 until well into the twentieth century [and they] offered seed for 10 varieties."[21] Certainly people in and around Berea would have had access to watermelon seeds if they could afford to purchase them and if they had space to cultivate them. Thus it seems unlikely that watermelon would be a culinary novelty. Instead, here Cady seems to play on long-established stereotypes of watermelon-eating Southern African-Americans, a trope also discussed in the previous chapter. In doing so, Cady implies an equivalency between African-Americans and "mountain whites," suggesting that although there are visual differences of color, when it comes to greedy consumption of a sweet melon, the two are one and the same. As we see elsewhere, it presumably does not occur to Cady that someone could be African-American *and* mountain. Even so, Cady's implication supports Berea's target student population—"mountain whites" and African-American students—who continued to study together at Berea College for eight more years. Students of color and mountain students were often portrayed as in equal need of education.

Cady's depiction of indulgence in lemonade seems more plausible: although lemonade is a hallmark Southern beverage, the lemons used to make it would have had to be imported to a climate like Berea's. But as food writer Ronni Lundy points out, "even those who might not have had actual lemonade would have had plenty of the version made of sumac."[22] Peanuts are also an interesting inclusion. A legume probably originating in South America and introduced to North America by Africans, the peanut was originally thought of as "slave food."[23] Moreover, foodways scholar David Shields explains that by the 1830s, the peanut was "a favorite city treat" and "an emblem of distinctly American urban foodways."[24] Read within this context, the list of foods that Cady describes signal an opportunity for people in the area surrounding Berea College to experience the exotic, to eat their way into a different, more civilized experience, if only for an afternoon. For college officials, the eager consumption they witnessed justified their outreach efforts.

Had Cady's comment stopped at the description of foods consumed, readers might be left with the impression that commencement provided a way for mountain people to enjoy a wider variety of foods than those typically available. But Cady soon assumes a voyeuristic tone: "As we watch the visitors, the grotesque appearance of many of them adds great zest to the occasion."[25] Suddenly the mountain people who have traveled to Berea for commencement day are described as "grotesque," rendering them a special kind of mountain spectacle who provide just as much entertainment for Cady as commencement day does for them. Those who do not have frequent access to imported foods thus become humorous oddities instead of curious travelers eager to try new things.

Thus although Frost seems at times to have described mountain diets without criticism and at other times to have defended them, the more public message that readers received—and the one that Berea promoted—was one in which mountain people subsisted on a limited diet, and when given the chance to consume different foods, they did so in record numbers, the most grotesque of them leading the way. But if the public message was one of mountaineers beleaguered by nature, the private one revealed in Eleanor Marsh Frost's diaries was far more complex.

As historian Deborah Blackwell explains, the chain of events that brought Eleanor Marsh Frost to Berea was anything but linear. She grew up on a farm in Wisconsin, later attending Oberlin College, where she worked as a nanny for William Goodell Frost, his first wife Louise, and their three children. After Louise died unexpectedly in 1890 and Eleanor graduated in 1891, she and William married. In 1892, William accepted the offer to serve as president of Berea. Blackwell explains: "Thus in 1892 Eleanor Marsh Frost, twenty-nine years old, only a year married to a widower nine years her senior, and stepmother to three small boys, found herself a college president's wife in a rural town in central Kentucky."[26] As private letters between Eleanor (or Ellen or Ella) and family members reveal, she had a difficult time adjusting at first. But as she and William became better established, going on to have two children together, Eleanor became an advocate for the college and was instrumental in fundraising efforts.

Since Eleanor was largely unfamiliar with the Appalachian region and its people, trips made into the mountains were crucial in helping her understand the area. In her diaries she documented three trips into the mountains, with the first one occurring in 1893, then again in 1906, and in 1914 she spent the better part of two months traveling through the mountains of Kentucky, Virginia, North Carolina, and Tennessee with her son Cleveland and Miss Olive Sinclair, a Berea English teacher. Special Collections at Berea College house not only the diaries that Eleanor kept while traveling but also the reports she wrote for college administrators upon her return. She was careful to document the state of homes she visited, including kitchens, meals served, and presumed health of residents.

The culmination of Eleanor's trips, both in private diary form and in report form, reveals what seems an honest portrait of a diverse region. During her 1893 trip, she details having a supper with Mr. Jimmie Click and his family, where she is served "cornbread, biscuits, ham, chicken, coffee, milk, jam, apple sauce."[27] During her 1906 trip, she depicts an even more prosperous situation at the home of Jake Terry, where she finds "on the table chicken, cornbread, plain biscuit, honey, apple sauce, chowchow, buttermilk, coffee, raw onions, sweet potato, boiled cabbage, beans," and even "steel knives and fork." And in Virginia in 1914, she describes Mrs. Emory Robinett's linoleum kitchen floors and revolving server "filled with pie (meringue), cake (layer), beans, chicken, tomatoes, molasses, three kinds jelly, everything well cooked." Eleanor's emphasis on steel cutlery and kitchen luxuries like a revolving table indicates each family's middle- to upper-class social standing, at least within their respective communities.

Conversely, she also writes openly about wrenching poverty, poor sanitation, and inadequate nutrition. During October of the 1906 trip, she describes one house in which the pillowcases were black, "kitchen awful. Everything filthy . . . I ate as little as possible of things sterilized by boiling." At another location later that month, she writes about dirty beds, mice "scurrying in the ceiling above," and "biscuit solid, cornbread unbaked, no meat, no eggs." Likewise, in July of 1914 she encounters a "three-year-old lying on dirty kitchen floor, sick [with] fever, covered with flies . . . dirt unspeakable" and another home with bedbugs in which it was "impossible to eat." But what is remarkable about these entries is that unlike many other reformers of her time, in the official reports Eleanor writes based on her diaries, she includes both perspectives.

In her report chronicling the 1906 trip, she writes, "In one valley there will be the extreme of poverty and degradation. The worst things ever said about the mountain people can be found in a valley, but in the next one are evidences of thrift and character. People struggling hard to maintain decency and good order." In reports from both the 1906 and 1914 trips, Eleanor recommends to administrators that anyone who teaches at Berea should immerse themselves in mountain travel as much as possible, wishing that every Berea worker could teach six months in a mountain school before beginning work. In her 1914 report, she concludes, "It seems to me far more important that northern teachers should know the mountains than that mountain teachers should go to northern schools, though this last is important."

At a time when publications were full of sensationalized, problematic depictions of mountain people, Eleanor's diary entries and resulting reports are a welcome departure from the norm. But we must also keep in mind that her audience was one of college administrators, a population presumably already committed to serving its mountain students. While some readers may need more convincing than others of the virtues of mountain people, her audience was far easier to convince than her husband's national one.

Their purposes were also entirely different. While William was trying to raise money for the school, Eleanor was trying to make recommendations about best practices for teachers at Berea. After her travels she also made pragmatic suggestions like how to best teach domestic science courses to women who would likely return to homes without electricity or running water. Even so, she aspired to prepare women for more modern conveniences as well: "I would like to have one house which could be visited by all departments which would have all the conveniences possible on a farm. I would like the Delco lighting system, and a water system not dependent on the main plant but with the creeks as a source of supply."[28] In other words, Eleanor did not need to try to convince her audience to feel sympathy for mountain people as much as she needed to spur them to action. But her husband needed to incite as much pathos as possible. Even though at times William wrote about abundance in the mountains, his primary message was one of deprivation. The same was true of other publications about residents in the mountains, and as a result, we are left with portrayals of grotesques gorging on bananas instead of people in need or prosperous women with linoleum floors.

John C. Campbell, Olive Dame Campbell, and Grace Buckingham Campbell

John C. and Olive Dame Campbell provide yet another fascinating case study of how one Progressive Era couple wrote about Appalachia and its food habits. The public message was one of depravity and limited options, while the private one was far more nuanced. Careful analysis of a variety of documents written by John, his first wife Grace, and his second wife Olive reveals that purpose and audience mean everything when writing about Appalachian people and their culinary traditions. In the case of John, the more public his writing becomes, the less it criticizes the efforts of other Progressive Era reformers, like Katherine Pettit and May Stone. For Olive, private diary entries illustrate a diverse food scene in the mountains, one that she often enjoys. And for Grace, her private entries depict her as a young, nervous wife eager to fit into the community in which she and John are living. If anything, she wants to please the women of her community with her cooking, not overturn their dietary habits.

Contemporaries of Pettit and Stone, the Campbells were every bit as interested in the state of things in the mountains as those two women, from the food mountain people grew to the way it was prepared. But as Hindman was being founded, the Campbells were at work in a much different way. John C. Campbell had finished a bachelor of divinity degree in 1895 from Andover Theological Seminary in Massachusetts, married Grace H. Buckingham, and moved to Joppa, Alabama, to serve as principal of a new American Missionary Association (AMA) school.

After Grace died in 1905, John took a therapeutic trip to Scotland in 1907, where he met Olive Dame, a well-educated woman from Medford, Massachusetts, who shared John's sense of adventure and impulse to help those in need. Soon after their marriage that same year, the couple secured a $3,000 grant from the recently formed Russell Sage Foundation, and in the fall of 1908 they began conducting a social survey of the Southern highlands, traveling through the mountains of Tennessee, Kentucky, Georgia, West Virginia, and North Carolina, concluding in the early months of 1909. Olive kept a diary chronicling her experiences, and together for the next decade she and John worked to assemble a book about their travels and observations.[29] After John died in 1919, Olive finished compiling the book, though it was published under his name in 1921 as *The Southern Highlander and His Homeland*.

This authorial detail makes it impossible to know precisely which sections were written by John and which by Olive, adding another layer of complexity to questions about authorial intent and audience reactions.

When we juxtapose portrayals of mountain cuisine from *The Southern Highlander and His Homeland*—a book clearly meant for publication—with more private documents written by John, Grace, and Olive, we uncover interesting similarities and contradictions. Although the book makes clear that John was largely critical of what he saw as unreasonable or problematic attempts to "civilize" mountain people—and even though early sections of the book clearly distinguish between classes of people and the food they consume—those nuanced distinctions essential in preventing the stereotypical homogenization of a region and its people become blurred as the book progresses.

In chapter 5, Campbell[30] distinguishes between three social classes, the first "made up of urban and near-urban folk," the second and largest "of the more or less prosperous rural folk," and a small third class of "those with small and usually poor holdings, in distant coves, at the heads of streams, and on the mountain and hillsides, tenants, and all who have found it impossible to adapt themselves to the changes taking place."[31] Campbell spends a considerable amount of time describing the foods consumed by each class, remarking upon the "pleasing picture of comfort and simplicity" one takes from a meal like one enjoyed at Uncle Big Jim Franklin's, who served a number of foods, including "pork . . . fried potatoes, cornbread, hot biscuits, honey, apple-butter and jellies of various sorts, canned peaches, sorghum, coffee, sweet milk and buttermilk, fried chicken, and fried eggs" (84). But in a home of the second class, the "less bountiful table" lacks "milk, butter, and eggs, breads made of white flour, jellies, and preserves" (86). Campbell concludes that the food of the third class "in quantity, variety, and preparation is much inferior to that found in even the more modest homes of the second class" (88). In this carefully edited book-length account of Appalachian people, Campbell painstakingly delineates varying food options available depending on socio-economic status.

Yet just one year after John and Olive conclude their tour of the highlands, in a letter expressing concern about early marriages and infant mortality rates among mountain people in mill towns, he writes the following to John M. Glenn at the Russell Sage Foundation: "My observation has been, in the mountains, that there is little difference, between poor and moderately well to do, in the kinds of food consumed."[32] Such a statement obviously contradicts the class divisions established in *The Southern Highlander and His Homeland*, and we are left questioning the difference between a public audience of many and a private audience of one.

Purpose matters a great deal in analyzing these statements: in his letter to Glenn at the Russell Sage Foundation, John tries to argue that food available in the mills is not superior to food in the mountains: "I have been somewhat perplexed by the statement of those who claim to have studied, impartially, the mill situation, that the health of the mountain people is greatly improved when they go to the mills, by better food."[33] He opposes the migration of people in the mountains to mill towns, so in this instance it is to his argumentative advantage to assert little difference in culinary habits between classes.

Campbell's private letter also reveals judgments that are less apparent in the much more public *The Southern Highlander and His Homeland*. When discussing the trend of early marriages in mill towns, he references a "certain animalism or unmoral condition" of mountain people.[34] Campbell also makes clear to Glenn that he does not deem mountain people capable of making good food choices once they have easier access to "more stimulating food and high priced canned goods," especially since "even the best food loses its value when improperly prepared, and the mountain women and girls do not change their method of food preparation when they go to the mills."[35] This last statement implies a perceived culinary deficit among mountain women and a general lack of domestic know-how. Although *The Southern Highlander and His Homeland* notes similar problems, its tone implies that with enough support, such wayward women can be reformed. We should also keep in mind that John wrote the letter in 1910, and between then and the time of his death nine years later, he may have developed a more nuanced view of the region and its class divisions, which is reflected in the book.

Even so, those nuances become less defined as the book progresses. Although the summary discussion about food near the end of the book recognizes those differences to an extent, the primary focus seems to be on "what food is eaten in the ordinary rural home in the mountains."[36] After providing a fairly extensive overview of those foods and preparation methods, including the praise that "A real attempt is made to provide a winter supply of vegetables and fruit," the book concludes that "Food is usually poorly prepared. Frying and boiling are the common methods of preparation, the former predominating largely . . . whatever is fried, is fried a long time, large quantities of grease being used both in preparing and serving" (200).

Whatever Campbell thought about the taste of fried foods, the paramount concern was almost certainly one of digestion. In the late 1800s and early 1900s, scientists began to understand more about calories as they applied to food, as well as the varying nutritional value of different foods. There were, of course, misunderstandings: historian Helen Zoe Veit explains that "As late as 1911, the U.S. government nutritionist Charles Langworthy argued that fruits and vegetables were nutritionally void."[37] But virtually everyone participating in conversations about nutrition agreed that American food generally—and mountain food specifically—contained too much grease. In 1860, for example, Dr. Jno. Stainback Wilson writes about the proliferation of pork on a national scale, especially in the South and West: "For in many parts of this region, so far as meat is concerned, it is fat bacon and pork, fat bacon and pork only ... but the frying is not confined to the meat alone; for we have fried vegetables of all kind, fried fritters and pancakes often, fried bread not unfrequently, and indeed fried everything that is fryable." He goes on to explain that consuming so many greasy foods poses quite the health risk: "Grease being the most indigestible of all things, it is not strange that dyspepsia, fevers, liver complaint, skin diseases, and various inflammatory affections be so prevalent among a people who have everything swimming in grease."[38] He insists that hog grease is not the nutritious elixir that many believed it to be, and he warns Southern white women in particular to avoid the substance.[39]

As discussed in the previous chapter, landscape architect, conservationist, and author Frederick Law Olmsted made a similar observation in 1860 about the popularity of grease, specifically in mountain foods. Near Murphy, in Western North Carolina, he describes enjoying a meal in which "the table supply was abundant and various. Yet every thing was greasy; even what we call simple dishes, such as boiled rice, and toast, were served soaking in a sauce of melted fat."[40] Readers find similar complaints about "too much fry" in both in *The Southern Highlander and His Homeland* and in Olive's private diary entries, each occurring respectively sixty-one and forty-nine years after Olmsted's trip. Read within the historical context in which these criticisms are made, reducing the abundance of fried food provided one important way in which Progressive Era workers could improve mountain people and their diets.[41] Likewise, the fact that the Campbells continued to report on the perceived problem of too much grease signals the continuation of a criticism that was well established before they began their trip through the mountains.

Yet near the end of *The Southern Highlander and His Homeland*, it becomes clear that depictions of greasy food do much more than alert readers to the presumed cause of mountain indigestion. The Campbells place the blame of insufficient or improper foods on the deficient moral character of mountain people: "It would seem likely that to the limitations of diet are due also some of the inertia and even apathy that are evidenced by many. Tall and lean the Highlander seems to have, when interested, plenty of endurance; he can walk long distances without apparent fatigue, and he is indefatigable on a hunting or camping trip.... By some, however, the indolence of the mountaineer is laid to lack of purpose, while others attribute it to hookworm" (202). Language linking height and body composition to endurance evokes uncomfortable connections to biological racism, and Campbell emphasizes that some—though the text does not identify who—insist the "indolence of the mountaineer" responsible for "limitations of diet" stems from either laziness or illness. Notably, there is no mention of economic standing, crop yield, farming know-how, or any number of other factors that would play a part in food availability.

Perhaps the most salient example of how audience and purpose shape the ways in which the Campbells write about food in the mountains does not reference food at all, at least not in its most public form. The beginning of *The Southern Highlander and His Homeland* is written in first-person-plural point of view, so readers learn about "our school," and John is called "the Professor," which raises even more questions about authorship.[42] The opening pages tell the story of a pupil named Myrtle who changed the way the Campbells viewed their work in the mountains. The narrator explains the many successes of their students, noting that some of their male graduates attended state universities, one went to Yale, and others "would become ministers and lawyers of promise" (6). But as Myrtle's story indicates, the outlook for female students was not so bright. She tells the Professor that she plans to quit school, and when he asks her why, she replies, "What's the use of educating me? I'm only a girl.... Don't you see what's happening? The best boys, the only kind I would want to marry, don't stay here when they finish school. There's nothing ahead fer me but to stay home and let my men-folks support me, or to marry someone I don't want now I been to school. (I'm wanting things I can't have. I'd better be left in my ignorance)." At the Professor's urging, Myrtle stays in school, but the narrator calls her case "a bitter failure" (6). Rhetorically speaking, Myrtle's story demonstrates humility, showing that not all of the Campbells' efforts were successful, while also laying bare the gross gender inequalities of the time. But what Myrtle's story does not do is criticize the kind of domestic instruction offered to mountain women at the time, particularly those who either could not attend school or did but found themselves facing the same dilemma as Myrtle.

In a conference paper entitled "Social Betterment in the Southern Mountains," delivered at the thirty-sixth annual National Conference of Charities and Correction June 9–16, 1909, and printed in full in the conference proceedings, John does just that. John begins the talk by stating, "My subject is one that presents difficulties at the outset."[43] He immediately criticizes popular portrayals of mountain people that cast them as degenerate hillbillies, admonishing his audience, "We cannot generalize. The mountain region of the Southern Appalachians includes in places wide and fertile valleys and other long trough-like valleys, occupied by people able to supply their own needs" (130). He goes on to distinguish between prosperous and needy groups in the region, reminding his audience that they, presumably other socially minded activists, had decided that "education was the 'cure-all'" (131). To make his point that education was not a simple antidote to the mountain problem, he recounts a story about opening a school in the mountains presumably based on his past experiences in Alabama, Tennessee, and Georgia. He boasts of the success of some of the male graduates, one of whom attended Harvard and another Yale, but then he tells the story of a girl named Amanda, who came to their desk and said,

> I am going to leave school. What is the use of educating me—I am only a girl, one of many in the family. . . . You have taken me and lifted me above the level of my family. You have given me a glimpse of better things— things that cannot be realized in my surroundings. The best boys of the community who have accepted what you have taught them have gone elsewhere, and I am left to become a burden on my parents, dissatisfied with my home, or to marry a boy above whom you have lifted me. You would have done better to have left me in my ignorance (132).

Though the names (Amanda instead of Myrtle) and the phrasing are different, the story is clearly a different version of the same one that appears in *The Southern Highlander and His Homeland*. As in the other version, John uses this story to interrogate the impact education has on people living in the mountains, particularly women, whom he compares to tapers left to burn themselves out.[44] To remedy the problem, he asserts, "Under the impelling logic of this girl's plaint, we persuade those in charge that something more ought to be done to prepare for the life that must be lived in the community" (133). At this point in the essay, John's advice—which falls squarely in line with gender norms of the time—seems sincere, until he continues, with apparent sarcasm, "and we perhaps secure a domestic science teacher, who instructs our girls that 'Pillsbury's best brand of wheat flour and fresh compressed yeast every day are absolutely necessary for successful housekeeping,' and she distributes to the women in the community who cannot read, a pretty magazine, 'The Kitchen Queen,' to teach them how to make macaroons and Charlotte Russe" (133). Instead of continuing, the paragraph ends abruptly, and John's audience is left to ponder the practicality of a dessert like macaroons, which calls for imported ingredients including coconut, or a molded cake requiring specialized baking equipment and the proverbial Maraschino cherry on top.

When compared with the version from *The Southern Highlander and His Homeland*, we see that not only was John dissatisfied with opportunities available to women who receive a formal education, but he also seems disdainful of the domestic instruction they received from Progressive Era workers. As foodways scholar Elizabeth Engelhardt has explored, Hindman Settlement School workers Katherine Pettit and May Stone were determined to rid mountain kitchens of cornbread and replace it with beaten biscuits, believing beaten biscuits represented higher civility.[45] Considered within that context, John's cutting remarks about "Pillsbury's best brand of wheat flour and fresh compressed yeast every day" seem an obvious criticism of the type of culinary instruction Progressive Era workers like Pettit and Stone promoted.

In a draft of that same paper—the most private rendering of the essay, available only through the Southern Historical Collection at UNC Chapel Hill—John abandons using implied sarcasm to criticize such efforts and instead does so openly, adding several more sentences to the paragraph about Myrtle/Amanda: "If the angels have a sense of humor—and Heaven would hardly be Heaven unless they have—a smile must lighten their tear stained faces to see illiterate women bending over a high class magazine to better their cuisine with high grade flour, that would be doubled in cost by its twenty mile haul from the railroad. May not the same pitying angels doubt the miracle of making Charlotte Rousse [*sic*] and Macaroons from salt meat and corn meal, the sole viands of these women?"[46] On the one hand, John's critique illustrates the absurdity of recommending that mountain women within a subsistence-based economy gather cash funds to purchase imported foods to make desserts that seem frivolous in comparison to meal mainstays like hog and hominy.

But on the other hand, John takes a superior tone here, turning the illiterate women about whom he is writing into a source of amusement, as though any efforts to sophisticate them are laughable since such people are clearly not redeemable. Perhaps John recognized the problematic nature of the passage and eliminated it from the conference version of the paper. The draft form differs from the final version in other ways, too, including, for example, this directive: "Imagine yourself tossing in fever on an unclean bed, the windows and doors shut tight at night to keep out the dangerous night air, and if you are fed at all, you are fed perhaps with pork or cabbage as a delicacy." Presumably he thought better of including dramatic portrayals like this one and several others in his final conference paper.

These three different versions of the same story illustrate well the impact that audience and purpose have on writing about Appalachia, its people, and the food that they consume. In its most private form, John's criticisms about culinary reform are explicitly clear. Although his portrayal of mountain women is deeply problematic, he recognizes the absurdity of recommending unattainable, impractical ingredients for everyday cooking. In a paper delivered to colleagues and published in the proceedings of the conference—a publication intended primarily for those in his field—John's criticisms are less scathing but still present. In *The Southern Highlander and His Homeland*, the most public and widely read account of his impressions about the region, the criticism is eliminated altogether. It appears that the more public these documents become, the less they question Progressive Era work, especially regarding domestic intervention, and the more they rely on generalizations palatable to a national audience.

In the examples discussed above, the same story takes on a dramatically different meaning in each version. Similarly, careful analysis of the private diary Olive kept during her highland tour with John from 1908 to 1909 provides a much more complex portrayal of food in the mountains than the one presented in *The Southern Highlander and His Homeland*. First, it is important to note that Olive seems unable to see the people with whom they stayed—who offered her and John a variety of foods that were often imported—as identifiable with the region, seeing only those who needed reform as "mountain." She seems to miss the point that people living in the mountains who functioned in a higher social class were not participating in a regional food economy but rather a global one. To Olive, her hosts did not seem to "count" as mountaineers, suggesting that a lower social standing and perhaps a long family history in the region was necessary for that categorization.

Another notable aspect of Olive's diary is that many of her descriptions of the food mountain people consume are based on secondhand reports, while her own observations of the food proffered are quite positive. For example, upon staying at the Dickey Hotel "on the other side of Knoxville," she remarks that "the food was excellent—heaps of fried chicken, hot biscuit, meat etc, etc."[47] Likewise, when she and John visit "Miss Berry's School," the precursor to Berry College, she describes their meal as "a delicious supper of fried chicken, toast, tea and jelly—gelatin with real cream and nice tea. A fire also in that room" (37). In instances like these and more, she depicts fried chicken as comforting food welcomed by the weary traveler.

One exception occurs with their stay at a "nice modern little hotel" in Williamsburg, Kentucky, with running water and "good table service (with too much fry as usual)," but for the most part it seems that she and John are provided with good meals at the same time they are noting deficiencies in mountain diets according to information they receive from their hosts (66). While in Williamsburg, for example, they meet with Mr. Hibbs and Dr. Ellison, who are running a school, and who note "a good deal of typhoid and great ignorance of the sanitary and culinary side. Need of teaching cooking especially. Had little food and did not know how to cook—that this is a great source of the sickness" (67). Through comments like these, Olive highlights a pressing need in the community, but she never seems to note the paradox that while portions of the population suffer from lack of quality food, others consistently offer a bountiful table.

Information about the need for culinary reform comes not only from their hosts but also from the larger social welfare landscape. In an entry dated November 13, 1908, Olive includes notes presumably taken during the Hearing of the President's Committee, Rural Research, at Knoxville, Tennessee. She notes U.S. Public Health and Marine Hospital Service geologist Dr. Charles Waddell Stiles's assertion that "Lack of ambition in mountain people and mill operatives is result of disease, hookworm, etc.—anemia" (59). Stiles's mention of lack of ambition echoes Campbell's statement about the "indolence of the mountaineer" in *The Southern Highlander and His Homeland*, signaling a common discursive trend when discussing Appalachia and its people.

Stiles also apparently also spoke on the great need to "send out women to teach cookery, food-chewing" (59). Such advice likely seems offensive or strange to contemporary audiences, as though food chewing is a skill that must be taught to adults. Instead, Stiles was almost certainly referencing the teachings of Horace Fletcher, a nutrition guru who instigated a national fad in the early 1900s of chewing one's food into obliteration. As food historian Harvey Levenstein explains, although Fletcher had no scientific training, his recommendation to chew food for an incredibly long time (at least one hundred times) became popular because it helped people chew more and eat less.[48] Fletcher even earned the nickname "The Great Masticator," and Dr. John Harvey Kellogg created the term "Fletcherize," which Kellogg promoted at his well-known Battle Creek Sanitorium.[49] Olive's inclusion of Dr. Stiles's recommendation illustrates that she was drawing from a larger national conversation about nutrition at the time and applying it to Appalachia. Certainly many people in the region John and Olive visited could have benefited from these domestic improvements, but what stands out about Olive's entries is the pejorative separation between "them" and "us." Although almost all the people with whom she and John stay offer pleasing food, like "a good breakfast of fried chicken and biscuit," these experiences do not alter what she writes about the social condition of the region, its people, and the food "they" prepare (90).

Even when writing about the food offered by those whom she clearly classifies as mountain, Olive seems unaware of or unwilling to recognize the fact that many people in the mountains are participating in a larger food economy. In one instance, this revelation comes through one man's propensity to suffer from indigestion. When staying in Crab Orchard, Tennessee, Olive writes, "Up for 7 and breakfast of fried pork, fried potatoes, and soda biscuit. I chewed carefully and felt no ill results" (56). Given her criticisms of "too much fry," it might seem that she is worried about consuming too much grease, but more likely she is concerned about the soda biscuit. In an earlier entry she describes their driver, Charlie Lance, as a "rather good looking mountain lad with a heart trouble [she lays] to indigestion," noting with horror that he "ate enormously of the [biscuits] which were strong of soda—poor weak heart!" (28, 32). As Engelhardt explains, during this time there was a prevalent "belief that soda biscuits were not a healthy food for long-term consumption."[50] In this instance Olive seems to have genuine concern for Charlie, and his penchant for soda biscuits also tells us something about his economic standing: he has the means to presumably buy the wheat flour used in making soda biscuits, as well as baking powder, soda, or a cheaper alternative like sal soda or saleratus. While it is possible that the flour used in his biscuits was produced locally, it is not likely.[51] This small detail signals that the hosts with whom she stays, as well as the mountain people whose lives she and John are chronicling, are not bound to a local food economy but rather participate in a larger food system.

In Crossville, Tennessee, for example, the Campbells visit a woman named Mrs. Music of whom Olive clearly disapproves. She comments that the room smelled, "five children . . . were playing in and out, and a large turkey and a number of hens kept invading the room." Despite the relative chaos of the visit, Mrs. Music still insists on serving her guests cornbread, coffee—which Olive notes is actually Postum—milk, and some "horrible looking meat" (57). Certainly, Olive's description of the foods offered deserves attention, but most important within the context of this argument is that Mrs. Music, who was apparently not wealthy, still offered her guests Postum, a coffee substitute first made available in 1895.

Made from roasted wheat bran and molasses, the product was created by C. W. Post and marketed as a healthy coffee alternative. An advertisement for the Bee Hive store appears in the December 10, 1908, issue of the *Comet*, a newspaper distributed from Johnson City, Tennessee, roughly 175 miles from Mrs. Music's home in Crossville, and Postum appears under the "New Cereals" category.[52] Olive's diary entry is dated November 1908, indicating that Mrs. Music had acquired Postum even before some stores, like the Bee Hive in Johnson City, were carrying it. Moreover, the product was not cheap. An advertisement for coffee in that same newspaper from August 12, 1909, lists prices for a pound of coffee ranging from fifteen cents to thirty-three cents depending on the type, whereas Postum cost fifteen cents for a small box and twenty-five cents for a large box.[53] In other words, Olive may not have approved of her living habits, but Mrs. Music clearly had access to imported foods and the means to purchase them.

While Mrs. Music offers a store-bought coffee substitute, the students at Carson Newman prepare a meal of "corn soup—cornpone—Hamburg steak coffee charlotte" (168). Although the ingredients of the meal are likely local, the form the steak takes is German in origin and the dessert choice of charlotte cake is European as well. Likewise, after attending church with a middle-to upper-middle class couple named Mr. and Mrs. Webb, the couples enjoy a snack of "hot tea and doughnuts and later grape juice, Roquefort cheese and crackers—all very convivial in appearance" (177). From the British origins of hot tea to the Dutch history of "oily cakes" (doughnuts) to a sheep's milk blue cheese originating from the south of France, the repast that the Campbells and Webbs enjoy is anything but locally inspired. Yet the entire premise of the Campbell's trip through the Southern highlands is to document the habits of the presumably isolated mountain people, including their dietary choices. Once again, examples like this one point to a dichotomous mentality not found in the reality that Olive and John experienced in their travels.

Perhaps the materials that most directly overturn the public statements about food in the mountains presented in *The Southern Highlander and His Homeland* are found in letters written by Grace H. Buckingham (John's first wife) to close family members after the couple opened a school in Joppa, Alabama, in 1895. First, the letters reveal that Grace was keenly aware of the class divisions between herself and many of the other residents of Joppa. She and John, both raised in Wisconsin, must have experienced significant culture shock upon arrival.

In a letter to her mother dated February 24, 1896, Grace writes, "O the sick people whom we visit in dirty rooms, in dirty beds, surrounded by dirty children. Night clothes they have none. When they are [sick] in bed they wear their dirty calico dresses and shirts. And still a great many of them are people whom you must handle carefully, and not let them think that you are disgusted with their ways. It is pretty hard to know how to help them except by example."[54] This excerpt reveals a host of attitudes about the people Grace and John were working among. Although she is sympathetic to their plight, she clearly places herself far above them socially, privileging her own way of living above theirs.

Yet Grace is not long able to maintain her sense of superiority. In fact, where food is concerned, she finds herself intimidated by the culinary know-how of the women of the community, inverting her standing in the community in a significant way. In one account, she writes about preparing a meal for local residents. She frets that she would be "under examination," so when Mrs. Ogletree, "a woman who has the reputation around [Joppa] of being a pretty good cook," asks Grace whether she uses sweet milk or buttermilk to prepare her biscuits, it is a loaded question.[55] When Grace answers that she uses sweet milk, Mrs. Ogletree declares that she and another woman, Mrs. Cordell, need to take lessons from Grace in biscuit making. Mrs. Cordell agrees and tells

Grace, "Yes indeed, they are- the- best- biscuits- I- ever- ate." Mrs. Ogletree goes on to compliment Grace's light bread as well (as opposed to cornbread), and Grace writes, "So I was quite delighted."

Foodways scholar Marcie Cohen Ferris interprets this exchange as a "true victory" for Grace, "given local resistance to 'uppity' foods associated with outsiders and domestic science."[56] Moreover, the fact that Grace feels vulnerable to the culinary scrutiny of Mrs. Ogletree and Mrs. Cordell suggests that at least in this situation, they hold sway over acceptable foods and preparation methods, not newcomers John and Grace. In other words, instead of writing about the deplorable eating habits of mountain people—as they were generally considered to be at the time—in this private entry, Grace chronicles her experience of introducing a new version of a food and its preparation method to matriarchs of the community, and she revels in gaining their acceptance.

Likewise, in another account Grace writes that Mrs. Cordell gave her and John "some of the nicest sausage [she] ever ate."[57] Later, she tells another local woman, Mrs. Fairchild, about how much they enjoyed it, and Mrs. Ogletree brings more. Grace exclaims, "I never ate such sausage in my life, it was elegant." Grace's word choice here functions as a noticeable departure from typical descriptions of mountain food as coarse, undesirable, and likely to cause dyspepsia, indigestion, and other digestive ailments.

Equally surprising is her admission to her father in a January 24, 1896, letter that she and John "can have meat every day, probably twice a day, and sometimes *three times*! It hardly seems possible."[58] While food scarcity was a problem for many people in Joppa during the time, such was not the case for the Campbells. Yet these depictions, which do so much to complicate the already established food narrative of mountain people, are never part of the larger, public story of food in Appalachia.

Considered together, what the Campbells wrote about food in Appalachia, whether in mass-distributed public form or private letters, reveals a keen awareness of complexity and nuance in the region. So why do those nuances not always surface? Is it because the Campbells were so steeped in the narrative they were trying to document and in fact change? Is it because admitting those complexities would make it more difficult to do the kind of work they intended to do? Or is it a tactic regularly employed during this time and today—that if you can neatly categorize a people and the food they consume, you can use that group's food habits to measure your own progress and civility? It is not possible to assert which—if any—of these possibilities is accurate, but what careful analysis of these materials reveals with certainty is that audience and purpose mean everything when writing about mountain people, and in this case, the food that they consume.

Late in *The Southern Highlander and His Homeland*, Campbell writes, "Better health required better food, better cooked," a true statement that no doubt would have benefited many people in the mountains (311). But what is missing in this most public document is John's damning, if problematic, critique of unreasonable attempts to uplift mountain women via complicated recipes and hard-to-procure ingredients; or Olive's sheer delight at some of the meals offered to her and John during their travels; or the respect that Grace Buckingham demonstrated for the culinary prowess of the women in Joppa, Alabama. Although the Campbells worked to overturn dominant cultural narratives about mountain people and what they ate, as they wrote and published for wider audiences they also contributed to those narratives. Food is messy. As the work of the Campbells demonstrates, so too is the process of writing about it. When food depictions come to represent an entire region and its people, the process becomes even more complex.

Thomas Robinson Dawley and The Child That Toileth Not

Around the same time that the Campbells were observing life in the mountains, Thomas Robinson Dawley was conducting his own kind of social survey that began in Asheville, North Carolina. Hired by the Bureau of Labor, Dawley conducted two investigations focused primarily in Western North Carolina, eastern Tennessee, and parts of South Carolina in which he tried to determine the extent to which children were working in the mills, as well as the resulting consequences of their employment. He had experience working as a journalist and war correspondent in the Spanish-American War.[59] The stylistic flourishes he developed in those positions continued to influence his writing; rather than a dry list of facts, his observations read like a sensationalist account of poverty in the mountains that may only be remedied by the presence of benevolent, opportunity-giving mill operations.[60]

His stance is noteworthy, since during this time most people writing about child labor instead found it deplorable. According to visual rhetorician Cara Finnegan, the National Child Labor Committee (NCLC) formed in 1904, and in 1907 a bill was introduced that would regulate child labor in the District of Columbia.[61] Representative Albert Beveridge of Indiana delivered a speech using stacks of evidence, including now-famous photographs by Lewis Hine, to illustrate the dire circumstances facing children who worked in the mills. But rather than pass the bill, Finnegan explains that "in January 1907 Congress approved a federal study by the Bureau of Labor and appropriated three hundred thousand dollars for it."[62] Dawley became one of the investigators for that study, conducting two investigations, and his resulting report, *The Child That Toileth Not: The Story of a Government Investigation That Was Suppressed*, is a behemoth text that falls just ten pages short of 500. In it, he advocates for the largely unpopular idea that life in the mills—especially for children—was preferable to life in the rural mountains from which many of the millworkers came.

At the time of its publication, the book was reviewed in the *New York Times* and *Washington Post*, while sociologist Roy William Foley wrote a scathing review of Dawley's polemic, charging that it "is not entitled to scientific recognition within the field of labor problems . . . the argument is illogical and weak," and "conclusions are reached without proof from premises which either assume the conclusions desired or are not directly pertinent to them."[63] Not surprisingly, Dawley's pro-mill report was not well received by the Bureau of Labor either, prompting him to seek publication elsewhere and subtitle it "The Story of a Government Investigation that was Suppressed." Scholar George Dimock consequently refers to Dawley as a "disaffected federal investigator."[64]

Dawley's work has received scant scholarly attention; what work has been done on *The Child that Toileth Not* focuses primarily on the book's photographs, exploring how Dawley uses images, especially those first taken by Lewis Hine that Dawley recontextualizes to support his arguments.[65] Dawley repeatedly juxtaposes presumably healthy children of the mills with impoverished, hungry children in the mountains; at one point he refers to mountain people as "specimens" and discusses "sampling" them.[66] He relies on this dichotomy between mill and nonmill children even when some mills are *in* the mountains, as in Marshall, North Carolina. Finnegan asserts that Dawley's rhetoric plays off of the notion of the "sacred child" around the turn of the twentieth century: "Contesting the visual fictions of the sacred child through the figure of the mountain child, Dawley rhetorically situated the mill child in a middle space between these two extremes, recognizing the value of appropriation for arguing for the value of child labor in upholding 'the soundness of a nation's children.'"[67] In other words, Dawley's representation of mountain children is so damning that the opportunities afforded by the mills offered a method of social elevation that would otherwise not be possible; according to Finnegan, Dawley implies that reaching the "sacred child" version of childhood in the mountains is not feasible, but producing healthy, responsible citizens who are not afraid of working hard is achievable with the help of the mills

One of the most fascinating ways in which Dawley conveys this message is through his descriptions of food. According to Dawley, although the foods available in mill towns are not always the epitome of a balanced diet, the situation there was far better than the foodscape from which the millworkers came. Early in the text he writes that he "could tell almost at a glance, upon entering one of their homes, whether they were recent arrivals [to the mill town] from the farms, or whether they were a longer or less period removed" (49). He goes on to explain, "At mealtime the various members of the family might be seen distributed around on the beds and in corners, especially near the fire place, munching pieces of yellow soda bread, with the big tin coffee-pot, covered with dirt and grease, somewhere near at hand" (49). As discussed earlier, soda bread was believed to cause indigestion, suggesting that one of the family's primary food sources was inappropriate and unhealthy. Dawley's description also suggests that they do not adhere to a particular mealtime or dinner ritual; likewise, the people he observes do not chew but instead "munch," like animals who use their paws to eat. Moreover, the only foods consumed seem to be bread and coffee from a dirty pot.

As seen here, Dawley initially criticizes the food practices of mountain people, insisting that they need redemption via millwork. But at other moments in the text, especially those in which mountain people seem eager to adopt the mill town lifestyle, he identifies with and even defends the "mountaineers." He makes exceptions for those who have embraced mills into their communities and who are making an effort at what he deems self-improvement. In such instances he defends their presumed culinary isolation, even pointing out that he can "remember the first banana that was brought into [his] own New England home" (143). In instances like this one, he encourages a personal rapport with the reader, one that suggests a shared experience between Dawley and mountain residents. Read in this way, his approach invites early twentieth-century readers in most of North America to consider when and where they (or if they have) experienced their first banana or other exotic, imported food.

Dawley also recognizes that mountain people are sensitive about written accounts depicting their way of life. He recounts what happened when a woman who visited the mountains wrote an article about her stay with an Episcopalian clergyman and it was printed in a local paper. Her statements caused an uproar, prompting a delegation to visit the clergyman to investigate her claims. When the clergyman failed to see how the article might be offensive, a local person explained, "She says there that we never saw a lemon! That's a lie right there! I can take you down the street and show you a whole box of lemons" (145). In instances like this one, Dawley presents a more well rounded view of the population he documents, but even when recognizing a "better" class of mountain people, he writes about them in ways that support his pro-mill stance.

In eastern Tennessee, for example, on his way to the Chilhowee Mountains, he meets a farmer's wife who is quick to condemn those around her who are poor. The woman tells him stories of families who exist "without a particle of food" in their cabins, until the father eventually appears "with a peck of corn-meal, some pork and coffee," at which point "the indolent mother" prepares the meal and "the children would ravenously devour the chunks of hot, barely-cooked dough, and drink the muddy decoction of cheap coffee without sugar or milk, as if they were literally starved" (245). In this instance, it seems important that the woman criticizing this family is a mountain resident, adding a level of credibility to Dawley's claims. He also writes about a few instances of prosperity in the mountains, like one section in North Carolina in which families preserve wild fruits and berries for winter use, or a meal in Chilhowee that he enjoys "immensely" (309, 252). Doing so helps qualify his otherwise entirely negative portrayal of foods available in rural mountain locations, and by extension, the quality of people living in those locations.

Later in the book Dawley draws a clear distinction between his intended audience and the people about whom he is writing. After an extended visit in rural locations, he returns to Asheville looking "like a veteran just returning from a hard fought campaign," after which he goes to Hendersonville (337). While there he boards at an upscale hotel and comments that "for the first time in weeks, [he] found himself quartered midst surroundings and people who are of no particular interest beyond the mere mention of the fact that they belonged to the class that we are familiar with in our usual walks of life, and who are rich enough to idle at least part of their time away at winter or summer resorts" (377–378). Here Dawley uses a first-person plural pronoun to imply that anyone reading his book would be of a similar class as those staying at the resort. Whether or not that is the case, the result is the kind of implied flattery meant to persuade readers to agree with his views.

Like in the documents John C., Olive Dame, and Grace Buckingham Campbell wrote, Dawley's intended audience seems to have much to do with how he represents food and what those foods mean in terms of proper citizenship. In *The Child That Toileth Not,* Dawley makes only slight mention of rural mountain farmers who are faring well and providing various foods for their families. But in a 1910 conference paper entitled "Our Mountain Problem and Its Solution," Dawley states that class distinctions exist in the mountains and that they impact foods available. Interestingly, Dawley delivered this paper at the fourteenth annual Convention of the American Cotton Manufacturers Association. Two years later, near the end of *The Child That Toileth Not,* he insists that such connections were not a contributing factor to his mill advocacy, but Finnegan points out that the NCLC believed he was working as "paid operative."[68] Regardless, his conference paper delivered to an undeniably pro-mill audience acknowledges socioeconomic diversity and its resulting food consequences, while his almost 500-page book downplays that diversity and instead emphasizes the impoverished culinary scene in Appalachia that, according to him, may only be remedied with millwork. Thus it seems that to a smaller audience that was already pro-mill, Dawley admits social complexity in the mountains, while to a larger audience that would likely need convincing that mills were the savior of the mountains, he de-emphasizes those complexities to present a much more one-sided view of the region. Though the contexts from which they wrote are quite different, Dawley's shifting representations of food function in the same way as the Campbell's: the more public documents become, the less nuanced their descriptions of food.

In his paper addressed to attendees of the cotton manufacturer's association conference, Dawley gives a brief history of settlement in Appalachia:

> We find in these mountains today different classes of people, strikingly different in their characteristics and mode of life. There is the farmer who produces good crops, lives in a well-built house, and usually rears a family of well-behaved children and sends them away to school or college. On the other hand, there is the tenant farmer, and the poor land owner, who in extreme cases live in miserable cabins or board shacks, having a single room

in which they rear their families of children, cook, eat and sleep, without ambition to improve either their own condition or that of their offspring.[69]

He even goes on to plainly state, "The well-to-do farmer, as a class, was soon eliminated from the course of [his] investigation, for it is not the farmer who owns a farm, and makes even a fair living, who takes his family to a cotton mill. [His] studies then had to do chiefly with the poor, the poverty-stricken, and in many instances the hungry and forlorn."[70] Such delineation is never as clearly stated in *The Child That Toileth Not*, leading readers of Dawley's book to surmise that most mountain people must fall into the latter category. In the conference paper, Dawley even clarifies that such cases of poverty are extreme, while in the book-length version these extreme cases come to represent virtually all mountain people.

Yet even in the more nuanced conference presentation, Dawley makes sweeping claims about the diets of mountain people. He explains that he has "found family after family huddled together in their miserable cabins all winter long, with no other food than coarsely ground unsifted meal, a little fat pork and black coffee, if we class coffee as a food."[71] Dawley's focus on "coarsely ground unsifted meal" urges his audience to think of the consumers of that food as equally coarse and "unsifted" or unrefined. Likewise, his description of fat pork is historically accurate, but it also carries with it unsavory connotations. In 1890, for example, journalist Clinton Montague wrote in *Good Housekeeping*, "As an article of food, pork, of late years, does not generally meet the approval of intelligent people and is almost entirely discarded by hygienists." Montague goes on to clarify that he is "neither going to condemn or advocate the use of pork. Eaten properly cooked and in temperate quantities it is no doubt as wholesome and nutritious as any other kind of meat," but for those with sedentary lifestyles, it is best avoided.[72] Thus Montague and others during this time implied that a lowly meat like pork may be appropriate for rough, working people but not for refined readers of the magazine who can presumably afford to avoid heavy labor. Finally, Dawley's mention of black coffee signals a lack of cream or milk, indicating the absence of a family cow. Considered together, these descriptions leave audience members pondering the culinary monotony and poor nutrition found in such conditions.

To further make his point, Dawley references a Washington judge who once said to him, "when discussing the conditions of these people, 'Why, they have corn-bread to eat, and that is the healthiest kind of food.' Well, I should like to feed that Washington Judge on that corn-bread, without butter, or vegetables, or fresh meat, or anything else but a little fat pork and black coffee, for just one week, and then have him tell me what he thinks of corn-bread as a healthy food."[73] In this instance, Dawley presents himself as sympathetic to the plight of mountain people, who are in need of opportunities provided by the mills. He draws on the pathos of his pro-mill audience to simultaneously cast mountain people as degenerates who consume the lowliest of foods but who also have the potential for redemption. Even so, in this condensed conference version of his pro-mill argument, audience members are still told that the neediest people Dawley discusses are only a subset of a larger, more socio-economically varied population.

Such is not the case in *The Child That Toileth Not*, his longer, more public version of the same argument. In a chapter that explores potential drawbacks of the mills, Dawley explains that when poor whites first came to work in the mills, many "had sunk to such a low state of degradation that they neither knew how to take care of themselves, nor properly prepare and eat the food which they suddenly found themselves supplied with in unstinted quantities. They gave it to their children barely cooked, or not cooked at all, and the children stuffed themselves with it and literally rolled up and died."[74] In comparison, the family he describes at the beginning of the book, that munches on yellow soda bread, seems to have adjusted to their new home rather well.

Even though Dawley admits that mountain people who have moved to mill towns require a period of adjustment, according to him the pains associated with that adjustment far outweigh the alternative of remaining on mountain farms. As previously discussed, whereas John C. Campbell so firmly believed that rural food choices were superior to those in the mills that he glossed over food variation according to social class when writing to Glenn, Dawley felt just as strongly about the opposite stance, insisting that conditions in rural locations were grossly inferior.

Dawley provides several examples to support his claims about the dire culinary scene in the mountains. In a chapter about his travels through Madison County in Western North Carolina, Dawley includes a photograph of three children with the following caption: "As many of them are before they get the advantages presented by the cotton-mill. . . . The gloom of their cabin is presented in the background. The baby is examining a piece of candy given her. She doesn't know what it is" (146). The toddler Dawley references may or may not have seen candy before he gives it to her, but the only conclusion we can draw from the photograph is that she is inspecting it.

Dawley also finds it repulsive that more than one mountain family he and his associates visit use varying household items for more than one purpose. Upon his return trip to Marshall with a new assistant, he writes, "Our first dinner was at a cabin where the mother of two half-scared, tangle-haired, grown daughters, prepared the meal while we looked on curiously. She swabbed out the frying-pan in which she cooked the biscuits, with a piece of fat pork, and she boiled a mess of sour cabbage that made the place smell as bad as a limburger cheese factory" (319). Rather than compliment this family on its resourcefulness, Dawley complains about the food offered to him and the methods employed to prepare it.

Even more unacceptable to Dawley is that at one point, his assistant helps a woman give birth and "had been obliged to wash the newly-born babe in the frying pan in which later the family breakfast was cooked," remarking dryly that "she refused to eat any of the breakfast" (305). In dramatic scenes like this one, Dawley emphasizes again and again that entering mill life would greatly improve the material conditions of the mountaineer. When discussing particularly isolated landowners, he even writes, "If I were obliged to live the lives they do, I would commit suicide" (277).

Dawley emphasizes that isolation produced boredom, both in life and at the table. In one home in the Dark Corner region of South Carolina, he complains that his "breakfast consisted of the same kind of biscuits as served for supper; more fat pork, a sauce-pan of boiled rice and a big tin pot of coffee," and after taking a big spoonful of molasses from a cracked jelly jar, he "saw that it evidently was a grave-yard for flies" (401). In a township called Egypt in Yancey County, North Carolina, Dawley visits a family that has just finished their breakfast and observes that "cracked cups and a broken saucer or two were on the table; a plate or two, a coffee-pot, and remnants of corn-bread—a few broken pieces, scarcely more than crumbs—and that was all. Black coffee slopped over in the saucers from the cups, indicated that the family cow, chewing dried cornstalks in the muddy yard fronting the cabin, had gone dry" (343). Such descriptions continue for hundreds of pages, pummeling readers with portraits of destitution that according to Dawley may only be remedied by millwork.

His representations are clearly one-sided, prompting the negative reception of the text at the time of its publication and likely explaining the dearth

of scholarship available on it now. But Dawley's text did make one lasting
contribution to an already existing conversation: even when critics like Foley
lambasted his biased, poorly supported claims, they often never questioned
his representations of mountain people or mountain life. For Foley, Dawley's
methods of investigation were questionable, as were his conclusions about
millwork, but Foley seems unable to turn that same critical eye on Dawley's
portrait of mountain people. Foley even writes that the book is "a valuable
contribution of detailed information upon the social life of the mountaineers," indicating that despite the book's many problems, it presented an accurate portrait of mountain life.[75] Foley's comments reveal that Dawley's 1912
representations continued already developing perceptions of mountain people as deprived, ignorant, and in need of culinary redemption.

Although Dawley's text exists as somewhat of an anomaly when placed
alongside writings by William Goodell and Eleanor Marsh Frost or John C.,
Olive Dame, and Grace Buckingham Campbell—certainly his work never received the recognition and acceptance that theirs did—the ways in which he
depicts mountain food and those who consume it functions in a remarkably
similar vein. Each representation seems eerily voyeuristic, even if that voyeur-
ism is meant altruistically, echoing the Local Color and travel writing depictions discussed in the previous chapter. Considered together, acknowledging
how culinary representations shift depending on a document's audience and
purpose helps reveal the many ways in which food descriptions have the potential to shape reader perceptions.

CHAPTER 3

Writers Respond

Critiquing the Live at Home Program

I MAGINE LIVING IN NORTH CAROLINA IN 1932. NEXT, IMAGINE YOU are a woman from the western part of the state who has moved east to work in the mills. Although your work is unceasing, you also help your father grow cotton in hopes of earning more income, all while providing meals for your family. You have plans to impress extended family with a special meal featuring flour-based breads instead of cornbread. Your only regret is that you have no fresh vegetables to prepare because instead of planting a vegetable garden, you used time not spent in the mills tending the cotton crop.

Next, imagine attending a banquet at the governor's mansion. You are seated among university presidents, important politicians, and Jane McKimmon, the state agent for home demonstration work. Menu items include shrimp cocktail, clam cocktail, a variety of pickles, fried oysters, turkey, multiple vegetable options, two bread options with butter, sweet milk and buttermilk, a dessert course with cheese and fruit as well as a candy course, followed by mints and cigarettes. Upon completing your meal, you are given souvenirs and party favors produced locally from counties all over the state.[1]

Although these scenarios seem disparate, they represent a problem and a theoretical solution. The first example is taken from Grace Lumpkin's 1932 novel, *To Make My Bread*, while the second describes one of North Carolina governor O. Max Gardner's banquets designed to promote his Live at Home program. Lumpkin's novel depicts the myriad reasons why a family living in the mountains of Western North Carolina in the 1920s would leave their farm to seek work in the textile mills. They soon discover that millwork does not provide enough income, and they supplement it by attempting to grow cotton. As a result, they have little time to grow their own food, as was the case for many farmers who relied on cash crops to sustain themselves. For Lumpkin's characters, the problem is neither that they do not know how to grow edible crops nor that they lack the mental capacity to plan for the months ahead. The problem is lack of capital.

Yet Governor Gardner's plan to ameliorate situations like the one Lumpkin describes targeted a perceived lack of knowledge; government programs like his strived to educate farmers about how to successfully grow cash crops while also producing enough food for one's own use. For the characters in *To Make My Bread* and many others discussed in this chapter, these programs did little to improve their situations, and the authors discussed here offer a resounding critique.

Historian Adrienne Monteith Petty explains that "From the late nineteenth through early twentieth century, 'live at home and board at the same place' was a widespread folk expression that captured the safety-first way of farming."[2] In other words, rural reformers were concerned that farmers, especially tenant farmers, were too focused on producing cash crops like cotton and tobacco and as a result neglected to grow enough food for their own consumption. Petty cites rural sociologist Samuel Huntington Hobbs Jr., who in 1922 heavily criticized the situation: "The simple truth is that thousands of our farms do not begin to feed the farm family and livestock. The people on these farms live on short rations, especially in lean years. Their diet is ill-balanced and insufficient. They are undernourished, their children badly fed and their physical development stunted" (quoted in Petty, 75). As Petty explains, this problem continued throughout the 1920s, when farmers were particularly susceptible to market fluctuations in cotton and tobacco.

The 1917 North Carolina Cooperative Extension Service Annual Report, for example, explains: "With tobacco, as with cotton, we have not urged an increase in acreage, but rather a decrease or reduction of acreage with the substitution of better methods in order to get larger profits, and also to allow larger acreages to be devoted to food and feed crops."[3] In 1929, O. Max Gardner became governor of North Carolina, and he "adopted the live at home slogan as the state's mantra" (Petty 90). Petty contends that the program did have an impact on the acreage that farmers devoted to growing their own crops, but she also provides a detailed explanation of why the Live at Home Program could be difficult for farmers to follow (94). Gardner's "minimum" recommendations for farmers "no matter how small his farm or family" included the directive to "raise at least $50 worth more food and feed stuffs and livestock products than he did last year" and to grow "a patch of cane, corn, spring oats, soybeans, a vegetable garden, chicken and eggs, hogs, and a cow" (quoted in Petty, 91). Although the Live at Home Program primarily targeted farmers in eastern North Carolina, its attention to tobacco, as well as literary depictions of characters' reactions to it, suggest that farmers across the state were aware of its initiatives.

As the last chapter discusses, Thomas Robinson Dawley's focus on conditions for Appalachian people in mill towns signaled a larger historical shift around the turn of the twentieth century, as many mountain families moved from a subsistence-based existence to one based at least partially on cash. In *Miners, Millhands, and Mountaineers*, historian Ronald Eller explores how and why mountain residents began leaving farms to work in coal mines, textile mills, and timber camps. Eller provides an extended discussion of the effects of extractive industry in Appalachia, all of which necessarily impacted what mountain people were able to grow, prepare, and eat.

Likewise, as historian Tom Lee explains, in late nineteenth-century Western North Carolina and eastern Tennessee, farmers began producing bright leaf tobacco, a fact that surprises many contemporary families with a tobacco farming history in the region, since these areas have long been associated with burley tobacco. According to Lee, the bright leaf variety, which must be flue-cured before being sold, "promised to be the commodity that would lift Western North Carolina from its economic doldrums."[4] Historian Katie Algeo explains: "The Flue-Cured Era lasted from the 1870s into the first decade of the 20th century. The Burley Era started in the mid-1920s," continuing to some degree in the present day, though the lack of federal price support programs has greatly curtailed tobacco production in the twenty-first century.[5] Algeo contends that recognizing the flue-cured era is worthwhile, because "flue-curing technology and bright tobacco varieties were adopted in the mountains nearly simultaneously with their diffusion through the Piedmont and Coastal Plain, testifying to Appalachian awareness of agricultural innovations, adaptability to changing market conditions, and readiness to adopt non-capital-intensive technologies" (48). Moreover, time spent cultivating tobacco meant, at least to some degree, less time growing edible crops, even though Eller argues that the effects of relying on a cash crop like tobacco were quite different in Appalachia from other "agrarian sections of the Midwest and nonmountain South that had moved steadily toward dependence on a single cash crop," explaining that "mountain family farmers remained essentially diversified and independent, producing primarily for their own use" (16).

Even so, conditions in the Mountain South and in Western North Carolina and eastern Tennessee specifically were not entirely buffered from the food-related consequences of tobacco production and certainly not from dietary changes that occurred upon moving to a mill town. Lee also makes the point that a "lack of sources" about Appalachian agriculture from this time period and location "may have kept scholars from digging in rocky ground" (194).

One fascinating way to focus such a sprawling discussion of extractive industry, cash crop production, and food in the mountains is to consider governmental initiatives designed to address nutritional problems associated with mill life or reliance on an inedible crop like tobacco and how authors writing both during and after this time responded to—and often critiqued—these initiatives in their fiction. Localizing the discussion almost exclusively to North Carolina allows us to consider historical context, including the 1914 Smith-Lever Act, the resulting boom of cooperative extension work, and the creation of the Live at Home Program in 1915 to interpret how writers depicted, and in some cases still depict, Appalachian food during such seismic economic shifts. At their core, these programs had roots in Progressive Era ideology, and these fictional portrayals may be read as both a response to the examples described in the previous chapter and a calling out of misguided or inept government aid programs contemporary to the time in which these writers were living. These fictional accounts teach us a great deal: readers learn about culinary variety and deprivation in the mountains, the difficulties characters encounter when attempting to make ends meet in a mill town, the obstacles they may face when trying to implement advice from a cooperative extension agent, and so much more. Considered together, these imagined scenarios convey a very real disconnect between government programs meant to improve and increase food availability "at home" and what may have been possible in the mountains. Just as important, these representations help till the "rocky ground" that Lee mentions, making clear that Appalachia is an integral part of the historical narrative often focused on nonmountain regions.

Novelists including Marie Van Vorst, Grace Lumpkin, and Olive Tilford Dargan (pen name Fielding Burke) created works of fiction in direct opposition to Thomas Robinson Dawley's claims: these writers depicted mill life—

and the sustenance it often failed to provide to workers—as a hellish existence. They also comment upon the difficulty of assuaging such industry-
induced hunger with growing one's own food, as when Granpap in Lumpkin's *To Make My Bread*, who after a long chain of events ends up trying to
grow cotton on a rented farm near a mill town, discovers that he is unable to
grow enough crops to eat, or a farmer named Abraham Beasley in Dargan's
Call Home the Heart criticizes the Live at Home Program. These novels also
provide unflinching portrayals of why characters would abandon farm life altogether in search of a better existence in mill towns, only to find that capital
was often lacking in both situations.

These literary depictions extend well beyond the time in which the shift
away from agrarian-based economies occurred: present-day mountain writers
also represent the effects these historical trends had for mountain people and
their diets. Novelist Julia Franks, for example, fictionalizes a couple's struggle
to raise tobacco in Madison County, North Carolina, in her 2016 novel, *Over
the Plain Houses*. The novel explores the tensions that emerge between local people and advice-giving cooperative extension and home demonstration
agents, while the protagonist laments the heavy focus on tobacco production
at the cost of her own garden. Though the novel was published in 2016, it
is set in the late 1930s; when put in conversation with archival cooperative
extension materials, it provides important commentary on how present-day
writers imagine mountain people, their food, and the control they do or do
not have over what appears on their tables.

When thinking about how these writers portray food against the historical backdrop of immense economic and social change, audience and purpose
remain central points of discussion. These fictionalized accounts of real-life
culinary circumstances detail the pain of food scarcity in radical criticisms
of exploitative systems; they lay bare the difficulty of breaking out of a cash-
based system once one has entered into it; and they depict nuanced portrayals
of subsistence-based economies. At times these writers romanticize "living off
the land," while in other instances they make clear that surviving on a mountain farm is extraordinarily difficult and often dependent on circumstances
outside of one's own control. Most of all, in this chapter we witness a continuation of some of the trends established in chapter 1: writing about food can
mean writing against injustice. Unlike some of the earlier writers discussed
in chapter 1, here we are not positioned as critical voyeurs, ready to mock a
character who has never seen a banana. Instead, as works by Frederick Law

Olmsted and Rebecca Harding Davis encourage us to do, these texts highlight the struggles of mountain people both on and off the farm, using food as a central vehicle for conveying that message. We should also keep in mind that the time frames discussed in chapters 1, 2, and 3 overlap, though writers considered here begin in 1904.

Depicting Empty Promises: Food, or Lack Thereof, in the Mills

Marie Van Vorst's 1904 novel, *Amanda of the Mill*, was published eight years before Dawley's *The Child That Toileth Not*, yet it may be read as a kind of prescient polemic against the argument Dawley would later make. In fact, the narrator directly references "Children of Toil" when personifying the frightening mill that "hummed, buzzed, whirred and sung its epic of Labour and Toil at the cost of brain and body and soul."[6] Although the novel is set in South Carolina and does not mention North Carolina's Live at Home Program, it introduces the tensions present between farm life and mill life. As Elizabeth Engelhardt explains, although Van Vorst came from a wealthy family, she disguised her upper-class pedigree and worked as a spinner in a Columbia, South Carolina, cotton mill, while her sister Bessie labored in a pickle factory.[7] Drawing from these experiences, the sisters published *The Woman Who Toils*, a kind of 1903 version of *Nickel and Dimed: On (Not) Getting by in America*, Barbara Ehrenreich's wildly popular 2001 exposé on life as a working-class woman from the perspective of an author who temporarily assumes the reality of a working-class existence. Van Vorst's experiences radically shaped her opinion about mill conditions, including the food offered there.

Although Dawley insists that workers had more and better access to different kinds and better quality of foods, Van Vorst's novel suggests otherwise. The narrator describes a meal taking place in a "six-roomed shanty" that is part of Jacob Grismore's mill property: "Tin plates bore the repast, and one presented fish-skin, bones, head and tail all cooked and served together with naive indiscrimination; another was stacked high with cold hominy; one bowl contained fat drippings. There was a pitcher of molasses and one of coffee" (79). The narrator goes on to explain that the fare provided at this boarding house is considered lavish, though Van Vorst's presentation makes clear that it is substandard. The lack of fruits or vegetables is noteworthy, but so

too is the opinion that only a cook with "naïve indiscrimination" would prepare and serve fish heads and tails together. Here Van Vorst indicates that not
only are foods provided by the mills inadequate, but her narrator also considers them poorly prepared, an indication that even Van Vorst's anti-mill stance
was colored by class-based judgments about how foods should be served.

Even so, the novel is adamant in its depiction of the horrors of mill-life
nutrition: lunchtime in the mill is a sad affair. Workers who are able to eat
elsewhere during their break do, but many eat in the mill. The narrator describes "one girl, seated on the floor in a nest of filth and grease, [who holds]
between her knees a piece of newspaper containing a bit of bread and pork,"
which she eats as she looks longingly out the window (96). A page later the
narrator calls the girl's food "wretched," and the novel's protagonist, Amanda
Henchley, spends all that she earns to "live on pork and beans and coffee, to
sleep on straw" (117). When Mrs. Grismore ventures into the mills to observe
the conditions under which her husband's employees work, she is horrified,
especially when she sees a "giant African huddled close to the wall" holding
and sucking on a piece of salt pork (124). This particular scene, as well as
other descriptions of African-American millworkers, signals to readers that
no matter how bad situations were for white workers, they were worse for
workers of color.

In 1929, twenty-five years after Van Vorst published *Amanda of the Mill*,
over a thousand textile millworkers went on strike in Gastonia, North Carolina. Although the strike was ultimately unsuccessful, historians consider it
one of the most significant uprisings in Southern labor history. Ballad singer,
mother, and millworker Ella May Wiggins became well known for her protest
songs that inspired workers to join the union. As punishment for her out-
spoken union activities, she was murdered, and her story, as well as the narrative of the strike more generally, inspired no less than seven novels.[8] Some of
these novels provide rich, evocative descriptions of life in the mountains pre-
and post-mill. Both published in 1932, Grace Lumpkin's *To Make My Bread*
and Olive Tilford Dargan's *Call Home the Heart* offer detailed portrayals of a
culinary landscape in the mountains and in the mills. Putting these depictions
in conversation with one another, as well as with Van Vorst's from two and a
half decades prior but set in South Carolina, gives us a sense of how these authors imagined food-related gains and losses experienced by mountain people
who left their homes in search of wage labor and a better existence. Despite
their efforts, their situations were seldom improved. Considered together,

the novels also provide a glimpse of how 1930s fiction taught readers not only about "the labor problem" down South but also about mountain people, their food traditions, and perceptions of both.

As Suzanne Sowinska explains in her introduction to the 1995 republication of *To Make My Bread*, in 1929 the Communist Party sent Grace Lumpkin to Gastonia with the directive to become involved in the textile mill strikes and to bring African-American workers into the union.[9] Lumpkin drew heavily from her Gastonia experiences when writing the book, and one has to wonder how her family background affected her reaction to working conditions for both white and African-American workers. Lumpkin was born in Milledgeville, Georgia, to a family with deep Confederate ties. Her father was a Confederate veteran, and as Sowinska discusses, Lost Cause ideology was an integral part of Lumpkin's childhood. Yet despite Lumpkin's adamant affiliations with the Communist Party—and the mostly positive praise that the novel garnered from left-wing radicals at the time of its publication—she later renounced the party and revealed the names of fellow comrades in an investigation instigated by Senator Joseph McCarthy (viii). Despite Lumpkin's seemingly abrupt turn away from Communism to religion in the 1950s, *To Make My Bread* provides significant commentary on the hardships that many mountain families endured during the Great Depression, as well as their disappointments in the false promises offered by the mills, social workers, and to an extent, governmental programs including the Live at Home initiative.

Whereas Van Vorst's characters do not teeter on the edge of starvation while in the mountains, Lumpkin's text urges readers to understand why the impetus to leave the mountains for work in the mills could be so strong. Lumpkin begins the novel in 1900 with a harrowing snowstorm and the birth of Emma McClure's fourth child, John. Readers soon learn that her husband has died, and she lives with her father, Granpap Kirkland, and her three other children (Kirk, Basil, and Bonnie). Early on, readers encounter descriptions of food scarcity. After a visit to town, Granpap expresses his wish for a glass window, and the narrator explains that "Emma caught her breath. Granpap could not understand how they needed money for food. A man did not watch the meal get lower in the bag and wonder where money for the next lot would come. He didn't see the slab of fatback get smaller until there was just a greasy end left for boiling with cabbage. And then no more" (23). The narrator's emphasis on a gendered awareness of how much food the family needs to survive is noteworthy. Although Granpap provides the bulk of the family's food, Emma shoulders the responsibility of keeping track of supplies and stretching them to fit their needs. Despite her planning, she is not always able to ensure that the family has enough, as when during one especially harsh winter they run out of potatoes and ammunition to hunt for wild game. Readers learn that "For the first time, John knew what it meant to have pains in his belly because it was empty. He had been hungry before for a day perhaps, but Granpap had always managed to provide something. Now his belly had been empty for three days. The pains were grasshoppers jumping from one blade of grass to another." John's sister's hunger pains are so great that she sits "in a corner with her arms pressed tightly over her belly." Emma witnesses her children's pain, but "there was nothing for her to do but watch" (29). In similar descriptions of mountain life, especially during winter, Lumpkin repeatedly highlights a lack of food and the stress it brings to the family, especially Emma.

Not long after the family's prolonged struggle to procure food, a peddler named Small Hardy visits the cabin, regaling Emma and her children with tales of prosperity in the mill towns. He tells them, "You get a house with windows and cook on a real stove—no more bending over a chimney" (39). Hardy's comment echoes Louise Coffin Jones's 1879 remarks about the warped bodies of women who have stooped over fireplaces for fifty years or more, suggesting that in addition to providing much-needed income, life in the mills would also render domestic tasks less burdensome.[10] Although Hardy does not state it outright, he implies that access to a cooking stove, one notably provided by the company, would also allow Emma to better emulate models of proper womanhood. The larger implication here is that a change in geography (from mountains to flatland) and occupation (from farmer to millworker) would make ideals of Victorian motherhood more achievable for Emma. As with Gertie Nevels, a character from Harriette Simpson Arnow's *The Dollmaker* discussed in the next chapter, these stovetop aspirations prove untrue.

When the family makes the difficult decision to relocate to the mills after having sold their land in a desperate attempt to acquire cash, the stove in their company house is anything but impressive. The family is unsure how to use it, and when John places a piece of iron where he thinks it should go, "the round lid fell off with a clatter and scattered soot in every direction" (161). Read metaphorically, the cooking implement that was intended to make life easier for Emma is instead in poor condition, a clear sign that the improved culinary conditions the family had hoped to find are not likely to appear. Later in the novel when Emma and Granpap move off of company property, Emma purchases her own stove on an installment plan, but it is repossessed when they cannot make the payments. The narrator explains that "Bonnie cooked on the fire as they had done in the mountains," emphasizing the hollow promise of all that mill life and its time-saving devices were going to provide. Lumpkin is careful to emphasize that her characters are fully aware of their situation, yet no alternative options are available, for when Emma and Ora "talked of going back to the hills," "they always remembered the terrible winters, sometimes without food . . . [and] always came back to thinking it was best to stay where they were" (213).

As in *Amanda of the Mill*, Lumpkin personifies the mill in *To Make My Bread*, and the McClure family becomes sustenance for a ravenous industrial beast. Lumpkin uses hyperbolic language to evoke children's stories about hungry ogres who grind bones to make bread. Emma connects those stories to her experience in the mill, for while "at first the throb of the mill had been like the throb of a big heart beating for the good of those who worked under the roof," "now to Emma the throb of a heart had changed. She was feeling the grind of the teeth. The mill crunched up and down—'I'll grind your bones to make my bread." Lumpkin also utilizes agrarian imagery to remind readers that the subsistence lifestyle that the McClure family once had, no matter how difficult, is rendered inaccessible by mill life: "The mill sat over them like an old hen and clucked to her chickens every day" (219). In this simile, Lumpkin urges readers to compare the family to eggs, marketable commodities that may be sold, broken open, and consumed.

Granpap finds such an existence detestable and returns to the mountains not long after the family's arrival in company housing. After saving enough money for a down payment, he returns and begins payments on a cotton farm not affiliated with the company. Considered within the context of Lumpkin's depictions of food, what matters about Granpap's return is his intention to try a combined approach of farming and mill life. He does not have the necessary capital to establish the first crop, so he tells Emma, "I must give the man who owns the place now a bale [of cotton] for the use of farm things and as part of payment. I figure if we make two bales, then one will go to us, and you can stop work in the mill." Emma's response is telling in that it foreshadows the unlikelihood that Granpap's plan will be successful: "I hadn't expected not to work in the mill. . . . For what would we do for meat and bread everyday otherwise?" (238). Emma's acceptance of her reliance on millwork signals to readers that she fully understands the instability of Granpap's proposed plan. Even so, she remains hopeful that it will work and is "very careful and saving of food" (239).

When she and Granpap invite Ora Mae and her family to the farm for dinner, Emma spends precious funds to purchase "sweet potatoes and rice, and a whole sack of flour, and a can of lard" (245). Presumably she plans to impress Ora Mae with flour-based bread as opposed to the more common cornbread the family regularly consumed. Despite the care with which she approaches the menu, the narrator reveals that she wishes she could provide more: "Her regret was that she had no garden of fresh vegetables. Granpap had plowed the ground and she had planted. Then they had all neglected the garden, for cotton was everything" (246). As mentioned at the beginning of this chapter, Lumpkin's emphasis on Emma's desire for a garden and inability to have one provides an almost textbook definition of how and why the Live at Home Program began in North Carolina.

Although Lumpkin does not directly reference the Live at Home Program, Emma's longing for a garden on the new farm, as well as the reasons why she does not have it, clearly depict the need for such a program. When put in conversation with the program, what Lumpkin's novel offers is a nuanced portrayal of a family's attempt to negotiate an existence caught between the improbability of a sustainable lifestyle in the mountains and the deprivations of mill life. Even when an enterprising character like Granpap takes the initiative to grow a cash crop such as cotton, and Emma accepts her fate in the mills to provide more income, the family is still unable to grow enough food for Emma to present a meal that she's proud to offer.

Lumpkin's novel highlights her characters' intelligence and awareness, while stressing the limitations of their circumstances. In the same way that Emma is keenly aware of the need for a garden, Bonnie (Lumpkin's stand-in for Ella May Wiggins) is similarly aware of current nutritional recommendations but is unable to meet them given her grueling work schedule in the mill and inadequate pay. Near the end of the novel, Lumpkin includes a woman named Miss Gordon. The narrator explains that "She had left college with the idea of working for the poor, and it was very hard that the people she was working for did not appreciate what she was ready to give" (301). Miss Gordon—who also tries to persuade John to report individuals, including family and friends, suspected of union activity to company administrators—

holds women's clubs in which she provides advice about cooking, nutrition, and other domestic duties. Lumpkin does not specify whether Miss Gordon is an extension agent or instead an affluent woman driven by Progressive Era ideals, but her affiliation with the company is clear, as is her judgment of the people she theoretically intends to help. Frustrated, she tells John that the mill women are either "stupid or else they are too lazy to learn anything. Many come once to club, and never come again. The girls think of nothing except their beaus and a drink of ginger ale, or chewing gum in their mouths" (305). Taken within the context of Emma's and Bonnie's lives, Miss Gordon's comments would be laughable were they not so offensively judgmental.

John is temporarily persuaded by Miss Gordon's estimation of reluctance among the women to devote themselves to her clubs. He criticizes his sister, Bonnie, for not giving them a chance, and she responds, "I did try at first. . . . But it seemed no use. [Miss Gordon] says, 'You must never have fried food,' as if hurrying home from the mill at dinner time a woman or little gal can do anything but throw together something in the frying pan." Bonnie continues, telling John that Miss Gordon doles out advice about consuming a variety of foods to stave off pellagra. John haughtily tells Bonnie that these recommendations are true, and crying, she tells him, "Of course it's true, . . . I'd like the best food . . . and everything for my young one . . . but how to get them . . . I don't know" (302). In this scene and in her depiction of Emma's longing for a garden, Lumpkin highlights the impracticability of implementing recommendations made by those not entrenched in situations like Emma's and Bonnie's. Historical documentation also supports the unattainable nature of some suggested improvements. The 1925–1926 annual report for the Cooperative Extension Service of North Carolina, for example, describes a statewide "Year-Round Farm Home Garden Contest" meant to "increas[e] the consumption of vegetables by farm families in North Carolina" and to teach families that growing their own food was cheaper than buying it.[11] These are not lessons that Emma nor Bonnie need; they understand the value of growing their own vegetables and long to do so; a contest will not "point out their value from a health and nutritional standpoint."

Although well outside the time frame of the discussion here, *Pressure Cooker: Why Home Cooking Won't Solve Our Problems and What We Can Do About It*, a 2019 book by Sarah Bowen, Joslyn Brenton, and Sinikka Elliott, illuminates a similar problem in contemporary America.[12] Through extensive field research and hours of interviews, the book chronicles the reality of nine families in the Raleigh, North Carolina, area and the challenges they each face when struggling to provide home-cooked meals. The difficulties Bowen, Brenton, and Elliott uncover are rooted in a variety of causes, from home insecurity to the hardships of juggling multiple jobs to immigrant children's dietary preferences that may differ from those of their parents to the stresses of juggling career demands with putting food on the table. Their research repeatedly reveals that the pressures many women—from diverse situations—face to provide home-cooked meals for their family are unsustainable. Their findings, published in 2019, echo several of the same dilemmas Lumpkin's characters faced almost nine decades earlier in 1932. Miss Gordon's advice to Bonnie to avoid fried foods seems about as achievable as present-day advice to avoid processed foods given to a mother working full-time whose family is living in a motel.

Likewise, one particular facet of the Live at Home Program provides a fascinating connection to contemporary discussions about Appalachian food and its increasing popularity nationwide. As Petty explains, Gardner "declared December 15–21, 1929 'Live at Home Week' [and] . . . hosted his own live at home banquet at the governor's mansion." North Carolina farm products comprised the entirety of the menu and Gardner invited "about 250 editors and state council members" to the meal (91). Gardner's wife declared that he was "as full of enthusiasm over [the program] as a young boy."[13] Gardner served as governor from 1929 until 1933, and the program from a Live at Home banquet held on December 16, 1932, mentioned at the beginning of this chapter, provides a fascinating look into how Gardner promoted the program. Guests received several souvenirs and party favors, many of which came from mountain locations. Champion Fibre Company in Canton (Haywood County), for example, provided stationery, while galax leaves came from Jonas Ridge in Burke County, and Beacon Manufacturing in Swannanoa (Buncombe County) supplied wool blankets.[14]

Most relevant to this discussion, though, is the actual menu, which is not altogether different from what one might find in a trendy farm-to-table restaurant today (figure 9). Although the 1932 Live at Home menu includes foods from across the state, dishes from the mountains are featured, indicating that while the program was aimed primarily at eastern North Carolina farmers, the governor wanted to demonstrate an investment in the well-being of farmers statewide. Ingredients for each dish are geographically located, and four items are sourced from the mountains. The kraut comes from the

Menu

COLD PRESSED SCUPPERNONG JUICE
Bladen County Council of Home Demonstration Clubs

SHRIMP COCKTAIL   CLAM COCKTAIL

CRACKERS

Shrimp from W. B. Keziah, Southport Pilot
Clams from Wilmington Star-News
Sauce made of tomatoes from State Farms by L. H. Harris, Steward

MIDGET PICKLES   PEPPER HASH   PEACH PICKLES

Pickles from O. F. Cates and Sons, Faison
Pepper Hash from Grover Britt, Clinton
Peach Pickles from Isaac London, Rockingham and Bladen County
Council of Home Demonstration Clubs

ROAST TURKEY   SAUSAGE
FRIED OYSTERS   BAKED APPLES IN HONEY

Turkeys from N. C. Producers Mutual Exchange, Durham; Durham
Mutual Exchange, Durham; Farmers Federation of Western
N. C., Asheville; Wild Turkeys from O. F. Crowson, Burlington
Times-News
Oysters from State Department Conservation and Development
Sausage from Hooker and Company, Kinston
Apples from State Department of Agriculture
Honey from R. L. Sloan, County Agent, Morganton

MUSHROOMS   SWEET CORN   WHITE POTATOES
CANDIED YAMS   SPINACH
KRAUT   WHITE ONIONS   SPAGHETTI

Mushrooms from Carolina Mushroom Growers, Inc., Charlotte
Corn from Grover Britt, Clinton
White Potatoes and Onions from John Gold, Wilson
Yams and Spinach from State Farms
Kraut from North State Canning Company, Boone
Spaghetti from Waldensian Baking Company, Valdese

BUTTER

HOT ROLLS   CORN PONE

Butter from Gilt Edge Creamery, Shelby and Mooresville Cooperative
Creamery, Mooresville, Caldwell Creamery, Lenoir
Rolls from A. & P. Tea Company, Charlotte; Whole Wheat Rolls, Royal
Baking Company, Raleigh
Flour from Eagle Roller Mills, Shelby; Austin-Heaton Company, Durham
Corn Meal from H. C. McNair, Maxton

COFFEE

SWEET MILK   BUTTERMILK

Sweet Milk from Leonard Tufts, Pinehurst
Buttermilk from Pine State Creamery, Raleigh
Carolina Blend Coffee from Woods Coffee Company, Greensboro, made
and served by Sir Walter Hotel

BLACK WALNUT ICE CREAM   FRUIT CAKES
CHEESE   DELICIOUS DOUGHNUT CAKES

Cheese from Brushy Fork Creamery, Boone
Ice Cream by Pine State Creamery, Raleigh
Black Walnuts from Madison County
Delicious Doughnut Cakes from Staudt's Bakery, Raleigh
Fruit Cakes made by Mrs. Effie Vines Gordon, Home Demonstration
Agent, Nash County

CANDY   SALTED NUTS

Candy from Lance Packing Company, Charlotte
Salted Peanuts from Roy Parker, Hertford County
Salted Pecans given and prepared by Lumberton High School Students
Black Walnuts from Marshall News-Record

AFTER DINNER MINTS   CIGARETTES

Mints made and furnished by Tom Bost, Raleigh
Lucky Strikes from American Tobacco Company, Reidsville
Chesterfields from Liggett-Meyers Tobacco Company, Durham

Fig. 9. Menu from the Live at Home dinner served at North Carolina governor Olive Max Gardner's mansion on December 16, 1932. North Carolina Cooperative Extension Service, Office of the Director Records, UA 102.001, Series 1.2, Box 3, Folder 4, Special Collections Research Center, NC State University Libraries.

North State Canning Company in Boone (Watauga County), cheese comes from the Brushy Fork Creamery (also in Boone), the black walnuts featured in black walnut ice cream are from Madison County, as are the black walnuts in the "candy" section.

Imagining university presidents, cooperative extension supervisors, and state representatives gathered around the robust meal in this chapter's opening in the same year that Lumpkin's novel was published highlights a startlingly disparate comparison of food availability. When placed in conversation with one another in this way, Emma's longing for fresh vegetables feels difficult to reconcile with a politically motivated feast featuring the bounty of the state. In a retrospective account of Gardner's term as governor, historian Joseph Morrison contends that "Nobody was deluding himself that 'Live-at-Home,' even where it was keeping the poorest sharecroppers alive, was any palliative for the grave crisis in cotton and tobacco."[15] As discussed in later chapters in this book, that juxtaposition does not feel so different from today's dichotomy between a long overdue celebration of mountain foods in expensive restaurants and the difficult economic conditions in which many mountain people live, conditions that can limit access to food at all, let alone desirable foods.

Granted, Lumpkin's novel presents a worst-case scenario for the McClure family. Perhaps comparing it to dinners like the one discussed above is unfair. *Call Home the Heart*, a novel by Olive Tilford Dargan (written under her pseudonym Fielding Burke), was also published in 1932, and unlike Lumpkin, Dargan does not cast pre-mill life in the mountains as an existence constantly threatened by lack of food. Yet the novel criticizes the Live at Home Program all the same, as well as other government programs designed to help mountain farmers. She depicts surviving on a mountain farm as unquestionably difficult, but Dargan imbues the novel's protagonist, Ishmalee (or, as her family calls her, Ishma), with an abiding connection to the mountains that extends to a culinary prowess not often seen in depictions of mountain women in the 1930s. In several ways, Dargan's nuanced portrayal of Ishmalee's abilities echoes the socioeconomic and culinary diversity that Eleanor Marsh Frost described in her diaries when traveling in the mountains of Kentucky in the early 1900s. Dargan also sets up a paradigm in which Ishma's intellectual curiosity—the narrator reveals that she is "easily a scholar" and that she believes formal speech is "a way to power and larger life"—results in exposure to mainstream depictions and understandings of food.[16] Throughout much of her time spent in the mountains, Ishma balances the reality of limited ingredients and equipment with her creative vision in the kitchen. Dargan portrays her as deftly creative; she does not just "make do" with what she has but instead prepares resourceful, imaginative meals.

Early in the novel, the narrator reveals that Ishma's great-grandmother, Sarah Stark, is also a talented cook who kept a collection of recipes, despite not being able to read. Dargan encourages readers to consider Sarah's talents and her husband's ability to provide for the family: starvation was not a concern under Sarah and her husband Frady's leadership. Instead, they work as a team to provide for the family. The narrator explains that Frady "could bring a ham into [Sarah's] kitchen" that he cured himself "and leave it, knowing it would be boiled in cider, tenderly skinned and given a new covering of baked sugar with just the right number of cloves" (9–10). Likewise, he helps her can tomatoes, and she grows "every kind of seasoning known to her day" in her garden. Conversely, after Frady and Sarah die, Ishma's sister Bainie and her husband Jim take control of the farm. Under Jim's so-called leadership, the family typically subsists on "fat-back, corn-pone, and coffee," while "supplementary dishes were entirely the concern of the women, if they cared about such inessentials" (10).

Two things of note occur here: first, Dargan subverts assumptions about gendered labor and food preparation by depicting the older couple, Sarah and Frady, as the more progressive one that shares the labor of food preparation. Frady presumably enjoys helping his wife in the kitchen, in addition to being an effective provider for the family. Second, the narrator's emphasis on garden-grown spices suggests that Sarah does more than put food on the table. She provides dishes that are seasoned with herbs and spices that she cultivates herself. Her household is not one of slovenly mountain folk with no culinary know-how or appreciation for well-seasoned food. But lest Dargan idealize the situation, making it potentially unbelievable for readers steeped in long-established misunderstandings about inadequate food in the mountains, Dargan is careful to juxtapose the bounty that Sarah and Frady provide with the meager offerings available under Jim and Bainie's care.

Ishma shares her great-grandmother's desire to prepare tasteful, interesting meals in the same way that she yearns for a formal education. When a teacher visits her family's cabin, he is dismayed to learn that at fourteen, Ishma has never been to school. Though he soon leaves the area, he subscribes to *Woman at Home* magazine for Ishma, and she swoons over the magazine's depictions of clean homes and smiling women: "They took her breath. But the most miraculous of all were the laden eating tables. Surely they were waiting for angels to sit down at them!" (11). She becomes so mesmerized by these images that she emulates them when playing alone in the woods: "She practiced arraying such a table as was in her heart," with galax for a service set, leaves for plates, and wildflower petals and baby oaks and maples for food (12). Notably, this emulation does not cease with pretend play in the forest. Later in the novel when she marries and must juggle work in the fields with never-ending domestic tasks, the narrator highlights not only her efficiency but also her inspiration: "She was deft in a kitchen, and she remembered much of her grandmother's teaching. Long ponderings over the *Woman at Home* had made her daring with materials at hand" (65). Although Ishma's primary goal is to put food on the table that will fuel necessary farmwork, she draws from two sources of inspiration: her great-grandmother and a popular magazine.

Literary scholar Margaret Beetham explains that *Woman at Home* was a "six-penny middle-class monthly" published between 1893 and 1920, when it merged with *Home* magazine.[17] According to Beetham, the magazine targeted middle-class British women, a focus that differed substantially from *Queen*, which targeted wealthy women who considered themselves ladies and certainly not domestics. Beetham's discussion of the magazine points out that "*Woman at Home* did not simply locate its readers in the middle class; it set up an opposition between them and their aristocratic 'sisters' where all the advantages were perceived to lie with the middle-class woman" (159). In other words, a primary rhetorical goal of the magazine was to bolster values and understandings of domesticity held by middle-class women and to validate them when compared with their elite counterparts. Considered within the context in which Dargan evokes the magazine, we see the magazine functioning in an entirely different way for Ishmalee. Instead of affirming her own way of life, it educates her about the comforts available to those with a higher social standing. The three-year subscription the schoolteacher provides for her "opened gates to a way of living so enticing in comfort, so engaging in form, so ravishing in color, that it seemed nothing short of celestial." She even clutches the magazine to her chest and whispers, "He has prepared me a table in the midst of mine enemies" (11). Using an overt biblical reference, the narrator positions the magazine as a kind of domestic scripture by which Ishma plans her meals and runs her household. Yet Ishma does not spend time lamenting unavailable ingredients or feeling ashamed about the foods she prepares;

rather, the magazine seems to prompt her to try new methods with what she has available. Dargan highlights Ishmalee's eagerness to learn new things, depicting her not as a backward mountain woman obstinate to change but instead as a bright, curious person who is open to new methods.

Ishma's creative capacities in the kitchen are most fully realized on Sundays, when the family takes a much-needed break from working in the fields. Before they have children, Ishma and her husband Britt prefer to spend Sundays walking in the woods; sometimes they go to church instead, and afterwards she would "apply her wits and skill to contriving a more interesting supper than the buttermilk and cold pone [her sister] Bainie had intended to set before the family" because she "would feel that something must be done to save the day." The narrator describes one rainy June Sunday when Ishma manages to find "a few handfuls of dried apples, which she picked over, scalded, and cooked to a healthy red" for turnovers. Her son finds "two little striped punkins in the hay in the barn," which Ishma identifies as mountain cymlings. According to Ishma's great-grandmother, a cymling is "near to nothin' as a snowball on the forestick when it ain't properly cooked, but cook it right, an' there's yer barbecue!" (67). The narrator continues with a detailed description of how to cut and prepare the cymling, but within the context of this discussion, what matters is Ishma's ingenuity. In an ideal cooking scenario, the narrator emphasizes that cooks would have brown sugar, rice, butter, and ham, none of which are available to Ishma. But she also knows that she can substitute molasses for the brown sugar, and she knows how to create a ham substitute by slicing fat-back, "rolling the slices in flour, and frying them crisp brown" (68).

Not only is Ishma able to improvise when necessary, but the novel also emphasizes her connection to the larger world and her willingness to follow current nutritional advice: "She knew from the Health and Food bulletins which the children brought home from school, that the corn product and milk made a wholesome meal," yet on days when they have gone to church, she prefers to prepare something more varied (67). Likewise, both Britt and Ishma educate themselves about best farm practices by reading farm bulletins and *Progressive Farmer*, which inspire plans to create pastureland and plant soybeans (69). Yet as time goes on, Ishma gives birth to a son and then twins. The couple wants to arrange a rent-to-buy agreement for a farm of their own but do not have enough money for a down payment. At the same time, their corn yield is down. Despite these hardships, the narrator explains, "They would have a large patch of turnip greens," and "Ishma made two barrels of kraut," while Bainie dried apples; sweet and Irish potatoes also grew well and would last the family through the winter (87). When considered alongside the likely postpartum depression that Ishma experiences, by this point in the novel readers begin to understand that despite an openness to learning new farming techniques, cooking methods, and education in general, without at least some cash income, it becomes increasingly difficult for Ishma and Britt to live. This is not a problem the Live at Home Program can solve.

When the twins die of croup, Ishma rallies, placing all hope in the soybean field they decide to plant. The couple does not have the funds to purchase the seeds, but the Wimble County farm agent tells Ishma that she can draw from a fund—which the narrator reveals is the agent's own money—to buy the seeds and pay it back when she is able (92–93). The agent "carefully explained the process of inoculating the beans with nitrogen bacteria," which Britt and Ishma painstakingly follow (93). The beans begin growing, along with their hope that the beans would generate income when sold in the spring, but before the beans mature, cows from a neighbor's farm find their way into the field and destroy the crop. The narrator reflects: "Farming—without tools, stock, seed. Nothing to pour into it but their strength. What had it brought them? Debt, sneers, injustice. Nothing to wear. The crudest food, and no time to prepare it. Nothing for study—books—trips. Just bare life" (106). Here Dargan highlights that while a bounteous table in the mountains is possible—as evidenced by Frady's and Sarah's leadership—starting with very little and creating a similar situation proves incredibly difficult. In this particular scenario, it matters not that Ishma is eager for education, both from books and farm agents, nor that she prefers to exercise creative agency in the kitchen with varied ingredients.

By her fourth year of marriage, Ishma is pregnant again and increasingly desperate to escape the continuous cycle of work, hardship, and insufficient funds in which she and Britt are caught. The narrator explains, "They had to have bread from something. And bread was about all they would make this year, in spite of Britt's hard labor. With no surplus, what would they do?" (142). Despite the fact that Britt does not want to leave the mountains to work in the mills, Ishma decides that she will go without him. After leaving and then returning, she tells her mother, "I couldn't go on living like an old cow. Fodder in the winter and grass in summer, and a calf every half year" (393). Not only is Ishma bound by her economic circumstances, but

her gender and reproductive capacity also clearly limit her options. Unable
to leave the mountains alone and pregnant, she pairs up with Rad, a man
who had always hoped to marry her, and they leave in a scandalous departure.

Dargan provides a nuanced portrayal of foods available in a mill town by
emphasizing the impact that different occupations have on available foods.
While mill life initially seems better for Ishma, Dargan soon complicates that
rendering. In other words, without enough capital, surviving in a mill town
becomes as fraught as "living at home." It matters that Rad does not work in
the mills; instead, his carpentry experience earns him a job as a builder. Rad
has "contempt for the mills," and his friend Pace Unthank agrees that work
outside of the mills is best (180). Rad's employment, as well as the wages he
earns, afford Ishma a higher social standing in the village than many of the
people who rely on millwork. As a result, she and Rad eat relatively well:
"With access to groceries, and a not altogether barren pocket-book, [Ishma's]
talent for cooking flourished, and Rad's lunches were the envy of his fellow
workmen." Ishma's ability to "stretch a penny" also puts Rad's mind at ease
about the cost of groceries (198). Later in the novel, Ishma teaches a young
woman how to make creamed eggs with cheese, "hot sally lunn with butter,"
and pork chops (276). Such descriptions might seem to support claims Dawley makes about improved life in the mills, but Dargan's portrayal of foods
available to millworkers suggests otherwise.

As Engelhardt discusses, like in Van Vorst's *Amanda of the Mill*, Dargan's
novel also depicts pellagrins. Ishma interacts with one woman named Mame
Wallace who appears to eat only cornbread and water. She claims to prefer
this diet but also pleads with her doctor, "Don't be hard on me. . . . There's so
many of us," making clear that food scarcity has much to do with her diseased
condition (201).

The longer Ishma spends in Winbury, the more aware she becomes of the
inequity that millwork creates. The meals she is able to prepare thanks to
Rad's wages no longer satisfy her, nor do the conveniences of her kitchen. The
narrator explains: "She looked at the hot kitchen stove that Rad was so proud
of, and thought of the meals she had cooked with no stove at all. Red-white
oak-wood coals under a hearth oven with a pone in it. A pot of vegetables
swinging over a fire, and milk from the spring-house" (219). Although Ishma's
longing for the mountains and its foods is somewhat romanticized—after all,
one of the reasons she wanted to leave was because it was so difficult to get
ahead—Dargan's description also reminds readers that while Britt and Ishma

were unable to buy their own farm and live independently (at least before she left him), they were not on the verge of starvation as are the characters in Lumpkin's *To Make My Bread*.

In addition to remembering and wishing for the lifestyle she had with Britt in the mountains, Ishma becomes heavily involved with millworkers and their plight for better working conditions. She helps organize meetings, and Dargan represents this newly discovered agency via food. Whereas Ishma viewed the repetitive food provided by Bainie as void of creativity, similar food takes on a new meaning when consumed alongside pro-union activists: "The dry bread that she ate at Mildred's table was sweet with life to come. The tri-weekly pot of beans, the ever recurrent potatoes—boiled in their jackets so that nothing should be lost, and eaten without butter—became an endurable prelude to the feast from which none would be turned away" (306). She helps provide food to striking families, even when the relief store is raided and all of the food supplies are purposely ruined. Here, resilient people like Ishma provide sustenance for one another, not government programs.

As the strikes and protests become more violent, Ishma begins to lose hope that justice can ever be achieved. She visits a farmer named Abraham Beasley, who, with his wife, was able to achieve what Britt and Ishma were not: a productive farm and land of their own that they purchased themselves. Initially she admires all that he has accomplished, but he quickly cures her of any illusion of success, telling her that such individualized struggle is a never-ending battle and their "life was just work" (343). He surprises her by insisting, "We've got to pool our farms, our tools, our labor; same as in any modern industry" (346). His recommendation for collective efforts echoes Dargan's communist leanings and the general political thrust of the book.

Beasley issues a scathing critique of farm agents, academics, and the ways in which government intervention has the ability to dictate what and how farmers produce:

Here's one game o'farm-doctors that's for years been sendin' out their demonstration trains an' bulletins an' college professors to tell us how to produce more an' work harder. . . . Learn how, an' go to it, an' you'll be all right, they told us. And when our big crops had to be sold for less than they cost us, along comes another gang an' says the trouble with you farmers is you're producin' too much. Cut it down an' you'll be all right. We'd worked too hard and ruined ourselves. An' we pay em' a big salary to ride around and tell us that. It's a spectacle, ain't it? Now they're beginnin' to talk about a live-at-home cure. We farmers are to go back to the days of Adam, while the rest o' the world rolls along into the twenty-first century. It makes me tireder than ever I was after workin' sixteen hours a day to save a crop that wasn't goin' to pay me half wages. (345)

In this passage, Beasley issues a resounding critique of the Live at Home Program, echoing food historian Megan Elias's point about "inherent tension between the bringers and receivers of knowledge" when discussing the work home economists did in rural communities in the 1920s.[18] Beasley seems frustrated not only by the inconsistent advice given by academics and extension agents but also by the spectacle of those who are not farmers "rid[ing] around" and giving advice to those working the land. Dargan's portrayal of Beasley's character subverts many well-established stereotypes about mountain men while simultaneously criticizing government programs: Beasley is hardworking, successful, and well aware of farming recommendations. But his many years of farming have taught him that efforts to achieve all that he has should be collective, not individual. Moreover, Beasley's criticisms of the Live at Home Program indicate that farmers would be better off relying on one another rather than on such initiatives, all of which supports Dargan's communist bent.

While Dargan's depiction of county agents, at least in this instance, is not positive, historical records illustrate Beasley's criticisms from a different perspective. The Cooperative Extension Service annual report from 1933, just one year after the publication of Dargan's novel, discusses the urgent need for crop reduction: "Surplus commodities had glutted the markets until prices fell to unlivably low levels. Farmers could not make ends meet. . . . Cotton was selling at about five cents a pound and tobacco at 10 cents or less. The farmer's plight was augmented by a lack of cash from former crops, and had not the balanced farming plans promoted in previous years been effective, the condition would have been of serious consequence."[19] In this excerpt, the extension service congratulates itself on balanced farming plans that helped offset the surplus goods problem. But from Beasley's perspective, the very attributes that the extension service boasts about are the elements he criticizes most, insisting instead that the solution lies in communal action, not programmatic intervention.

Yet rather than depict the collective action Beasley suggests, Dargan has

Ishma return to the mountains, where she finds Britt running a profitable farm that he was only able to begin with seed money earned from a brief stint in the music business. Although Ishma embodies ideals of collectivism, her vision of what the farm can be—far from the mills—is also quite idealized. She imagines "Britt as the last farmer in history, safe on his rock ledge with its fertile spots and patches, feeding his family out of his hand; while humanity swirled past him in the wake of great tractors, combines, combustion engines of all sorts" (429). The isolation of the mountain farm that initially drove Ishma to the mills is now what draws her back, but she has plans to bring mill children and families to the farm in the summer to "give them plenty to eat and turn them loose on the mountain to get strong" (430). Although Ishma's decisions do not square with Beasley's recommendations, Dargan's overall commentary on collective efforts resonates within the text. Government programs do not address Beasley's complaints, nor does Ishma rely on them to fuel her vision of a mountain utopia populated with well-fed children.

Connecting the Dots: Millwork, Tobacco, Government Programs, and Fiction

Investigating how government programs represented their work during these same years in which major economic shifts occurred provides crucial context for better understanding Lumpkin's and Dargan's critiques, as well as representations by present-day authors such as Julia Franks. As explained by the National Archives Foundation, the 1914 "Smith-Lever Act established a national Cooperative Extension Service that extended outreach programs through land-grant universities to educate rural Americans about advances in agricultural practices and technology."[20] Even so, cooperative extension documents housed at North Carolina State University reveal that such work was occurring in North Carolina well before 1914: on November 18, 1907, James Butler began work as the first county agent in the state.[21] Petty points out that as early as 1915, county agents like "Robert J. Johnson encouraged farmers 'first of all to raise their home consumption and then all the cotton and tobacco they could'" (76). By 1918, annual reports indicate a heavy emphasis on encouraging farmers to grow enough crops to feed their families, while still focusing on improving yields and profits from cotton and tobacco.[22] At least in the case of tobacco production, the years during World War I were productive and profitable, though they preceded a major downturn: "Many tenant farmers became farm owners while thousands of families got out of debt for the first time in their lives. . . . And then came 1920. In North Carolina and Virginia tobacco fell from an average of 50 cents in 1919 to about 20 cents a pound in the fall of 1920."[23] These dramatic swings in market value continued to plague farmers until the Agricultural Adjustment Act was passed in 1933. Part of Roosevelt's New Deal program, the act was intended to "offer farmers subsidies in exchange for limiting their production of certain crops [including cotton and tobacco]. The subsidies were meant to limit overproduction so that crop prices could increase."[24] But the act benefited those who owned more acreage, not those functioning within the sharecropping system.

In order to understand what all of this meant for tobacco farmers in Western North Carolina—and in the Madison County setting of Julia Franks's *Over the Plain Houses*—we should first recognize the shift from flue-cured tobacco to burley tobacco mentioned earlier in this chapter. Madison County was a major producer of both kinds of tobacco, but in different time periods: from the "1870s until the first decade of the twentieth century," flue-cured tobacco reigned, while the "Burley Era started in the mid-1920s" and continued throughout the twentieth century and into the twenty-first century.[25] In 2004, President George W. Bush initiated the Tobacco Transition Payment Program, a ten-year federal program that ended the quota system that had been in place since the Great Depression. Farmers received payments during this ten-year period, after which price supports for tobacco ended. In other words, after 2014, growing tobacco became financially precarious since the price-support system that had been in place since the New Deal was no longer available.

Algeo's nuanced discussion of the shift from flue-cured to burley tobacco in Madison County highlights the progressive tendencies of mountain farmers, emphasizing a consistent willingness to try new techniques. Algeo explains that in the late nineteenth century, Madison County farmers were eager to expand flue-cured acreage and resulting profits. Even though pinpointing precisely how to properly flue-cure brightleaf tobacco took years of experimentation, "Madison County farmers . . . adopted flue-curing and bright tobacco during the same period in which these innovations transformed the North Carolina piedmont and coastal plain."[26] Algeo continues to point out that these developments—which illustrate a clear desire to participate in cutting-edge agricultural practices—were ironically occurring at exactly the same time Local Color writers and philanthropists were establishing conceptions of mountain people as isolated, backward, and un-willing to change (41–42). Likewise, by the 1920s, burley tobacco, which was air-cured instead of flue-cured, had "almost completely replaced flue-cured tobacco in Madison County" (44). The air-curing process meant farmers did not have to worry about barn fires from the flue-curing process or cut down scores of trees to fuel the fires required for curing the brightleaf variety. As Algeo discusses, although the burley variety was in many ways desirable, it also meant that farmers had to learn about proper soil type, which often involved using just the right amount of lime and fertilizer. In the same way that the area's adoption of flue-cured tobacco signaled progressive awareness and acceptance of current agricultural trends, so too did the adoption of bur-ley tobacco. Though not immediately apparent, these historically contextual distinctions factor into how we read present-day representations of Madison County, burley tobacco, cooperative extension agents, and depictions of the culinary consequences of tobacco production and government intervention. It is a different conversation from one centered on literary depictions of mill-work, but it is linked by a common thread in which authors consider govern-ment intervention, the perceived success of that intervention, and how food factors in.

Imagining: Burley Tobacco, Madison County, Cooperative Extension Agents, and Culinary Consequences

In her 2016 novel, *Over the Plain Houses*, Julia Franks fictionalizes what happens when one cash crop—in this case, tobacco—replaces subsistence farming, especially when that transition is encouraged by the U.S. Depart-ment of Agriculture (USDA) and its home extension agents. But the novel's statement about reliance on cash crops—if such a statement may even be deduced—is complexly rendered. The novel is set in 1939 in Western North Carolina and chronicles the oppressive, abusive relationship between Brodis Lambey and his wife, Irenie Raines Lambey. Franks casts Brodis as a fun-damentalist preacher whose domination over his wife is troubling from the start, and by the novel's end, so unbearable for Irenie that she leaves him to seek an abortion for a rape-induced pregnancy. While describing the constant power struggle between Brodis and Irenie, Franks also weaves in the back-story of USDA extension workers Roger and Virginia (Ginny) Furman, a his-torically accurate addition since the first farm agent began work in Madison

County in 1925.[27] In my conversations with Franks, she said that she did not use Virginia's last name to remind readers of Hindman Settlement School worker Lucy Furman, but for those schooled in Progressive Era history, the comparison is difficult to ignore. Virginia Furman functions as a role model for Irenie, demonstrating a brand of confident independence that was initially inconceivable to Irenie. While Roger Furman reaches out to farmers in hopes of increasing their tobacco yields, Virginia holds classes for women in the community that cover topics ranging from "The Efficient Kitchen" to "The Science of Nutrition" to "Cooking with Electricity" (99). Yet despite Irenie's admiration for Mrs. Furman, much of Irenie's agency is bound up not in modern kitchens but instead in tending the earth and overseeing food production on her family farm, though as the narrator points out, technically only Brodis owns the land.

Franks uses limited third-person point of view to narrate the novel, revealing both the beginning and the violent ending of the USDA presence in the county on the first page: "It was the week before Easter when the lady agent first showed up to church. . . . [before] the agent and her husband were dead and the Department of Agriculture had closed its extension office for good . . ." (3). Right away, Franks alerts readers to two things: first, that this government intervention will not have a happy ending, and second, that Brodis and Irenie have very different views of the extension work offered to them. Even so, what unites them is their shared loathing of the way that tobacco has taken over their farming practices in the three years they have been growing it.

Thanks to the novel's point of view, at times readers are aligned with Irenie's perspective, while at other times we are uncomfortably close to Brodis's. Such character alignment reveals perceptions that would otherwise be inaccessible unless spoken directly. These shifts are sometimes clear and sometimes subtle, but after the narrator explains that "From the get-go [in 1934] they'd been selling the idea of tobacco. . . . Not that any of the agents had ever farmed a day in their lives," readers understand that these criticisms are Brodis's. The narrator continues with a declaration that echoes Brodis's views: "And you couldn't trust their interest. It was the looking-down kind, the kind that made a body to take in a stray dog or an idiot child. The kind born of vanity" (10).

As the novel continues, readers become more familiar with Brodis's fragile ego and insistence on having an overruling hand in his church and marriage. He sees the extension office as a threat to his agricultural methods and to his carefully cultivated dominance over his wife. The narrator, again aligned with Brodis, describes Roger Furman as a "soft fellow," someone who has never performed "real work" except to fill out paperwork, and whose paycheck comes from the taxes that people like Brodis pay. In this particular section, long sentences list one criticism after another: when read aloud they sound like a sermon Brodis would deliver to his parishioners. As the rant builds toward its climax, the narrator exclaims, "It was all about making more money in the here and now and do what the Department of Agriculture tells you because they have your best interest at heart" (246). Such sentiments are rooted in reality. In her discussion of the history of home economics, foodways historian Megan Elias cites an article from 1911 in which a farmer exclaims, "These fool colleges have always got a lot of high-falutin' notions about better living," echoing Brodis's thoughts as well as Abraham Beasley's from *Call Home the Heart* (quoted in Elias, 79).

After Irenie leaves to seek an abortion in eastern Tennessee, Brodis visits the extension office looking for her, where he makes his views even clearer by speaking directly to Roger when referencing men in line at the office: "Can't you *see* these *men*? Every single one of them was living close to the bone before you come. And now they've plowed their fields and set their crops and put every last ounce of their labor into a crop they can't even *eat*" (255). Ironically, Brodis's rationale in this scene parallels the impetus for the Live at Home Program, another instance of government intervention. But his awareness of an increased pressure to grow tobacco is historically accurate. The 1937 North Carolina Cooperative Extension Service annual report states, "Tobacco has become the State's greatest cash crop and extension workers were kept busy last year aiding growers in their efforts to produce higher yields of better quality leaf at less expense."[28]

Later on, the narrator emphasizes Brodis's damning view of modernization, industrialization, and extractive industry. In just one paragraph the narrator laments—clearly informed by Brodis's perspective—the timber industry, its resulting environmental consequences, reliance on store-bought goods, and loss of generational knowledge about how to produce one's own goods, ending with the declaration, "People had brought-on appliances in their homes, but they'd all at once become poor when they'd never been before" (123–124). Brodis's sexism and violent tendencies make him an unlikely candidate for reader empathy, but his views here echo the situations that characters in *To Make My Bread* and *Call Home the Heart* find themselves in: new cookstoves may be preferable to fireplace cooking, but they do not automatically translate to prosperity, economic or otherwise. Despite his problematic character traits, Brodis gives readers insight into how it must have felt for farmers to receive conflicting advice about a cash crop that many, like Brodis, were reluctant to try in the first place. Considered within the historical context of tobacco production in Madison County that Katie Algeo discusses, Brodis represents resistant farmers, while Algeo's findings highlight more progressive farmers willing to try new crops and techniques if they had the potential to become profitable. In both cases, however, an increased reliance on tobacco as a cash crop takes precedence.

While Irenie does not share Brodis's criticisms of Roger and Ginny, she does lament their family's increased reliance on tobacco and its resulting food consequences. At times, the narrator reveals that Irenie finds her culinary responsibilities stifling. In a description of Irenie's time spent inventorying food in the root cellar while Brodis "roam[ed] the ridge," readers learn that "She'd come to hate the root cellar. . . . Cull the apples, unwrap the sweet potatoes, put the potatoes by, set the squash out for cooking before it was too late. . . . But she as the keeper of the house and the yard and the fields. She'd cooked and put up all manner of food" (20). Here the root cellar functions as a metaphor of entrapment that encourages readers to compare Irenie's confinement with Brodis's relative freedom.

Even so, Irenie also recognizes the importance of producing their own food, suggesting that the Live at Home Program's recommendations would not have told her anything she did not already know. As a coping mechanism for dealing with an unsuccessful first pregnancy, Irenie focuses more than ever on gardening. The narrator's description of her planning highlights not only the care with which she approaches the task but also the agricultural know-how she applies to cultivating crops to sustain the family throughout the year. The 1937 annual report referenced above states that "one objective [for the year] was to see that every family farm had a year-round garden," but Franks's novel imagines that, at least for Irenie, such a garden was already in place:

> Potatoes needed setting in the ground by the end of the March moon in order for them to make by September; corn during the growing of the April moon when the whippoorwill sang; squash, cucumbers and mush melon in the May bloom days of Virgo. If you paid attention, you had it in your head the way things would turn out. There would be lettuce and rhubarb

in May, radishes, peas, and onions in June, beets, cucumbers and melons in July, corn, tomatoes, peppers, and lima beans in August, cabbage, apples and walnuts in September, and then, in October enough squash, collards, sweet potatoes, and rutabaga to last the winter. (52)

The above passage also illustrates a cycle of crop production that would help cushion the unexpected loss of one crop. In other words, if one crop failed, the others would hopefully help mitigate that loss. Conversely, the novel depicts tobacco as a fragile, labor-intensive, "all or nothing" venture that one hard frost could render pointless.

In the paragraph following the description of Irenie's gardening prowess, the narrator states, "But in the past three years, it had been all about tobacco" (52). Later in the novel, the narrator emphasizes the point again:

Nor was there planting of cane or flax, nor cradling of wheat, nor bundling and stacking, nor mowing of hay. In place of it all, the shaggy mops of tobacco lined the fields, row after leafy-headed row, as if all the growing world had put its energy into this one lurid plant. The sameness troubled her. Where once there'd been whispering cane and melon vines, the heads of tobacco pushed up in absurd formation, greedy for water and potash and food. Their leaves grew broad and white-veined and springy. But Irenie knew the lie of that abundance. The roots were shallow and gave up life to the hoe or the wanderings of deer and pigs. (95–96)

Descriptions like "lurid" and "absurd" signal to readers that the family's shift to growing a cash crop was a mistake, perhaps one they should have known better than to make, yet their trust in government programs presumably led them to do so. Unlike the McClure family in Lumpkin's *To Make My Bread*, Irenie and Brodis do not experience food insecurity before they begin growing tobacco. Lumpkin's characters seek millwork and eventually cotton farming because they are being pushed out of their land and are barely able to eke out a meager existence, but with Irenie and Brodis the impetus seems to lie with government intervention.

The novel takes its critique of tobacco a step further by metaphorically emphasizing its life-killing rather than life-giving properties. When packing her son Matthew's belongings for his trip to school, Irenie lines his trunk of clothes with tobacco leaves to deter bugs from the trunk's contents. When preparing his winter coat, she removes it from the pennyroyal and tobacco leaves she used for storage. Irenie also uses pennyroyal—a toxic plant—as the first ingredient in a homemade abortion tea that nearly kills her (137). Franks's pairing of pennyroyal with tobacco to deter pests from damaging clothing sends a clear message to readers about the literal and figurative toxicity of tobacco.

But if tobacco occupies an unhealthy space in Irenie's life, Ginny Furman—despite her husband Roger's promotion of tobacco production—is an antidote. Midway through the novel, readers have repeatedly witnessed Brodis's domination over his wife, as well as Irenie's desperate need for a supportive network of women in whom she can confide. Although not local, in many ways, Ginny fills that role: "The other women in Irenie's life were like biscuits and butter. They were what you expected, and you needed them to survive, but Virginia Furman was like muscadine wine, something delicious and out of the ordinary that you looked forward to" (165). Ginny teaches Irenie what independence can look like, and she helps her escape Brodis's clutches in a dramatic escape to eastern Tennessee. But what matters within the context of the argument that this chapter establishes is that in some ways, Ginny echoes Miss Gordon—the judgmental woman who tries to teach nutrition and other domestic classes to millworkers—in Lumpkin's *To Make My Bread*. However, the key difference between Ginny and Miss Gordon is that Ginny realizes her mistake and seeks Irenie's advice about how to make amends to the women Ginny has offended.

Irenie manages to convince Brodis to allow her to attend Ginny's class on "The Efficient Kitchen." Right away, Irenie feels uncomfortable because she is the only woman present who does not live in town. Though not instructed to do so, all of the women bring food to the class: Irenie carries a baking dish of turnips in a cabbage sack, and the "smell of butter and fried food wafted from beneath colored cloths" (107). The women are eager to share their dishes with one another and assume that they will eat first, then have the class. Instead, Ginny insists that they have class first and eat later. The narrator explains: "The ladies sighed and mumbled and relocated all the dishes to the edge of the stage. The manila folders were returned to the table" (108). The irony of this passage is that the folders contain "floor diagrams of kitchens with counters in the middle of the room" and visual depictions of efficient kitchens that "allowed a woman to move from stove to sink with less wasted effort. . . . Each had electric stoves and light bulbs. Indoor faucets curled over the sinks" (108–109). The fact that the women in attendance bring food with them to the class signals that they are already proficient cooks, adept at using what resources they have to produce dishes fit for community sharing. Ginny acknowledges that "not everyone had plumbing or electric, but . . . those things became more accessible every year" (109). In this scene, Ginny's belief that she is teaching these women knowledge they need parallels Miss Gordon's misguided conclusion that the mill women she teaches need her advice, when in fact, characters like Bonnie are already well aware of proper nutritional guidelines but have no way to achieve them. Though the situation in Franks's novel is different, the similarities are worth noting.

Franks's novel emphasizes the ways in which the women, despite socioeconomic and urban/rural differences, come together to acknowledge the feelings of shame that Ginny's class elicits for them. When they finally eat the food that has grown cold during Ginny's lecture about appliances many of them cannot afford, "the women were extra kind to one another . . . and all exclaimed over the richness of the cobbler and allowed as how [one woman's] biscuits would float away if you didn't hold them down" (109). Although Ginny's recommendations about efficiency may have saved these women time in preparing meals, what it really teaches them is to feel ashamed of their kitchens and the food that comes out of them. As a response, the women come together to bolster one another's confidence.

Irenie's confidence continues to grow after she leaves Brodis. After the dramatic scene in which he dynamites the USDA office, killing Roger, Ginny, and himself, Irenie returns to the farm after Brodis has died, joined by her son Matthew on his break from school, and the novel gives a clear indication that they will cease growing tobacco and instead grow their own food once again. "For the three weeks of harvest break, Irenie and Matthew dug potatoes and rutabagas. They plucked the apples into a wire basket atop a long pole. They wrapped and buried the cabbages, and they braided the long green tops of the onions into ropes. They bleached and dried the apples, strung what beans there were, and put up the sweet potatoes and the turnips" (267–268). They also slaughter a hog and put up the meat, and Irenie is saving onion, bean, cucumber, squash, sweet potato, tomato, and pepper seeds (269–270). Unlike the idealized ending of *Call Home the Heart*, it seems possible that Irenie can raise enough crops to sustain life on the farm—she already knows how to "live at home." Notably, in the novel she is only able to achieve this level of self-sustenance once the government office has literally exploded.

Yet while Ginny's classes unintentionally shame the women they are meant to help, she serves a much more important role than extension agent in this text: she functions as Irenie's savior, adding a complex layer to this chapter's discussion of government intervention programs and how authors imagine their reception and effectiveness. As foodways scholar Marcie Cohen Ferris explains, "The impact of Southern-born, black and white female extension agents on rural women was profound."[29] Like the characters in the other novels discussed, Irenie did not need instruction in culinary techniques, but she did need a strong woman to help find her way out of a detrimental relationship. Considered alongside novels depicting millwork, as well as the Live at Home Program, Franks's twenty-first century reimagining of 1939 tobacco dependency in Western North Carolina serves as an important reminder that those programs may have brought with them much more than recommendations about crop production and culinary advice.

CHAPTER 4

"Feeling Poor and Ashamed"

Food Stigmas in Appalachia

M OST LITERALLY CONSIDERED, FOOD IS WHAT NOURISHES us. Whereas the last chapter focused on the ability to produce enough food for one's own consumption, this chapter asks what various foods consumed may represent. It seems almost counterintuitive to imagine that the very sustenance our bodies demand might also evoke feelings of shame for the consumer. Yet as previous chapters in this book have discussed, food—and the social judgments associated with it—can act as a kind of cultural shorthand. Certain dishes become marked as belonging to a particular race, ethnicity, class, or region, which then signals the possession or absence of power in varying degrees. For most Americans in the twenty-first century, citing caviar as one's favorite food sends a much different cultural message than pork rinds: both deliver calories to the body, but the cultural associations for each are vastly different. The first generally signals a wealthy consumer with refined tastes, while the latter might suggest a working-class Southerner who prefers a quick, porky snack. As food scholars Peter Naccarato and Kathleen LeBesco explain, food can function as an "economic and cultural commodity," one that can give consumers "a sense of distinction within their communities" that is not always tied to expensive food choices.[1] Naccarato and LeBesco call this kind of value associated with particular foods culinary capital, noting that these assigned values shift depending on time and context.

To understand the concept of culinary capital, we must start with French sociologist Pierre Bourdieu. He wrote famously about these dynamics, albeit within a French context, in the late 1970s, with the first English translation becoming available in 1984.[2] Bourdieu discusses the concept of cultural capital, the idea that one's familiarity with and knowledge of various cultural trends can—and often does—function similarly to economic capital. According to Bourdieu's framework, cultural capital becomes valuable to individuals when the cultural knowledge they possess is deemed valuable by hegemonic understandings of what is "worthy" in any given society. Cultural capital is often "inherited" when families pass on their tastes and judgments to the next generation; formal education also often has much to do with one's valuing of various kinds of cultural knowledge. Classical music taught in a music appreciation class, for example, may be viewed more highly than 1960s classic country. These understandings are hugely dependent on time and place, and the hierarchies implied that separate caviar from pork rinds or opera from Merle Haggard are generally understood implicitly, at least within the circles in which they function. The fact that these judgments often go unspoken makes pinpointing them difficult, yet the identity conflicts that frequently emerge when one realizes that the cultural knowledge they possess does not align with what others deem valuable provide critical sites of inquiry. Using the slippery idea of cultural capital to discuss food in Appalachia reveals a great deal, especially when we consider how these understandings have evolved over time. The same dishes that Local Color authors used to denigrate mountain people are sometimes used in the contemporary moment to venerate them. When we take this long view of how representations of mountain food have shifted and continue to change, one dynamic remains static: firmly entrenched power structures that dictate the worth of a region and its people.

Historian Katharina Vester draws from Bourdieu's ideas about power to examine "how American culture has employed representations of food to create subject positions."[3] For Appalachia, a region that has arguably occupied a subject position since writers and philanthropists began conceptualizing it as a place apart in the late eighteen hundreds, considering food's role in that creation matters. Vester asserts, "As food helps to nourish the individual, food discourses aid in producing the subject," since "identity is not simply created in the process of eating—you are what you eat—but within the discursive structures surrounding it."[4] As demonstrated in previous chapters, the discursive structures surrounding Appalachia have, for the last century and beyond, narrated a relatively narrow view of region, race, and food. For people in Appalachia, the long history of cultural stigmatization extends to its cuisine, a process that often lumps consumers together in one indistinguishably inaccurate blob of whiteness.

As one example, the most indigenous grain of all—corn—became affiliated with white hillbillies through moonshine and cornbread, obscuring its native roots while ignoring the role that corn also played for African-Americans during and after enslavement. In 2008, for example, historian Rayna Green lamented that although she observed a national interest in native foods, such was not the case in the South at that time. She writes that the deep and abiding "history [of native food] seems irrelevant today—as do Indians themselves—to popular conceptions of the South."[5] In the years since Green published her article, native foodways have slowly garnered more attention, at least in discussions of Southern (not necessarily Appalachian) food. In 2014, the Southern Foodways Alliance created a project called "Lumbee Indians of NC: Work and Cook and Eat" that featured interviews with various community members who discuss how Lumbee tradition, culture, and food are intertwined.[6] Likewise, at the beginning of the Covid-19 pandemic, one of Vivian Howard's early episodes of *Somewhere South* featured collard sandwiches at Lumbee Homecoming in Robeson County, North Carolina.[7] In the summer of 2020, undergraduate researcher Arcade Willis published an article about community gardens, food, and their inclusion in the curriculum at the Snowbird Day School in the Tuti yi "Snowbird" Cherokee community.[8] Despite these developments in acknowledging the indigenous roots of Southern food, and corn in particular, much work is yet to be done in recognizing the role that native foods play in Appalachian cuisine.

If we continue tracing the corn example and its curious alignment with the white hillbilly stereotype, then we must also ask how its importance to African-American communities in the South and in Appalachia has been obscured. As historian Sam Bowers Hilliard explains, during the antebellum period, corn was essential to all Southerners, whether free, enslaved, wealthy, middle class, or poor.[9] Yet in "areas where [enslaved people] made up a large portion of the population, they undoubtedly were the major corn consumers."[10] Scholars, including Jessica Harris and Frederick Douglass Opie, have written at length about the prevalence of corn in an enslaved person's diet.[11] And yet where ideas of Appalachia are concerned, for much of the twentieth century and often still today, corn—a food with a complex, multiracial history—signals whiteness, poverty, and shame. The menu rotates, but the meanings often remain stagnant.

As chapter 1 explores, writing by some popular Local Color authors, as well as travel writers, was instrumental in establishing these deeply embedded misunderstandings about the region, its people, and its cuisine. As chapter 2 discusses, Progressive Era reformers shaped their representations of food available in the mountains to serve their own goals; the larger the audience, the more blunted their representations became. By the twentieth century, writers, including those discussed in the previous chapter, explored how a shift from a subsistence-based lifestyle to one dependent on industrialism, cash crops, or both, affected what people were able to grow and eat. While depicting these changes, authors such as Olive Tilford Dargan (Fielding Burke), Grace Lumpkin, and contemporary writer Julia Franks, used their fiction to explore—and often critique—government food initiatives like North Carolina's Live at Home Program. In each of these examples, food shaming is present, sometimes overtly and sometimes symbolically. By the twentieth century, many mountain writers seemed to take it as fact that certain foods associated with the mountains would be deemed inferior. In Dargan's *Call Home the Heart*, for example, Bainie remarks that Ishma's children are "too uppity" to take molasses to school, preferring jelly instead.[12]

As with virtually every food reference discussed in this book, the meanings here are manifold. Although Bainie cites molasses, she almost certainly means sorghum syrup, or what some people call sorghum molasses. Food writer Ronni Lundy explains that many mountain residents shorten the term, calling the syrup "molasses," which creates quite a bit of naming confusion.[13] Molasses, derived from sugarcane, is not likely to have been in Bainie's household since sugarcane does not grow in Appalachia. Conversely, as Lundy and other food experts explain, sorghum syrup has an entirely different origin. "Sorghum seeds were part of the cargo of the slave ships that came to the Americas as early as the seventeenth century" (12). According to Lundy, these seeds did not produce the sorghum high in sugar content that is used to make syrup; instead, they were likely used as a grain to feed enslaved Africans. Lundy explains, "So far as we know, sweet sorghum cane was not grown in the United Stated until the 1850s," when farmers began growing South African imphee grass in the South and Northern growers cultivated a variety known as Black Amber (12). Lundy provides a fascinating account of how sorghum became the nationally preferred sweetener during the Civil War, explaining that defunct sugar trade routes created a need for homegrown sweetening (13). Even in the years following the war and Reconstruction, some mountain farmers grew sorghum as a cash crop, and many poorer mountain families produced the syrup for home use (14). In comparison, imported sugar would have been considered a luxury alongside homemade sorghum, also known as long sweetening.

When Bainie comments that Ishma's children are too "uppity" to take sorghum to school, the assumed social hierarchy is clear: for her children, sorghum would signal a lesser-than mountain identity, while jelly would indicate a higher standing, one that includes access to sugar and other ingredients necessary for jelly making. Notably, although Ishma does have homemade blackberry jelly to use in her children's school lunches, the previous summer she traded extra berries for sugar. It was not an ingredient she had on hand.

Moreover, in calling the syrup molasses instead of sorghum, the complex origin story of how a seed from an African grass not originally used for sweetening morphed into a variety of cane that could be made into a sweet syrup is lost. Bainie is not knowingly calling the syrup molasses as a slight to its history; presumably she calls it molasses because that is the term used by family and community. As Lundy points out, when people began making sorghum syrup, they were already familiar with molasses, and the connection seems logical even if the ingredients and resulting tastes were different. Even so, this term conflation signals a connection between poor white and African-American communities. Whether molasses (made from sugarcane) or sorghum syrup (made from sorghum), both homemade sweeteners suggest a lower socioeconomic class and the inability to buy imported sugar for regular use, though some may have been purchased for special occasions and dishes. Molasses has long been associated with poverty generally and African-Americans specifically: it "was the sweetening most frequently issued to" enslaved people, though poor Southerners across the board often relied on it.[14] As discussed in chapter 1, historian James Klotter contends that in the fifty or so years following Reconstruction, popular descriptions of Southern African-Americans and mountain whites shared striking similarities. These depictions marked mountain people as "Other," and while the molasses/sorghum example is not nearly as overt as the watermelon depictions examined in chapter 1, the connection remains. In this case, the naming confusion almost certainly developed naturally, but whether associated with poor African-Americans or poor white hillbillies—and whether you call it sorghum syrup or molasses—it was a food that could incite shame.

Examples like this one illustrate the crucial point that food shaming is incredibly dependent upon context. A dish that evokes gut-wrenching shame in one instance may become a source of pride in another. After all, sorghum is now a highly sought-after item by foodies intent on re-creating mountain dishes deemed "authentic," yet another slippery term as food scholars Carrie Helms Tippen, Ashli Quesinberry Stokes, and Wendy Atkins-Sayre have explored.[15] Similarly, depending on the context in which the shaming occurs, significant nuances about a food's origin or history—understandings that often disrupt too-easy stereotypes about Appalachia—may be lost.

It is not possible nor productive to attempt to chronicle every instance of food shaming that occurs in Appalachian literature since the turn of the twentieth century. Instead, what this chapter strives to do is illustrate key examples of such shaming, examining how and why particular foods are shameful in one scenario but not in another. As Vester contends, "How food and identity interact is determined by cultural narratives and the specific historical moment."[16] Works by Cratis Williams, James Still, and Crystal Wilkinson provide rich examples of the ways in which food, shame, and identity intersect. Investigating these representations in memoir (Williams) and fiction (Still and Wilkinson) provides a fascinating glimpse into both "real life" and fictional representations of how the sustenance one's body demands can also make one feel inferior. Williams's and Wilkinson's works also reveal troubling connections between sexuality, shame, abuse of power, and perhaps unexpectedly, food. In Wilkinson's *The Birds of Opulence* in particular, food metaphorically links women's bodies, land, dietary sustenance, and generational shaming in a fascinating account of how in that book, a squash is not just a squash.

Cratis Williams

Though robust now, the Appalachian studies movement likely would not have developed in the way it has had it not been for Cratis Williams. Scholars, teachers, grassroots organizers, and others familiar with the Appalachian Studies Association know Williams's name well, though most others probably do not. His contributions to the field were seismic. He was an avid collector of ballads and folk tales; he had a lifelong interest in linguistics and mountain speech; he helped found the Appalachian Consortium in 1971, whose press published many works integral to the field; he served as an advocate for mountain students and as an administrator at Appalachian State University; and Appalachian literary critics are forever indebted to him. In 1961, he completed the first dissertation about Appalachian literature—"The Southern Mountaineer in Fact and Fiction"—to fulfill doctoral requirements at New

York University. It was over 1,600 pages long and has served as a crucial start-ing point for literary scholars for the last sixty-plus years.

Upon his death in 1985, Williams left behind a staggering amount of writ-ten records, including memoir-like excerpts. The following year, Cratis's son, David Cratis Williams, teamed up with Carl Ross, then director of the Cen-ter for Appalachian Studies in Boone, to work on compiling a publishable memoir, despite the fact that Williams left no indication as to how the chap-ters should be ordered, a detail that looms large when analyzing the text. Ross died in 1988, and the project stagnated until Patricia Beaver, then di-rector of the Center for Appalachian Studies, took it up again in 1997.[17] In 1999, David Williams and Beaver published *The Cratis Williams Chronicles: I Come to Boone*, a text about Williams's first year in Boone (1942–1943), and in 2003 they published *Tales from Sacred Wind: Coming of Age in Appalachia*. For the latter, David Williams and Beaver made important decisions about how to arrange the excerpts, doing so based primarily on chronology. These editorial decisions matter within the context of this chapter's analysis, since chronological order does not necessarily indicate a potential argument about rhetorical presentation. Consequently, tracing identity shifts represented through food becomes even more complicated when the original author did not provide an organizational framework for the memoir. Even so, following a loose chronology reveals much about Williams's journey from a young boy in eastern Kentucky to a university administrator and leader in the Appala-chian studies field. David Williams and Beaver contend that Cratis Williams "never detached himself from his cultural roots, although it did take him many years and no doubt much agonizing before he was able to embrace with pride his Appalachian heritage, even as he ascended through academic ranks" (4). Williams's descriptions of food throughout his life reveal these struggles clearly, especially upon leaving his home community, when he begins learning about new customs, dishes, and eating etiquette.

Williams was born in 1911 on Caines Creek in Lawrence County, Ken-tucky. At that time, Local Color and travel writers had been publishing ac-counts of Appalachia as a place apart for thirty-plus years; John Fox Junior's best-selling novel, *The Trail of the Lonesome Pine*, had been in print for three years; and John C. and Olive Dame Campbell had concluded their socio-logical survey trip through parts of Appalachia just two years prior to Wil-liams's birth. His adolescent years occurred during the height of Progressive Era initiatives that routinely focused on Appalachian residents: in 1920, when

Williams was nine years old, William Goodell Frost served his last year as president of Berea College. Though Williams does not mention these situational contexts overtly, they are nonetheless crucial to our understanding of how his representations of food fit into a larger narrative occurring in the United States during this time.

Careful consideration of Williams's food depictions illustrates three things. First, Williams was keenly aware that a potential audience might view mountain culinary options as scarce, inferior, or both, and he took great pains to dispel the preconceived notions about Appalachian food he suspected readers would bring to his work. Second, despite Williams's painstaking attention to representations that indicate a veritable horn of plenty in Appalachia, at times he also writes unflinchingly about the food scarcity that his family sometimes experienced. Even so, Williams repeatedly points out that no matter how hungry his family might be, someone else always had fewer food options available to them. Third, in multiple passages, Williams indicates shame when he encounters an unfamiliar food, constantly lamenting his dearth of culinary knowledge and proper mealtime etiquette. If we consider the historical context in which ideas about Appalachia were becoming more firmly entrenched, we see that Williams was deeply influenced by previous portrayals of mountain foodways and their association with negative stereotypes. He fought hard to combat these misrepresentations, but in many ways he internalized judgments about mountain food, which in turn produced shame and longing when traveling outside of his immediate family circle. In short, he came to believe the dominant narrative about the inferiority of foods associated with the Mountain South at the same time he wrote in defense of them.

Williams's Defense of Mountain Foods

In an initial chapter, Williams describes his childhood on Caines Creek, explaining that "The Sunday visits to the homes of relatives and neighbors were gala affairs. Chicken and dumplings, vegetables in season, pies and cakes all laid out on the table together were standard fare for 'company' dinner" (30). Later he asserts without qualification, "We ate well as mountain farm people" (59). In these early textual references to food, readers do not encounter descriptions of food shortages or shame associated with any of the items available. Instead, Williams effectively dispels notions of hungry mountaineers who want for nutritious fare by describing a hearty, yet typical, Appalachian breakfast: "Always there were homemade biscuits . . . gravy, bacon or smoke-cured ham, butter, and all the milk one cared to drink" (61). While these items seldom varied from day to day, Williams points out that "Seasonal varieties of what was served beyond the basics included fried white ('Arsh') potatoes, baked or fried sweet potatoes, jams, jellies, and preserves, syrup, molasses, or honey, and tomato, apple, or grape juice. During hunting and fishing seasons squirrel or fish might be served in addition to pork" (61).

His descriptions continue, including several lines about boiled molasses, none of which indicate the slightest hint of shame. He even takes pains to explain the order in which items were eaten and how they were prepared on the plate: "Juices were not drunk prior to beginning a breakfast but along with it as was milk. One began with a biscuit broken open on his plate, a generous serving of potatoes, enough gravy to cover both, and a piece or two of thick but well done bacon or ham. He then proceeded to the sweet, which was eaten with buttered biscuit and bolstered with more bacon or ham if one wanted it" (61). Here Williams seems to emphasize the phrase "more bacon or ham if one wanted it," indicating that no one left the table hungry, because if the diner wanted more food, it was available, and there was no shame in eating one's fill.

In this same chapter, Williams carefully explains regional foodways to readers who would likely not be familiar with them. This didactic approach includes loving descriptions about culinary practices in Appalachia, as when he explains the concept of dinner, lest anyone confuse it with supper, which occurred at the end of the day: "The main meal of the day was 'dinner,' our midday meal. Like breakfast, dinner consisted of certain basic foods supplemented by others in season. Cornbread, beans, potatoes, gravy, stewed pork or fried sausage, pickles or relishes, butter, and sweet milk, skimmed milk ('blue john'), or buttermilk ('sour milk') were basic." In a few short lines, Williams twice emphasizes that this wide array of foods was basic. He goes on to comment, "In season, we had, in addition, 'sallet' greens, mustard, turnip greens, boiled cabbage, boiled pumpkin, roasting ears (corn on the cob), radishes, green onions or sliced onions, lettuce wilted with hot bacon grease and sprinkled with vinegar, turnips, parsnips, sliced tomatoes, sliced muskmelon. For dessert there were fruit pies, cobblers ('sonkers'), stewed fruit, cakes (including 'stack cakes'), gingerbread, and cookies" (62). As with his description of breakfast, Williams ensures that readers understand his family was not relegated to these same foods: "From time to time such special dishes as tomato dumplings, vegetable soup, potato cakes, or crackling bread might be included among the wide variety of foods served. In the late winter and early spring months dried, pickled, and canned foods were dominant among the supplements to the basics. Pickled beans, shucky beans ('leather britches'), or canned beans, sauerkraut, pickled corn, canned corn, dried pumpkin, and canned mustard were served along with the more enduring 'side meat' and jowl, shoulder, and ham produced from the smokehouse" (63). These passages and many more not only celebrate mountain fare but also effectively anticipate—and respond to—representations of Appalachian people as continually hungry, void of culinary know-how, or lacking in appreciation for good food.

Williams also emphasizes his family's ability to prepare foods appropriate for guests, including "canned meats, biscuits in addition to cornbread, [and] special cakes coated with icings and decorated with coloring" (63). In other words, they were not entirely lacking in cultural capital and understood which foods were "basic," which seasonally available items could liven up a meal at home, and which dishes were fit for guests. Bourdieu writes specifically about the importance of self-presentation when offering a meal; Williams's family was aware of how guests might view them based upon the foods they offered.[18] As mentioned earlier in this book, foodways scholar Elizabeth Engelhardt has explained the social stigmas that Progressive Era women like Katherine Pettit and May Stone ascribed to cornbread while elevating beaten biscuits and all of the race- and class-based baggage that accompanied them.[19] Williams does not indicate the specific kind of biscuits his family offered to guests, but he references an established hierarchy of bread in which cornbread occupies the lowest standing, one that must be supplemented with biscuits. His mention of cakes adorned with colored icing is also notable, suggesting that his family either knew how to use plants to make their own food coloring or were able to purchase it. Imported ingredients necessary for baking a cake, including white flour and sugar, likewise indicate a fairly comfortable social standing.

A More Complicated, Less Bountiful Portrayal

In the examples discussed above, Williams mounts a kind of culinary defensive. His food descriptions read like insistent catalog descriptions that leave no room for arguing: his family "ate well as mountain farm people" (59). But even in this assertion, Williams qualifies the good eating with "as mountain farm people," implying that someone from a different region with a different occupation might not agree. In the same paragraph that Williams describes his family's typical, hearty breakfast, he also reveals that "Eggs, a main source of family income, were used sparingly except at Easter time. Only when there were guests or on an occasion considered special for some reason were eggs served for breakfast" (61). Williams embeds the detail that his family could not afford to eat eggs on a daily basis in elaborate descriptions of a variety of foods that they could enjoy. He also points out that eggs were a special treat served on Easter morning (369).

Even when describing what they ate when the potatoes were gone or too old to be edible, he explains that if they made enough money from the sale of eggs, they ate "rice as a cereal, sweetened with sugar when we could afford it or with molasses when we had no choice" (61). Williams's preference for sugar instead of molasses (almost certainly sorghum syrup) echoes the previously discussed preference Ishma's children have for jelly instead of molasses. For Dargan's characters, their preference stems from social-class implications and the subsequent shame of taking molasses to school, but Williams does not make clear whether his preference is one based on taste, social inferiority associated with sorghum, or some combination of both.

Williams also uses humor to represent the cost-saving measures his family took to make food items last as long as possible. He explains that his mother roasted her own coffee beans "and ground only what she needed each morning" but reused the grounds every morning for a week, adding to them each day. He jokes that "by Thursday or Friday her coffee was black and strong enough to spin the uninitiated into a . . . dance" (62). Although making readers laugh deflects attention away from the fact that his mother could not afford to buy already-roasted coffee beans and use fresh ones each day, Williams also subtly indicates that his family's abundance is not so great they could avoid being frugal.

Likewise, Williams is careful to clarify that while his mother does cook some of their meals in the fireplace, he casts the activity as one of nostalgia rather than necessity. He writes lovingly of the cold winter days when his mother would

sometimes cook the dinner . . . in the fireplace and bake the cornbread for the evening meal in hot coals on the hearth. Dried beans with ham hock cooked in a black pot slowly over the coals, corn meal mush prepared in a cast iron skillet, sweet potatoes baked in the ashes, cornbread baked slowly in a mound of live coals on the hearth, pumpkin ... all served in plates that we held on our knees and glasses that we set beside us on the floor as we arranged ourselves around the fireplace and took us back to the "old days" that our grandparents remembered from their childhood when people living on Caines Creek were only two or three generations away from the pioneer ancestors who had settled there shortly after the War of 1812. (64)

Williams even states, "We felt as if we were reliving the history of our valley," emphasizing the "intimacy and reassurance of such an experience" (64). The fact that Williams remembers these experiences long after they occurred has the potential to soften the edges of a difficult reality. Even if his mother did choose to cook in the fireplace when the weather was especially cold, doing so placed physical demands upon her that stovetop cooking did not. What functions as a fond memory for Williams may well have been a reminder to his mother to be grateful for their stove, a detail that he neglects to mention. As noted earlier, Louise Coffin Jones asserted in 1879 that "Fifty years' cooking by a fireplace, stooping over the hearth an hour or two three times a day, was enough to warp any form."[20] Williams emphasizes that even on those cold days, she used the stove to cook breakfast. Though not stated explicitly, Williams seems aware that romanticizing fireplace cooking is only possible when a family is not relying upon it as their only means for food preparation.

As Williams's narrative continues—and again, we cannot know the order in which Williams intended it to be presented—clues appear that suggest a less abundant situation. In a section entitled "Starting Elementary School," Williams references a picture of himself as a six-year-old boy, writing that the photograph "shows [him] as a thin, frail, and hollow-eyed child with an enormous wedge-shaped head too big for [his] slight body" (84). He weighed only thirty-five pounds. Such descriptions suggest malnourishment, though Williams's previous descriptions of abundance indicate no shortage of a variety of foods. In a different section, Williams writes about the effect that World War I had on food supplies in his community, explaining that his family used molasses instead of sugar, and "until autumn 1918 [they] had flour only occasionally," but once they had it they "had flour for gingerbread, stack cakes, molasses cookies, pies, and biscuits but ... had little sugar for white cake and sugar cookies until after the war was over" (95). Yet even in these descriptions that explain the effects of the war on food supplies in Lawrence County, Williams does not indicate that his family was actively hungry. They may have gone without luxuries like white cakes and refined sugar, but they could still treat themselves to sweet treats and were able to maintain the bulk of their food options, despite the shortages. In both instances, Williams teeters on revealing a lack of food without actually doing so.

What Williams does point out, however, is that despite these shortages, his family was still in better standing than others during this time. He notes that his family "heard reports of starving children in Europe," as if this was not the case for Williams and his family. Likewise, in a section about the Nipperses, a traveling family that seeks room and board with Williams's family, readers understand that the Nipperses are the impoverished ones, people meant to be pitied and even reviled once readers learn about the father's dishonest behavior. Williams recalls his family being "flabbergasted" by their number, the mother's "ghostly" appearance, and the barefoot children. When offered food, "they ate ravenously" (116). Williams's emphasis on this family's need is significant: they are hungry; his family is not. They do not know proper table etiquette, while his criticism of their behavior implies that he does. At this point in the narrative, Williams sees his family as economically and socially superior to the Nipperses. The clear indication that they occupy a space on the social ladder many rungs lower than Williams's family points to the ever-evolving schema of food-based hierarchies. Within his own community, Williams sometimes feels superior, but that position shifts dramatically when he lives in different geographic areas and attempts to enter new social circles that likely see him as he saw the Nipperses.

Navigating New Culinary Territory

In 1920 the Williams family moves to Ohio to work as tenant farmers for a landowner named Mr. McDormin, an arrangement Williams's father believes will be preferable to their current situation since Grandpa Williams remains unwilling to give or sell them the land on which they live. Williams's father initially attempts to use the possibility of tenant farming as an incentive to change Grandpa Williams's mind, but instead, it prompts Mr. McDormin's son, Paul McDormin, to visit and inquire about their intentions. McDormin arrives well dressed and driving a red convertible sportscar, all of which greatly impresses Williams and his siblings, who rush home from school to inspect the visitors. When they enter the kitchen, Williams describes his mother as "red faced and weeping" as she tries "to prepare extra food for the guests." Williams explains that his "mother was weeping out of shame for our poverty, our shabby house, its meager furnishings, and the coarse food she was preparing for dinner" (127). With the arrival of a well-dressed man in a spiffy car, gone are Williams's descriptions of a bounteous table overflowing with chicken and dumplings, cornbread, and buttermilk. Instead they are replaced with the descriptor "coarse," evoking language Local Color writers frequently used to describe food in the mountains. In this context, Williams feels anything but socially superior, as opposed to his description of the Nippers family. Presumably the food his mother prepares is similar to what the family eats on a regular basis, food that when cooked in the fireplace evokes nostalgia for the old ways. The seemingly abrupt shift in sentiment signals one of this chapter's primary assertions: the way Williams feels about the food his family consumes is largely dependent upon context. What one might be proud to serve—and consume—in one setting may produce shame and embarrassment in another.

An even more dramatic inversion of Williams's culinary hierarchy happens when the family moves to Selma, Ohio, and travels there by train. Upon arriving in the depot, Williams recalls travelers eating foods they had purchased, while his family brought their own meal. Although his father bought milk for the children, they "ate fried chicken, ham biscuits and jellied biscuits, feeling poor and ashamed as [they] watched others eat strange things they had bought at the concession at the end of the room" (133). Here an almost immediate transition takes place: what would be considered good food at home suddenly becomes the source of shame in a train station, notably a space where travelers and bearers of many food traditions converge. Suddenly the homemade jelly Williams considers superior to molasses—and that Ishma's children in Dargan's novel prefer to take to school for lunch—is not adequate when compared to purchased foods. Instead, Williams sees the protein and carbohydrates that nourished the family in Kentucky as markers of shame and poverty, despite the fact that having fried chicken meant the family had a bird to spare for the trip. A dish usually reserved for Sunday dinner in Kentucky evokes embarrassment in an Ohio train station.

Williams's father presumably realizes that his family feels ashamed of the food they have brought, so he buys bananas (or "banannies") for the family, the first that Williams ever sees or eats. He recalls that his father bought six, and each family member ate one, with his mother saving the last one in her basket. As discussed in chapter 1, within the context of mountain foodways depictions in the nineteenth and early twentieth centuries, bananas often represent a cultural exoticism or worldliness. As a once difficult-to-procure fruit that must be imported, within the context of an Ohio train station in 1920 bananas embody a certain cachet. The mere consumption of them in a public space sent several unspoken messages: the ability to purchase a nonnative fruit, the knowledge of how to consume it, and the implied culinary appreciation for a food item not typically found in traditional diets in that place and time. If we put Williams's enjoyment of and appreciation for bananas in conversation with James Lane Allen's piece from 1886 discussed in chapter 1, Williams's portrayal seems to talk back to Allen's demeaning portrayal of the mountain man who supposedly mistook bananas for beans. In Williams's telling, he may not have eaten a banana before, but he was eager to do so and keenly aware of navigating a new social space.

Such culinary discoveries continue when Williams encounters light bread (yeast bread made from white flour) for the first time. In the same way that different sweeteners occupy different rungs of a culinary hierarchy, with refined sugar at the top and molasses at the bottom, a similar system applies to bread, especially in Appalachia. As mentioned earlier, foodways scholars have long acknowledged this phenomenon. As Elizabeth Engelhardt and Marcie Cohen Ferris explain, Progressive Era reformers like Katherine Pettit and May Stone, founders of the Hindman Settlement School in Kentucky, were horrified by the cooking methods they observed. They viewed cornbread, which appeared regularly on mountain tables, as nutritionally and culturally inferior to light bread.[21] Likewise, whether store bought or homemade, breads that required imported ingredients (like flour) and demanded labor-intensive baking methods (like beaten biscuits) were also considered superior since they signaled funds to buy difficult-to-procure ingredients, and for some, the means to hire domestic workers. As Engelhardt points out, those hired to complete time-consuming recipes were often African-American women, signaling that much more than baking bread was at stake. Considered within the context Engelhardt establishes, the kitchen functions as a site where gendered and racial politics play out with each task given and performed.[22]

For Williams, his first encounter with light bread is a memorable one. Although Williams includes cornbread in his memoir, he writes more often about his family eating biscuits, as when they take them on the train trip to Selma. These are presumably not labor-intensive beaten biscuits, but they still require flour as a primary ingredient. Socially speaking, they would be considered preferable to cornbread, but even they make Williams feel ashamed when he encounters light bread. The family's trip requires a few stops and one night spent in a hotel; across the street, the children spy a bakery with a large window facing the street. Williams describes the awe with which he and his siblings observed bakers rolling out dough for light bread, a delicacy he emphasizes that none of them had ever eaten. At their final stop, the family connects with relatives named Uncle Willie and Aunt Sarah. Williams spends pages describing every detail of their lavish home, from their sofa to the ornate rug on the floor to the towel used for hand drying. Aunt Sarah prepares a supper for them that includes light bread "cut from a long loaf wrapped in a brightly decorated wax paper," strawberry jam, and "yeasty loaf bread." Williams remembers his childhood reaction: "How wonderful I thought it would be to be rich enough to afford light bread as a replacement for the cornbread and the big rough biscuits that we had been eating on the farm back in Kentucky" (141). These are the same "big rough biscuits" described with admiration in an earlier part of the memoir, indicating once again that the way he feels about the foods he consumes is situational.

When he describes the breakfast Aunt Sarah served the next morning—juice, milk, oatmeal sweetened with brown sugar, eggs, bacon, and light bread toast with butter and strawberry jam—he writes that "I had never eaten such a fine breakfast before" (141). This statement prompts him to remember the "big rough biscuits, fried potatoes, gravy, thick bacon or rusty ham, sorghum molasses, and milk still warm from the cow that we usually had for breakfast back on Caines Creek" (140). Whereas we are led to believe that the family was happy with—and even proud of—their food in Kentucky, once they are exposed to different items, that estimation begins to shift. Williams makes clear that even as a child, he conflates economic privilege, material goods, and food, all of which make clear to him that these new foods should be seen as superior.

Yet Williams also indicates that such hierarchies are not static and may be inverted in some situations. In 1920, when the family returns to Kentucky "to stay," he describes their "hardest summer" (167). After their return, Williams's father works in Columbus, Ohio, and Williams's pregnant mother is left to fend for herself, him, and his siblings. Even though Williams's grandfather lets them have a daily supply of milk, Williams writes that "Our diet was inadequate and monotonous," producing "heartburn, for which we took bicarbonate of soda." Here again readers see that despite Williams's initial declarations, the table is not always bountiful. During this same time, Williams's father stays at a boarding house in Columbus and longs for the food he was accustomed to eating in Kentucky. Williams writes, "He enjoyed rooming at the Caudill's place, but wished Rose [the caretaker] would put a square of cornbread in his lunch bucket instead of the two thin slices of light bread" (169). In this instance, light bread—the very food item that Williams viewed as the height of culinary capital when in Ohio—has fallen *below* cornbread for his father. Ironically, cornbread is one of the few staples Williams, his mother, and his siblings are able to eat regularly in Kentucky. Williams does not give readers a clear sense of whether his father and other family members experienced shame related to foods consumed, but here he emphasizes that while cornbread may evoke shame in one context, it produces longing and nostalgia in another.

Although the culinary shame created by their move to Ohio seems partially absolved by their return to Kentucky and the restoration of a more plentiful table, Williams continues to feel embarrassed that he lacks a certain culinary prowess, especially once he moves to Louisa, Kentucky, to attend high school and enters a new social sphere. While there he delivers papers for the *Cincinnati Post*, and a field representative of the newspaper, whom Williams identifies only as "Mr. W___," takes Williams to lunch and a movie to thank him for increasing subscribers. Mr. W makes Williams quite uncomfortable by touching him unnecessarily, observing him keenly, and even telling him he is a "pretty boy" three times (283). Williams also becomes flustered by Mr. W's question about where he would like to eat, and he "could not find the courage to say that [he] had never eaten in a restaurant." Williams manages to choose a restaurant that he has admired from the street, and once they are seated, the menu presents his next challenge because it was "the first [he] had ever seen" (281). Although written from a 2015 perspective, linguist Dan Jurafsky's claim is readily applicable to Williams's dilemma: "Every time you read a description of a dish on a menu you are looking at all sorts of latent linguistic clues, clues about how we think about wealth and social class [and] how our society views our food."[23]

Williams remembers thinking that "eating in a restaurant was an expensive proposition that only quite well-to-do people could afford," and he orders only items familiar to him, with the exception of breaded pork chops (281). Even that partially familiar food produces anxiety (he recognizes pork chops but is not sure what it means to "bread" them) and feels embarrassed when confronted with a small dish of peach cobbler: "I had not yet used the spoon, so I assumed that one ate cobbler properly with a spoon. Always before, I had taken cobbler from a big bowl directly into my plate. Was I supposed to rake the cobbler from the little dish onto my plate? If not, was I supposed to set the little dish in my plate and then eat the cobbler from the little dish?" As he ponders these questions, Mr. W abruptly stops eating his meal and begins eating his cobbler, presumably to show Williams what to do, which in turn makes Williams feel even worse (282). Yet Williams perseveres, engaging in what American studies scholar Margot Finn calls aspirational eating, which she defines as "a process in which people use their literal tastes—the kinds of foods they eat and the way they use and talk about food—to perform and embody a desirable class identity and distinguish themselves from the masses."[24] Like Jurafsky, Finn writes from a contemporary perspective, but her examination of how class anxiety produces significant shifts in mainstream hierarchies of desirable foods and culinary lifestyles applies as well to Williams's discomfort in 1920 as it does to the present day. Williams makes clear that while initially uncomfortable, he aspires to function within the new culinary sphere introduced by Mr. W. Williams observes him carefully, noting the slowness and precision with which he eats, as well as the rare beef he orders.

The shame Williams feels about his dearth of mealtime etiquette, as well as what he comes to consider a limited culinary repertoire, is not particularly surprising given his entrance into a new social setting, especially one in which people like Mr. W have the economic means to dine at a restaurant. But Williams also emphasizes that Mr. W makes him feel ashamed because of his inappropriate, sexually abusive behavior: he quizzes Williams about his virginity, offers unwanted sexual advice, and even hugs Williams tightly "like a sweetheart." This unexpected and troubling revelation calls attention to the multiple ways Mr. W attempts to establish control over Williams. Mr. W is no doubt aware that Williams may feel flattered to receive the attention of a cultured adult, and Mr. W capitalizes on that potential admiration. By introducing Williams to unfamiliar dishes and restaurant culture more generally, Mr. W implicitly incites shame for Williams. Likewise, by behaving inappropriately, he explicitly incites another kind of shame since Williams does not know how to process Mr. W's actions; he only knows that he "felt guilty and demeaned by having been hugged . . . by a full-grown man" (285). Mr. W's infatuation with Williams is one driven by a desire for dominance, from advising him to avoid sex with women to exposing Williams to unfamiliar foods and social settings in which Mr. W acts as teacher and benefactor. He establishes a warped cultural and physical control over Williams that leaves readers disgusted. As discussed later in this chapter when exploring Crystal Wilkinson's *The Birds of Opulence*, the politics of food, shame, and fertility sometimes intersect in surprising and uncomfortable ways.

The incident with Mr. W also seems indicative of a larger trend that develops during Williams's high school years. Reflecting upon that time in his life, he writes, "I doubted my self-worth. I realized the poverty in which my family lived and felt ashamed of myself and kin. I was beset by anxieties that were to remain with me for fully ten years and by feelings of inadequacy and low self-esteem" (307). His feelings about food are obviously not the only source of this shame, but they are an integral part of the identity conflicts he experiences and often function in similar ways for other mountain people, both real and fictional.

Culinary Shame Fictionalized

Analyzing Williams's memoir provides important insights about food, cultural capital, and the effect shifting hierarchies of that capital have on consumers. Fictional representations of that same phenomenon likewise reveal the potential shame that consuming certain foods, depending on situation and context, may produce for characters. The texts discussed here represent only a small portion of Appalachian works of fiction that could be discussed in an evaluation of food shaming, yet one trend persists that Williams emphasizes in his memoir: food shaming—especially when related to bodily dominance—is about power. Analyzing which foods evoke shame, the cultural messages that they carry in that time and place, how consumers feel eating those foods, and how authors imagine those scenarios on the page tells us much about structures that have routinely disempowered mountain people, and in many cases, still do.

James Still's 1940 novel, *River of Earth*, occupies an important place in Appalachian literary studies. Whereas literature published about the region in the late nineteenth and early twentieth centuries was largely, though not always, written by nonnative authors, Still embodied a perspective much more closely aligned with the mountains. Literary scholar Claude Lafie Crum contends that Still worked hard to cultivate and maintain that image, but even so, reading Still's portrayal of Appalachian characters in 1940 must have been a welcome change for readers weary of tired plot devices featuring moonshiners, feuds, and beautiful but intellectually stunted mountain women. Instead, *River of Earth* presents believable, empathetic characters trying to survive in a changing landscape characterized by an ever-present struggle between agrarian and industrial ideals.

Crum notes that the novel did not begin to receive widespread critical attention until the late 1960s, but despite its "uneven publication history," it is arguably one of the most important fictional portrayals of Appalachia.[25] Narrated from the perspective of an adolescent boy who does not fully comprehend all that is happening around him, the novel provides a beautifully wrought account of the warring ideals between agrarian and industrial lifestyles. The boy's mother, Alpha Baldridge, may be read as a stand-in for Agrarianism—she longs to establish a permanent homestead where they can grow their own food—whereas the boy's father, Brack Baldridge, functions as a stand-in for industrialism—he prefers coal mining instead of farming and is willing to move in order to find work. During one discussion between the couple about whether or not to move, Alpha laments, "Forever moving yon and back, setting down nowhere for good and all," saying that she wants "a place certain and enduring, with room to swing arm and elbow, a garden-piece for fresh victuals, and a cow to furnish milk for the baby."[26] Despite Alpha's longings, the novel makes clear that a life dependent on the land is not always food secure. In the first few pages, readers learn that Alpha is struggling to cook for eight people, including two of Brack's cousins who take advantage of the family's generosity. She becomes so desperate that she burns down the family's house because there is only room for the immediate family in the smokehouse. Starvation is a very real possibility, and Baby Green presumably dies of malnourishment.

Even though having enough food is a paramount concern for the characters, the social meanings embedded within that food still matter. When Brack begins working at a nearby mine, the family is elated when he brings home bags full of store-bought food purchased on credit. Likewise, when the children start attending school, the narrator explains the relief he felt when his mother was able to send what he felt was an acceptable lunch. The narrator and his sister, Euly, "laughed when [the lunch box] was opened, amazed at what was there. Fried guinea thighs and wings, covered with a brown-meal crust. Two yellow tomatoes. A corn pone, and a thumb-sized lump of salt . . . We had turned our backs on the others before looking into the box, but now we were not ashamed of what we had to eat" (86). It seems unlikely that Cratis Williams would have been proud of such fare in the train station in Ohio, but likely he would have felt that way at a schoolhouse in his home community. We see yet another contextual shift when the Baldridge family moves to the mining town and "old neighbors . . . stare at the dried, pickled, and canned victuals [the family] had brought" (184). Unlike at the beginning of the novel, when food was scarce, by the time the Baldridge's move to the mining town, they are able to bring surplus food with them. And when Baby Green dies, Alpha insists on having a funeral, saying, "I ain't ashamed of what we got" (174). The shifts in meaning associated with particular foods are not as drastic in *River of Earth* as they are in Williams's memoir, but food still functions well outside the bounds of sustenance, evoking both pride and shame for characters.

Another Kentucky writer, Crystal Wilkinson, presents a fascinating account of food, women's bodies, land, and generational shaming in her award-winning 2016 novel, *The Birds of Opulence*. As an African-American woman and founding member of the Affrilachian Poets, Wilkinson brings an essential perspective to Appalachian literature. Her work features love of place as a core value for her characters, despite the fact that popular representations of Appalachia often deny the reality of their existence, instead misrepresenting the region as monolithically white. In the same way that the book can expand reader perceptions of racial diversity in the mountains, it also expands the way we can—and should—think about food in literature. Certainly the novel contains examples of the kind of literary food shaming discussed thus far in this chapter. For example, at one point the narrator explains why Yolanda, one of the novel's main characters, dreads visits from her city cousins: "They always snarl their noses up at what she wears, how she styles her hair, and what she and her family eat," deeming oxtail shamefully rural.[27] The narrator makes clear that such judgments are not limited to Yolanda's cousins but are instead common for those who have moved away from Opulence, the town where the novel takes place. When former residents make their annual trip home to attend Dinner on the Grounds, "They bring candy that they claim is the best of the best," but the children spit out the "bitter chocolate" and go in search of familiar sweets at the local grocery store (103–104). What is notable about these instances is that instead of feeling ashamed, whether about oxtail or supposedly inferior candy, these characters feel indignant. They are resistant, indicating that if anyone should feel ashamed, it should be those making such judgments.

Judgment functions as one of the central themes in the novel: mothers judge daughters, neighbors judge neighbors, and gossip fuels steady debates among townswomen about who is sleeping with whom, who fathered whom, and what so-and-so's daughter or son has done. The novel presents Opulence as a firmly rooted community that provides a grounded sustenance for its characters, but that rootedness also proves suffocatingly toxic when generational shaming seems inescapable. One of the primary ways Wilkinson represents that inescapability is through food, and more specifically, squash and the vines that propagate it.

But first, she issues a clear directive to readers. The second line of the novel instructs, "Imagine yourself a woman who gathers stories in her apron" (3). From the beginning, we are cast as collectors, presumably collectors who know our way around the kitchen given our attire. Read metaphorically, Wilkinson links storytelling and food from the novel's genesis, emphasizing the reciprocal relationship between the two. The novel's first chapter also stands out as the only one narrated in first-person point of view, while the rest are told in third-person point of view. Here, Yolanda, the youngest member of the Goode line of women, narrates the circumstances surrounding her birth in a squash patch. She even explains that her great-grandmother, Mama Minnie, "thumped Mama's belly as if it were a melon" (4). This familiar comparison of a pregnant woman's stomach to a melon also evokes ripeness, soil, and growing things pushing their way out of the earth, or a woman's body. Only a few pages later, readers learn that one Sunday afternoon Mama Minnie, Granny Tookie (Yolanda's grandmother, whose formal name is Nora Jean), and Lucy (Yolanda's mother) visit the garden at the old homeplace. Although no longer occupied, the family house still stands, and the women tend the garden, suggesting a connection between women, land, and fertility. The narrator emphasizes that these connections to the land extend far beyond the living for Mama Minnie: "A feeling seeped into Mama Minnie's bones, a feeling like the return of everything lost. Old-time people from across the waters gathered all around her. She put her bony hand on her hip. Everything yesterday converged" (9). The garden becomes a site of generational remembering, and as the women work in it, Lucy performs the dualistic labor of gathering squash and giving birth to her daughter, Yolanda.

Yolanda's birth in a squash patch among three generations of women is significant and metaphorically suggestive. At the 2021 Appalachian Studies Association conference, I participated in a panel with Crystal Wilkinson and Ronni Lundy. During that conversation about food, shame, and Wilkinson's work, Wilkinson said that she was "fascinated by squash as a child," remembering that they "looked like bab[ies]" to her.[28] As we talked more about the connection, she said, "There's something very . . . feminine about the shape of the squash to me." Lundy added that hollowed squash and gourds—undeniably yonic symbols—were and are used as vessels from earliest native cultures well into twentieth-century Appalachia. Read in that way, the squash become suggestive markers of rooted fertility and motherhood.

Moreover, although not stated explicitly, the scene evokes a connection to the land that seems indigenous. Mama Minnie even buries the afterbirth, an act that connects land, fertility, and generations of the Goode women. While Mama Minnie, Tookie, and Lucy all clearly identify as African-American and are of different generations (not sisters), readers familiar with Cherokee agricultural practices cannot help but think of the Three Sisters: beans, corn, and squash, a planting practice that relied on the symbiotic relationship between the three food sources to provide sustenance in a space- and nutrient-efficient way. The narrator does not specify the kind of squash the women harvest but describes the "yellow bodies curved, [and] long-necked," suggesting yellow crookneck squash. In scientific and historical terms, *Cucurbita pepo* (almost certainly the variety Wilkinson describes) "was apparently the most widespread of the cultivated species in North America . . . [whose] seeds and rind date as early as 2700 B.C. in the Eastern U.S."[29] The vegetable's long history in North America combined with Mama Minnie's feeling of "the return of everything lost" indicates that the connections these women share exist in the past, present, and future (9). Not unlike a squash vine extending its tendrils as it grows, the ties that bind the Goode women are firmly rooted in the soil they tend.

The narrator's emphasis on the color yellow, in addition to the novel's overall focus on shame, sexual abuse, and bodily autonomy (or the lack thereof), also carries a sinister reminder for readers attuned to the horrors of enslavement. Historians have long documented the family lines white plantation owners established with the enslaved women they owned. The story of Thomas

Jefferson and Sally Hemings, for example, is one familiar to many Americans. White women married to these promiscuous masters often lamented their husbands' indiscretions in private diaries, and Harriet Jacobs' 1861 account of living in constant fear of her monstrous master and mistress repeatedly reminds readers that although her situation as an enslaved woman was horrific, others endured even more hardships.[30] Sexual abuse and trauma marked the lives of many enslaved women, and laws of enslavement in Southern states ensured that children followed the condition of the mother. This system of abuse and ownership not only granted male plantation owners dominance and power, but it also increased their wealth, since their own racially mixed children were also their property. Wilkinson's book is set long after slavery was a reality in the South, but the novel's repeated emphasis on history, rootedness, and generational connections emphasizes that the past is never too far behind.

Considered within this context of ownership, abuse, and shame, the narrator's description of Lucy's awareness of her surroundings during labor takes on another, heavier meaning: "Suddenly [she] smells squash. The blossoms, the yellow bodies curved, long-necked, and graceful, their fullness heavy on the vines by her head as she pushed her baby girl out" (19). In these passages the repeated emphasis on yellow connects to the squash that surrounds Lucy, but it also connotes generations of sexual assault that resulted in racial mixing, resulting in lighter-skinned bodies that were sometimes described as yellow. Although not applicable to Wilkinson's characters, the term "high yellow" describes a kind of racially based colorism within the African-American community in which lighter-skinned people place themselves above darker-skinned people. In this example, though, the narrator's emphasis on curved yellow bodies and long necks sexualizes the description of an otherwise ordinary vegetable. In doing so, a vegetable ripe for consumption becomes a metaphorical stand-in for women's bodies. Notably, squash grow all around Lucy, suggesting a great number of women who have endured trauma. Read in this way, Lucy's labor in the squash patch becomes a singular act that is part of an already long-established trend. Likewise, the fact that her daughter, Yolanda, is "gold as egg yolk" signals an enduring future connection (13). During our panel discussion about the significance of squash in the novel, Wilkinson stated she "became sort of obsessed with it in [the] book," contending that it functions as "a haunting vegetable that stays with these characters."

As the novel progresses, readers learn that these women are plagued by shame. Tookie, Yolanda's grandmother, is raped as a young girl and becomes pregnant as a result. Instead of offering support, her mother, Mama Minnie, beats her for shaming the family. When remembering that time in her life, the narrator explains that Tookie was "a long-necked girl again with her belly six-months swollen . . . shame washes over her still" (28). The comparison between the long-necked squash that surrounds Lucy as she gives birth and Tookie's description as a long-necked girl further emphasizes not only the rootedness to place these women experience, but also the deeply embedded shame that seems equally permanent.

In a heartbreaking scene near the novel's end, Lucy's mental state continues the decline it began after Yolanda's birth. The narrator explains, "She rubs her arms against the squash vines growing through her elbows down to her finger tips" (187). She repeatedly says to herself, "Mama gone, Granny gone, roots still here," before taking her own life and completing the trinity of three evoked at the novel's beginning (183, 187, 195). Though Yolanda does not seem tormented by the same feelings of shame the women before her endured, she suffers from presumed depression, anxiety, or both. In other words, the trauma passed down through the Goode women seems generational and rooted in the land that also sustains them.

References to food function differently for Francine Clark, a widowed neighbor whose unexpected pregnancy surprises her as much as it does the community. When she goes into labor in her kitchen, she is making fudge from "black walnuts, cocoa, confectionary sugar, and butter" (39). In some ways, the recipe's decadent ingredients foreshadow her impending tendency to hoard food once her daughter, Mona, is born, as though an accumulation of calories might offer some kind of protection, at least against hunger. The novel's narrator remains noncommittal about the circumstances of Francine's pregnancy, but the possibility of sexual assault is clear. The narrator states that Francine could be one of the "women who don't know where their babies come from, who have menstrual cycles all through their pregnancies, women who refuse to remember tragedy, women who were raped," or she could be one of the women "who live one life by day and another by night" (44–45). Either way, "each resident in town puts her where they want her," and readers insistent on hypothetical conclusions are forced to do the same.

This connection between readers and townspeople highlights Francine's reliance on food as a coping mechanism, illustrating the effect such town gossip can and does have. She refuses the meals supposedly well-meaning community women bring her, instead driving to a grocery store in Lexington where she will not encounter anyone she knows. She buys so much food that she must cram "pot pies in the box freezer on the porch," rearrange frozen goods to "make it all fit," and force another gallon of milk into the refrigerator even though it already contains two that are souring (53). No matter what forces exist outside of her control, she knows that she will have plenty of food for herself and Mona. As she puts away the groceries, "memory comes rushing in" and "shame is buried beneath the folds of soft tissue around her stomach. She rubs her fat hands through the sweat on her neck and fidgets with her bra, where sweat drips down to her navel" (53). In this passage the quick succession of memory, shame, and folds of abdominal flesh suggests a connection between memory, possibly of sexual trauma, fertility, reproduction, shame, and food. Her body becomes a receptacle for each of those elements and one that depends on the collection and consumption of food to combat the feelings of shame that threaten to overwhelm her. The narrator explains that Francine is "smothered beneath her own skin, smothered beneath all this worry. So she hoards food in the house, in her body, just like a mother squirrel inside the wall" (55). Her tendency to stockpile food is also presumably in response to her own mentally ill mother's inability to provide consistent meals.

Generational shame continues for Mona, Francine's daughter, when she becomes pregnant and leaves Opulence shortly after graduating from high school. The narrator explains, "And for a moment she regrets any additional shame that she may have brought on her mother's head, . . . Shame can't last always. Can it? Everyone in Opulence knows her, and she is glad to be going somewhere where no one does" (155). Mona hopes that uprooting herself from her home community will allow some distance from the shame that seems firmly rooted in Opulence. For her mother, it results in procuring more food than she can consume before it spoils, while for the Goode women, the metaphorically loaded image of squash haunts them. In both cases, Wilkinson's novel suggests an uncomfortable correlation between the cultivation (in the case of the Goode women) and the consumption (in the case of Francine) of food and women's bodies. For the Goode women, squash becomes the symbolic vehicle through which readers are reminded of assault, trauma, and shame, as well as the resulting new life, growth, and abundance that can occur. For Francine, food is stored and consumed in apparent response to feelings of shame. But in both cases, the consumption of women's bodies results in shame, echoing Cratis Williams's response to his mentor's inappropriate behavior.

Yet Wilkinson also imbues the novel with hopeful signs, ones that indicate the possibility for positive change. As she noted during our panel conversation, the African Sankofa, an Adinkra symbol, graces the cover of *The Birds of Opulence* and is also included in the text. The meaning of the Sankofa Adinkra varies, but according to Wilkinson, the main idea is to "go back and fetch it," or "you have to know where you come from in order to know where you're going." When talking about these symbols and their importance, she said one theme the book explores is "what is in the blood that we carry forward to the next generation" and "what's not," pointing out that some harmful traditions may be stopped or changed.

Other Shameful Stories

Plenty of other examples of shame connected to food exist in Appalachian literature. For example, Jim Wayne Miller's 1989 novel, *Newfound*, includes a heart-wrenching scene in which the semiautobiographical protagonist, Robert, is shamed by his teacher for not eating what she deems nutritionally appropriate foods for breakfast. As an adult looking back on the incident, he remembers, "I never grew accustomed to feeling shame. Each time, it flared up hotter than before, and raced from the center out, popping and cracking like a brush fire, leaving everything black and smoldering inside."[31] Likewise, as discussed in greater depth in the next chapter, in Denise Giardina's 1987 novel, *Storming Heaven*, another teacher, Miss Radcliffe, speaks condescendingly to the children she invites to her home for tea and cookies.

A primary organizing principle of this chapter is that social meanings associated with food shift depending on time, geography, and a myriad of other contextual factors. Equally important to note is the fact that someone made to feel culinary shame may use a similar schema to shame someone else: feeling the sting of shame does not preclude one from extending that feeling to others. As discussed earlier in this chapter, Williams's memoir reveals the shifting food hierarchies he experienced in his life, even poking fun at his own lack of understanding. When his family moves to Ohio, they work as tenant farmers for the wealthy McDormin family. While exploring the McDormin property, Williams and his brother Ralph come upon "a patch of what looked

like 'spargrass' planted in the hills" (156). They later learned "that the Mc-
Dormins ate them as [Cratis's family] did sallet" (156). He goes on to explain,
"In Kentucky spargrass was used in flower pots and arrangements taken to the
graveyards on Decoration Day. No one ever thought of eating it, but we knew
there were people who would eat anything. . . .We felt especially blessed that
we had . . . plantain, poke, dandelion, whitetop, sorrel, and lamb's quarter for
sallet instead of squirming spargrass" (156). According to memoirist Zetta
Barker Hamby, along the North Carolina/Virginia state line, "spargrass" (or
spar grass) is a regional term used in rural mountain locations to mean asparagus.[32] Hamby's assessment of the vegetable echoes Williams's adolescent
view of it: the only person in her family who would eat "that weed" was her
grandmother (22). Presumably the McDormins viewed asparagus as a vegetable well suited for the dinner table, but to a young Williams, he viewed asparagus as repulsive fare that only someone desperately hungry would consider
eating. He places other foraged greens—ones that the McDormins would
almost certainly see as markers of poverty—including plantain, poke, dandelion, whitetop, sorrel, and lamb's quarter, above asparagus.

It is also worth noting that Williams does not define these potentially unfamiliar wild greens for readers. His refusal to do so could be read as an incentive to readers take it upon themselves to self-educate about mountain
foodways. But for those who do not, confusion seems likely; the plantain
Williams references, for example, is not the tropical fruit readers might imagine but rather a wild and nutritious green. Likewise, Williams does not explain sallet: he does not mean salad comprised of raw vegetables but rather
a category of greens cooked in grease and consumed hot. There are multiple
levels of knowing and not knowing functioning in this description: as an adolescent, Williams did not view asparagus as an edible and socially elite vegetable, though his retelling gently highlights his naïveté. And in the same way
that he illustrates his not knowing, Williams also pokes fun at readers who
may envision his family eating cold salads and tropical fruits.

Yet in 2022, readers are more likely to recognize and understand terms
like sallet. Despite the pandemic's wrenching blow to the restaurant industry, foodies spending a lot of time at home seem more invested than ever in
learning about and practicing what they deem traditional, authentic mountain foodways. As the next chapter explores, this relatively recent recognition and celebration of mountain food was already a trend in a number of

important works of Appalachian fiction. In other words, venerating local cuisine is something mountain writers were doing by the mid-twentieth century, though the rest of the nation just now seems to be paying attention. In turn, twenty-first-century writers like Robert Gipe are watching with interest and providing their own postmodern commentary.

CHAPTER 5

"The Main Best Eating in the World"

Responding to Past and Current Food Narratives

FOR TELEVISION VIEWERS WHO ENJOY HIGH-INTENSITY COOK-
ing shows, chef Gordon Ramsay is a household name. His long-running
hit series, *Hell's Kitchen*, pits aspiring chefs against one another as they
complete various culinary challenges "in the hope of winning big." The National Geographic Channel carries Ramsay's more recent series, *Gordon Ramsay: Uncharted*. When describing the third season that began airing Memorial Day weekend, 2021, Ramsay said he wanted "to reposition the view of
a region's cuisine, and show that by peeling back the layers, we can get to
the root of its reputation." He continued, "What are the pieces that people
have forgotten or taken out of context? At the end of each adventure, I think
about how I can put respect back on the table with everything I've learned."[1]
The third season includes visits to Portugal, Croatia, Puerto Rico, Iceland,
Mexico, Finland, and four U.S. locations: Texas, Maine, Michigan's Upper
Peninsula, and the Smoky Mountains. In episode 304, Ramsay visits Western
North Carolina, where he cooks and fishes with Asheville-based chef William Dissen, searches for mushrooms with forager Alan Muskrat, makes liv-
ermush with butcher Matt Helms, turns corn into hominy in Cherokee, and
learns about moonshine from Cody Bradford of Howling Moon distillery.[2]
The episode sensationalizes various activities in a thinly veiled attempt to cap-
tivate viewer attention: instead of wading into a trout stream, Ramsay rappels
down a waterfall to access the stream; instead of safely driving to a distillery
in a nondescript car, Ramsay careens around curves in a souped-up muscle
car with Bradford. Despite these obvious plays to garner viewer interest, the

episode praises foods associated with the mountains, and Asheville chef Will Dissen wins the concluding cookoff.

It is striking that the food of the Great Smoky Mountains warranted an episode. Certainly the region's foodways are delicious and deserve celebrating after such a fraught history of denigration, but the show's website makes clear that part of its intent is to capture Ramsay's "journeys to some of the most incredible and remote locations on Earth in search of culinary inspiration, epic adventures, and cultural experiences he will never forget."[3] Casting the Smoky Mountains as one of "the most incredible and remote locations on Earth" sounds like a direct quote from problematic Local Color literature of the late 1800s and early 1900s examined in chapter 1 of this book. Yet Ramsay makes clear that part of his purpose is to "put respect back on the table," signaling that the show's producers are aware that the culinary history of the Mountain South is not one generally met with respect or admiration. The Great Smoky Mountains episode functions as one example of a larger trend: mountain food is finally receiving its due. Yet with that recognition comes continued categorization as Other. Chefs across the nation and world are interested in learning more about the culinary traditions of the region and the ways in which they may be incorporated into their kitchens. But as this book's conclusion argues, while welcome, this celebration should be tempered with a fair measure of caution. Asking which ingredients and dishes come to be associated with the region, whose are left out, and in what context the foodways of the region are made available are all important questions.

If the rest of the world has just begun to recognize the merits of mountain cuisine in the last decade or so, authors from the region have been venerating these foods, as the song goes, before country was cool. Writers, including but not limited to Harriette Simpson Arnow, Jean Ritchie, and Wilma Dykeman, wrote lovingly about foods associated with Appalachia in the midtwentieth century. Likewise, contemporary authors, including Denise Giardina, Crystal Wilkinson, and Michael McFee, capture the depth and meaning of emotion embedded in foods they connect to the region. In *Trampoline*, *Weedeater*, and especially in *Pop*, Robert Gipe presents a brilliant postmodern treatment of the processed convenience foods that have come to represent a demographic of people impoverished by third-party land ownership and coal mining–induced environmental destruction. In *Pop*, Gipe fictionalizes the current foodie obsession with mountain cuisine in a way that invites readers to examine their own obsessions with certain foods and to ask how their fetishization could affect the connection mountain people have with their own foodways, culture, and heritage. Most of all, the texts considered in this chapter invite readers to see the joy associated with Appalachian food. These authors remind us that not all representations are problematic literary portrayals, reform efforts characterized by oversimplifications meant to garner funds, government programs advising farmers on what they already knew, or tales of shame. These books show us an ebullience and love for place that endures, all the while commenting on and critiquing the context in which that celebration occurs.

Mid-Twentieth Century Celebrations and Critiques

As discussed in the previous chapter, James Still's 1940 novel, *River of Earth*, became a watershed text for Appalachian studies as the first book about Appalachia published by an Appalachian. From that point forward, mountain writers began gaining more critical acclaim on a national level. Harriette Simpson Arnow is perhaps one of the most important mountain writers of the mid-twentieth century, yet the critical attention her work has received is uneven. Her best-selling 1954 novel, *The Dollmaker*, was nominated for the National Book Award in 1955 and was a favorite among critics. Yet in 1971, Joyce Carol Oates wrote, "*The Dollmaker* is one of those excellent American works that [has] yet to be properly assessed."[4] Then in 1978, feminist, author, and social activist Tillie Olsen published *Silences*, a genre-bending book that celebrates women writers whose voices had been silenced but Olsen thought were worth hearing. Arnow was one of the writers Olsen featured, and in a 1972 reading list, Olsen includes *The Dollmaker* alongside works by George Eliot, Kate Chopin, and Virginia Woolf. In the 2003 twenty-fifth anniversary edition of *Silences*, literary critic Shelley Fisher Fishkin asserts, "*Silences* changed what we read in the academy, what we write, and what we count."[5] As just two examples of Fishkin's claim, in 2011 Appalachian studies scholar Emily Satterwhite used reader response theory to examine fan mail sent to Arnow and other authors of best-selling works set in Appalachia to determine the appeal of such works to readers across the nation.[6] In 2012, *Appalachian Heritage* published a special issue devoted entirely to Arnow and guest edited by Arnow biographer Sandra Ballard.[7] It included one of Arnow's previously unpublished short stories ("Crazy Blanket") as well as articles focused on Arnow's life, teaching her work, and literary criticism.

Arnow's best-known work remains *The Dollmaker*, a novel that depicts the heart-wrenching tale of the Nevels family's relocation from Appalachian Kentucky to Detroit. The book's sprawling plot touches on the pleasures and drawbacks of creating art for profit, as well as the identity conflicts that often ensue when characters transition into a new discourse community. *The Dollmaker* also functions as a love letter to the foods available and produced in Appalachia. Yet in a 1982 interview with literary critic Danny Miller, when asked if she felt "comfortable being labeled as a regional writer or an ethnic writer, an Appalachian's writer, a women's writer," Arnow responded, "I suppose I'd rather be referred to as a writer."[8] Likewise, when Miller asked her if she considered herself an Appalachian person or a hill person, she replied, "I must still feel I'm a hill person. I don't know. I can't always identify myself with certain backhill people or certain Appalachian writers, like the man who wrote *Yesterday's People* [Jack Weller], or sociologists who study a small group and from this draw conclusions about the whole."[9] Here Arnow does not reference the actual people of Appalachia but rather problematic depictions of them. Weller's text is a notoriously problematic War on Poverty depiction of the region, and Arnow's criticism of sociological conclusions drawn from one group of people and applied broadly make clear that her discomfort likely stems from inaccurate portrayals of mountain residents rather than the residents themselves.

In a similar vein, Arnow's depictions of the foods available to the Nevels family in Kentucky, as well as protagonist Gertie's continual longing for those dishes after they have moved to Detroit, reposition the way many authors prior to Arnow wrote about mountain cuisine. *The Dollmaker* presents Appalachian food not as something to be derided or pitied but rather something to be celebrated and missed when far from home. The novel is undoubtedly a dark one, and Gertie's remembrances of better food in Kentucky could be attributed to homesickness and nostalgia, except that more is at work here. The foods available to the family in Detroit are noticeably inferior; Gertie's husband, Clovis, hopes to provide a better life for his family in the city, but that hope fails in several ways. Moreover, the novel's narrator repeatedly references the exorbitant cost of poor-quality food in Detroit. In this way, Arnow not only valorizes Gertie's culinary and creative talents—in Kentucky she was able to create delicious meals despite a constant need for money—but she also highlights the failures of a capitalist system that promised prosperity to the Nevels family, only to deliver an expensive refrigerator that damages their food, a stove Gertie has trouble using, and rotten bananas. Within the larger context of this project, the urban environment that proves so detrimental to the Nevels family is one where Appalachian food is currently flourishing at farm-to-table restaurants and tailgate markets. Yet families surviving on an income equivalent to what Clovis and Gertie earned in Detroit likely cannot afford to dine at the restaurants serving the foods Gertie longs to have again.

Early in the novel, Arnow highlights tension between Gertie and Clovis: Gertie secretly longs to buy her own land and weighs each expenditure carefully as she accumulates savings Clovis does not know about. Conversely, Clovis dreams of living in a less rural environment with modern conveniences including electricity and running water. In one scene, he wonders out loud to Gertie, "Wouldn't it be something now to have it like th people in Town—th electric lights and bathrooms," to which Gertie retorts, "Electric lights and runnen water won't make a empty belly full."[10] Even before the family moves to Detroit, Gertie knows that the lifestyle Clovis wants does not ensure food security for the family. To further emphasize the point, the narrator describes a delicious, robust meal Gertie provides to her children with "a great platter of hot smoking cornbread . . . and other bowls and platters within easy reach . . . [and] new hominy fried in lard and seasoned with sweet milk and black pepper. It was good with the shuck beans, baked sweet potatoes, cucumber pickles, and green ketchup." The narrator continues, "Gertie served it up with pride, for everything, even the meal in the bread, was a product of her farming" (86). Notably, the narrator makes no mention of Clovis's farming but instead highlights Gertie's. Readers soon learn that Gertie follows Clovis to Detroit at her mother's prodding, and we wonder whether she will be able to provide as well for her family in a new, urban place.

In Kentucky, sweet potatoes serve as a nutritious side dish Gertie grows and prepares herself, but in Detroit they become an emblem of unattainable, expensive food. Upon arriving in Detroit, Gertie immediately notices the strange, red mud at the train station. She wants "very much to touch it, to know what it was and from where it came." The narrator comments, "It looked as if it would grow sweet potatoes and peanuts," and an African-American woman from Georgia remarks the same (144). But Gertie never has a chance to see if this assessment proves true; instead, she is left to buy food from street vendors, including a man named Joe who sells food in her neighborhood. In one scene, the narrator explains that Gertie attempts to buy "the things she might have had this time of year at home" but "only looked longingly at the sweet potatoes," since "at two pounds for twenty-five cents, a mess of baked sweet potatoes would cost almost a dollar. Back home she'd sold near twenty bushels for fifty cents a bushel" (214). When Gertie splurges on sweet potatoes "as a treat one night," they are "all black in their hearts, yet showing no sign from the outside" (351). Not only is the expense of the potatoes difficult to justify, but they are also rotten and a waste of hard-earned money. Metaphorically, the sweet potatoes represent the false promise of prosperity that Gertie was given as enticement to move to Detroit. The meals she prepared in Kentucky were superior, and after Cassie's death, the cost of her funeral, and Clovis's injury from a union dispute, the family experiences a financial crisis far greater than their concerns about money in Kentucky.

Like authors discussed in chapter 3, Arnow complicates the idea that a modern kitchen is a superior one. The difficult-to-use appliances Gertie encounters in their Detroit apartment hardly function as the beacons of innovation that Progressive Era reformers like the ones discussed in chapter 2 had hoped would elevate domestic spaces and goods produced within them. When Gertie and the children arrive after a grueling journey, the children beg Gertie to light the gas kitchen stove so it can warm the frigid apartment. She immediately notices the stove is "hardly a fourth as big as that of her range cookstove back home" and had "no warming oven at all" (167). The stove also endangers Gertie when she nearly catches herself on fire trying to light it. Even after she has used it for a while, the narrator reveals that it "turned out to be a contrary thing: [Gertie] was always turning the wrong knob, and twice she burned her fingers on pot handles that had got across the next flame" (179). Likewise, the expensive Icy Heart refrigerator Clovis purchases on credit damages food the family tries to store in it. The name "icy heart" makes clear metaphorical commentary on the material and emotional consequences of succumbing to the pressures of a capitalist-based economy. Clovis spends money the family does not have to purchase what he believes is a superior appliance, but it does not work well, and the family becomes further entrenched in debt. Meanwhile, Gertie longs for the foods she was able to prepare and store in Kentucky.

These so-called conveniences also carry heightened expectations: Clovis assumes ample ration points combined with modern appliances translate to better meals, but the narrator repeatedly emphasizes his flawed thinking.

Early in the family's time in the city, Clovis tells Gertie he's "starved fer some a [her] good cooken" and he has been "figgeren on some good eaten." But the ingredients Gertie procures are inferior and "the eggs had stuck for lack of grease and the bread, badly baked to begin with, was dry and hard and life-less, as the meal that had gone into it" (181). Similar scenarios play out as the novel progresses, and the narrator comments, "None of them ate the way they had back home" (206).

Despite the difficult conditions in Detroit, Gertie continues to save money for an eventual return to Kentucky. Her meal planning operates on a strict budget, prompting Clovis to complain, "That grub wasn't fitten fer a dawg" (266). He insists she should spend more on their meals, but as the book later reveals, doing so does not equate to higher-quality food. Gertie remains re-luctant to spend money in a way she deems frivolous because "she had to have something more than the money she'd saved for land ahead when they went back home. She had to have a mule—a cow and chickens" (267). Even when living in an environment that demands reliance on store-bought goods, Ger-tie remains devoted to creating a self-sustaining lifestyle for herself and her family.

Gertie's insistence on frugal grocery purchases combined with her own discomfort buying food—as opposed to producing it herself—results in consistently poor purchases. Gertie laments that she "wasted Clovis's money for rotten bananas and poor meat and all the other things they didn't know about—the box of pepper half full, the rotten eggs, the rotten oranges," and the metaphorically loaded rotten sweet potatoes. The narrator summarizes Gertie's dilemma in an urban area where families are dependent on wage-based labor: "She could raise a bushel of sweet potatoes, fatten a pig, kill it, and make good sausage meat, but she didn't know how to buy" (351). In other words, Gertie is not a "good consumer," and yet she holds herself to the same domestic standards she was able to meet in Kentucky. The narrator reveals that Gertie "was ashamed when meal time came. The food was worse than they'd ever had back home" (548). This time of supper preparation, "the time she had loved back home," becomes "the time of day she had learned to hate the most" (261).

Embedded in these stark criticisms of the havoc wrought on a family trying to achieve one version of the American Dream, Arnow implicitly celebrates mountain food as well as Gertie's independence in her home environment. In the same scene where we learn that Gertie has come to loathe suppertime, the narrator includes a vivid food memory when Gertie sees "herself back home." There, "the new milk was cooling on the porch . . . Clytie fried fresh pork shoulder in the kitchen. On the stove hearth was a big pan of baked sweet potatoes, and pulled back on the stove where they wouldn't burn was a skillet of fresh-made hominy and another of late turnips. It had been a good fall for the turnips she had planted" (261). Here, not only does Gertie long for the foods of home, but she also longs for self-sustenance. Rather than making better foods available to the family in Detroit, Arnow emphasizes that foods available in Kentucky are preferable, both in terms of cost and taste. Gertie exhibits no shame related to the foods of Kentucky, whereas she frequently feels guilty about the tasteless meals she prepares in Detroit.

In 1955, one year after Arnow published *The Dollmaker*, folk singer and songwriter Jean Ritchie published *Singing Family of the Cumberlands*, a memoir about growing up in the Cumberland Mountains. Ritchie tackles difficult topics, including one particularly disturbing scene where Ritchie's perceived insolence at supper prompts a violent attack from her father. Yet she also writes about loving family interactions, especially those related to food. Unlike *The Dollmaker*, Ritchie's text does not carry an underlying political agenda: she is not criticizing the food-related consequences of a cash-based economy, but it is also worth noting that her family does not relocate. They remain in Kentucky; the kind of harmonious culinary utopia she describes occurs far outside the parameters that Arnow describes in her novel.

If Katherine Pettit and May Stone deemed cornbread inferior, then Ritchie's text may be read as an emphatic corrective. In addition to uplifting formerly denigrated foods, like corn-based breads, Ritchie also celebrates other dishes considered distinctly Appalachian. Many of the foods Ritchie praises are now receiving equal amounts of attention from foodies nationwide. When discussing the family's corn crop, Ritchie notes that the family was able to use it to feed the family and livestock through the winter. She also emphasizes, "The bread from our corn was good" and was "ground into the best kind of meal [she knew] of."[11] She continues, describing the delicious corn mush made in the iron kettle, which they "all loved . . . especially on a cold snowy night" (72). In other chapters, Ritchie describes shucky beans "with garden onions and hot corn bread," remembering, "That supper sure tasted good" (90). Likewise, she mentions "sweet molasses [sorghum] from last fall's stir-off;" a gingerbread stack cake made with dried apples, cloves, and cinnamon sticks; and black walnuts (119, 165, 181). Ritchie explains that the walnuts were delicious in fudge, but "The very best taste of all, though, was to crack out a handful of black walnuts and eat them with a piece of cold bread, first a bit of nut and then a bite of bread. That's the main best eating in the world!" (181). Readers expecting some mention of shame or deprivation will be disappointed. Ritche unequivocally celebrates the food traditions of her childhood.

To fully understand Ritchie's elevation of mountain cuisine and those who prepare it, readers must bring a fair bit of knowledge to her text. Corn mush, for example, is not a ubiquitous food, nor is it the same as grits. Food writer Ronni Lundy explains: "Following Cherokee tradition, mush was made simply by mixing salted ground meal with hot water," though if allowed to cool until solid, it could be fried.[12] Using cornmeal not only to bake bread but also as a hot breakfast cereal signals a kind of resourcefulness that characterizes many of the dishes Ritchie mentions. Unless readers know that molasses is a colloquial reference to sorghum, they may mistakenly believe that Ritchie's family was growing sugarcane (instead of sorghum) in the hills of Kentucky. Readers unfamiliar with the term "shucky beans" (often called leather britches in other parts of Appalachia, like in Western North Carolina) will not understand the craft and ingenuity involved in drying protein-packed varieties of big, fat green beans using needle and thread, nor will they appreciate the patience and know-how it takes to reconstitute those dried beans and transform them into a delicious side dish. Likewise, readers who have never tried to crack a black walnut will not know the skill involved in knowing when one is dry enough to crack and which tools to use for the job. Ritchie does not take on the role of culinary instructor in her memoir; rather, she celebrates the joy and deliciousness of the dishes reminiscent of her childhood. Readers with some level of background knowledge about these dishes will better understand that Ritchie celebrates not just these foods but also the genius of the people who created them, but even readers who know nothing about Appalachia will understand that these are culinary traditions to admire.

In 1962, Wilma Dykeman continued in this vein of culinary celebration with the publication of *The Tall Woman*, a novel set during and after the Civil War. Protagonist Lydia McQueen endures a husband and marriage changed by war, as well as the hardships of childbearing and survival on a mountain farm. Like with *The Dollmaker*, Dykeman's text seems an unlikely one in which to find celebratory descriptions of food, yet the novel highlights the resilience of food traditions in a way that echoes Lydia's strength as a character.

Combined with Dykeman's comments about her own food preferences, it becomes clear that for her, hardship and mountain food are one in the same.

Dykeman's novel details food shortages that plagued many families during the Civil War. Early in the second chapter, after outliers attacked her home and mother, Lydia and her brother Robert are relieved to confirm that the raiders did not find and take the family's meat hidden in the loft. The narrator also mentions coffee, sugar, and salt shortages that affected so many families. By the time Lydia's male family members return, their garden is producing vegetables, and the narrator calls the food "bountiful," explaining, "The table that had been so light all winter and early spring now grew heavy again with steaming cabbages and sweet potatoes and beans. The rich, satisfying smells of their boiling and frying filled the house and spilled out into the yard."[13] Even so, after marrying Mark McQueen and setting up a homestead on the mountain, Lydia "pickled and dried and saved every scrap of food available" (101). Ritchie's family likely did the same given her frequent mentions of dried apples and dried beans, but in both cases, resourcefulness also produced tasty foods. At one point in the novel, when Mark travels out West to decide whether the family should move there, Lydia uses dried apples to prepare small fried pies as treats for her children. Eventually she runs out of grease and cinnamon, but the treat soothes her children all the same (162). In a conversation with cookbook author and writer Sidney Saylor Farr, Dykeman tells Farr about a favorite scene of hers from *The Far Family*, where one of the characters prepares everyone's favorite foods. Dykeman comments, "I was trying to show that food is not just a matter of staying alive. It's also a matter of relating to each other and to the land and to the world around you."[14] Lydia demonstrates these family connections through food on a regular basis.

Even so, Dykeman indicates a certain unwillingness to identify too closely with mountain foods at the same time that she tries to convince Farr that beneath her worldly façade, she is just a country girl. When she tells Farr that her mother combined cooking methods she learned from her Northern in-laws with her Southern mountain heritage, Dykeman mentions standing rib roast. She says that it would be one of her favorites "if it wasn't so darned expensive" (160). She also tells Farr that when she was studying at Northwestern University, she would request that her mother make "beans and corn bread and onions and buttermilk," telling Farr, "You see, I was just an old country girl at heart" (163). Certainly these food preferences may be accurate, but Dykeman also tells Farr that "one of the things [she has] always liked is just plain old dried beans," but when she does not "want to horrify someone by telling them about dried beans and soup beans," she tells them she is serving cassoulet. Cassoulet, a dish famous in French cooking, is also considered peasant food and is based on beans, but telling dinner guests they are having cassoulet is less horrifying to Dykeman than telling them she is serving soup beans. In this way, she celebrates mountain food, even emphasizing to Farr that dishes like homemade butter, cream, cobblers, and ketchups are authentic. Still, she is careful to insert a degree of separation between herself and that authenticity, lest someone associate her preference for those foods with the hardship she implies in the interview and describes outright in *The Tall Woman*. This separation also signals that for Dykeman, calling a dish "cassoulet" instead of "soup beans" carries more cultural capital for both the cook and consumer, rendering the food more acceptable. In other words, the celebration of regional identity via food occurs at a distance.

Celebratory Depictions in the 1980s, 1990s, and 2000s

By the late 1980s and early 1990s, West Virginia writer Denise Giardina not only continued to uplift mountain cuisine in *Storming Heaven* (1987) and *The Unquiet Earth* (1992), but she also revealed how food choices can signal resistance to historically derogatory portrayals. At the same time, Giardina's work diversifies common understandings of what "counts" as mountain food. Readers come to understand that depending on the cook, olive oil and garlic may be deemed as essential to a West Virginia kitchen as soup beans and cornbread.

In *Storming Heaven* and its sequel, *The Unquiet Earth*, Giardina creates rich, provocative stories that bring real historical events, including the Battle of Blair Mountain and the Buffalo Creek Disaster, to life. She imbues her fiction with myriad other realities as well, especially those related to food. In both novels, characters are keenly aware of the culinary capital (or lack thereof) associated with the foods they consume. Yet rather than producing the feelings of shame we witnessed in chapter 4 or causing the characters to hold their love of mountain cuisine at arm's length, Giardina's characters use their affiliation with mountain foods as a proud form of resistance. In this way, her novels demonstrate clearly for readers what it means to know that the rest of the world sees your food as inferior and what talking back looks like in the form of proud consumption.

Union organizer Rondal Lloyd narrates chapter 2 of *Storming Heaven*, recalling childhood memories of growing up in a coal camp in a house owned by American Coal Company. His narration emphasizes his family's ingenuity, strong work ethic, and pride in their home: his mother grows her own beans in the company garden and gently washes coal dust from the petunias that beautify her porch.[15] Despite the stability of his home, Rondal's third-grade teacher, Miss Radcliffe, tells Rondal and his classmates that they have "the obligation to raise [them]selves above [their] parents and save [their] mountain people from ignorance" (26). She makes her perceived superiority clear to the children in several ways, including the invitation to her home for tea and cookies mentioned in the last chapter. Miss Radcliffe lives in the company clubhouse, an elaborately furnished building reserved as a living space for certain company employees. Almost immediately, Rondal feels uncomfortable upon entering the space, remembering that he "tiptoed" across a special rug and sat in "miserable silence" (25). When Miss Radcliffe serves the tea to the children, she does so in "delicate cups with handles so small that even a child could not get a proper grip without being burned." Rondal remembers that he was unable to eat his cookies without spilling his tea, which he fears would prompt Miss Radcliffe to call him "slovenly," a term she uses often to describe the mountain children she teaches. As a solution, Rondal wraps his cookies in his bandana with the plan to share them with his brothers. As soon as he enters his family's company house, he smells grease from the gravy his mother is preparing. He describes the "gritty wood floor, sprinkled with coal dust despite [his mother's] daily scrubbings," providing a stark juxtaposition to the opulent clubhouse where Miss Radcliffe lives. Although Rondal seems proud to share the cookies with his siblings, his relief upon going home is clear: "I sighed, lay back on the bed, and was glad to be home" (26). Although he does not confront Miss Radcliffe's unacceptably derogatory behavior, his actions signal limited agency nonetheless. He takes the cookies she offers to share with his family, and he remains proud of the food his mother prepares and the space in which she prepares it.

In *The Unquiet Earth*, sequel to *Storming Heaven*, Giardina begins the novel with an even more overt example of culinary resistance through consumption. Dillon Freeman, Rondal Lloyd's son, narrates the first chapter of the novel. He provides a brief family history to orient readers, and right away we learn that his mother, Carrie, raises him very differently than her sister (Flora) raises her daughter, Rachel. He states that Rachel is "raised more proper" and "at school Rachel has fried egg sandwiches on lightbread with store-bought mayonnaise or sometimes mayonnaise by itself which nobody else has."[16] Dillon explains the bread hierarchy referenced multiple times in this book: "A poke of sliced lightbread is prized for it means you can afford to spend money to replace the biscuits and cornbread people bake themselves." Likewise, store-bought mayonnaise signals the ability not only to purchase goods from a store instead of making them at home but also a condiment meant to enhance flavor rather than a meal staple. Dillon seems impressed that Rachel "doesn't take on about it," meaning that she does not flaunt her higher social standing. On the other end of the spectrum, Dillon's mother, Carrie, "will not have lightbread in the house... [and] says even if [they] had the money it's just as tasty as a handkerchief," and she sends Dillon to school with cornbread. In this passage, readers learn that unlike Flora, Carrie cannot afford to buy light bread for her family. Carrie's criticisms of the bread could be rooted in her inability to purchase it, but Dillon's pride in eating cornbread at school suggests otherwise: "Some youngens who bring cornbread hide what they have because they are embarrassed to be poor but I won't do that because it would shame my mom" (5). Here Dillon remains more concerned about preserving his mother's integrity than he does about what his cornbread consumption signals to others about their economic status. In this scene, cornbread is not yet elevated to the foodie status it enjoys today in restaurants serving Appalachian food, but Giardina's portrayal emphasizes a kind of talking back to the dominant system that assigns more cultural capital to store-bought items like light bread and mayonnaise.

In other scenes in both novels, Giardina includes loving, celebratory descriptions of foods associated with Appalachia. In *Storming Heaven*, Carrie Bishop proudly describes the food preservation methods used in her community to prepare for winter. She mentions women "putting up their fruit, vegetables, and apple butter," a corn shucking that will provide food for farm animals and meal for making bread, a hog killing, and a molasses (sorghum) making, all of which meant "the winter could be faced with security" (56). Likewise, in *The Unquiet Earth*, Dillon describes women who "stand over the cast-iron stoves in the heat of summer and stir the great boiling pots of tomatoes and beans... slice the apples and sun-dry them into leather-sweet strips... [and] take a needle and thread to the beans and hang them in rows to dry from the porch rafters" (5). These summer labors mean that the family will have preserved tomatoes, beans, and apples for winter. Notably, this description follows Dillon's ruminations about cornbread, suggesting his pride in the know-how of community women to prepare for winter instead of relying on store-bought goods.

Giardina also highlights an abundance of foods and an outright joy associated with their consumption. When Carrie describes the molasses making in *Storming Heaven*, she describes the process—one that produces "mighty fine" syrup—in detail. Likewise, she catalogues foods served after the process concludes: "fried chicken and salty ham, mashed potatoes swimming in butter, green beans cooked with hunks of fatback, hot pickled corn, biscuits, yellow cornbread, boiled cabbage, sweet potatoes, green poke sallet in bacon grease, fresh kale, squirrel meat with dumplings, venison steaks, groundhog, red-eye gravy, milk gravy, stack cakes, apple pies." She lists several foods often associated with the mountains, including pickled corn, poke sallet, wild meats, and stack cakes. There seems to be an easy companionship between cultivated foods and those that were foraged or hunted, including poke and wild game. Unlike Dykeman's concern that her love for soup beans would horrify a dinner guest, Carrie simply states, "When we were done eating, it was difficult to stand up" (57). Likewise, when Carrie prepares a meal for Rondal earlier in their courtship, she serves pork chops, cornbread, potatoes with wild onion, and poke (117). In her recounting of the meal, she indicates no shame or discomfort related to the foods served, a departure from examples discussed in previous chapters, as when Cratis Williams's mother feels ashamed over the fare she has to offer the McDormins. Similarly, in *The Unquiet Earth*, Carrie uses food to console Dillon after his relationship with Rachel ends. Carrie picks tomatoes, cucumbers, and corn from her garden and serves them with "beans cooked with ribboned fatback and chunks of steamed potato, and . . . crusty hot cornbread" (192). After a dessert of blackberry cobbler, Dillon spends the night in "the same featherbed [he] slept in when [he] was a boy" (193). The food Carrie serves him comforts him, providing not only delicious sustenance but also a salve for his broken heart.

Although Giardina's characters frequently reference foods traditionally associated with Appalachia, including stack cakes, poke sallet, soup beans, cornbread, and wild onions, they also work to overturn the misperception that those are the only foods found in the region. Both *Storming Heaven* and *The Unquiet Earth* depict the racial and ethnic diversity that characterized many coal mining towns in the twentieth century. In her book about African-American migration into and out of the coalfields of eastern Kentucky between 1910 and 1970, sociologist Karida Brown explains that around the turn of the twentieth century, the coal industry "transformed [the region] into a hotbed of industry, contestation, and international mass migration."[17] Brown elaborates, writing that coal "companies . . . deployed an army of labor agents to foreign countries such as Poland and Yugoslavia, Hungary, Italy, Germany, and Greece to recruit the base of their workforce."[18] She points out that company agents also recruited African-American workers from the South, though as Thomas Wagner and Phillip Obermiller explain, "African Americans have a long history in the Appalachian mountains."[19] This combination of workers from the mountains, Deep South, and various foreign countries resulted in an incredibly diverse mix of languages, worship practices, and, of course, food, creating an eclectic mix of cultural traditions often obscured in mass media depictions that portray a monolithically white version of Appalachia.

In *Storming Heaven*, Giardina describes African-American baseball leagues in detail, paying homage to a history seldom associated with the region. Likewise, Carrie remembers that in Justice town she loved to "poke [her] finger into a fresh octopus or squid at the Italian grocery, or buy a strange-smelling cheese to carry back to [her] room" (101). And in *The Unquiet Earth*, when Rachel begins dating Tony Angelelli, an Italian bookkeeper for the coal company, he takes her to meet his mother. She remembers that "the coalfields seemed exotic" to her, and she notes "stone walls and bridges carved by Italian masons," as well as "a Russian church with an onion-shaped dome of gold leaf," and later, her daughter, Jackie, references Hungarians, Russians, and Czechoslovakians living in a segregated area called "Hunkie Hill" (24, 106). When Rachel enters Tony's mother's home, she remembers, "The walls were covered with dozens of crucifixes, calendars, . . . pictures of Franklin Roosevelt, the Virgin Mary, and the Pope." These markers of Italian Catholicism seem strange and foreign to Rachel, but she is drawn to the smells of the kitchen, remembering she had "smelled nothing like it, and only later came to identify the garlic, the oregano, the olive oil" (24). As food writer Courtney Balestier explains, the official state food of West Virginia—the pepperoni roll—was created by Giuseppe Argiro, an Italian immigrant living in Fairmont in the 1920s. She goes on to state, "There are actually a lot of Italians . . . in West Virginia—so many, in fact, that for a time, Italy ran a consulate office in the northern part of the state."[20] That the pepperoni roll became so ubiquitous in West Virginia makes Italian influence on culinary traditions there abundantly clear. Giardina's inclusion of Italian foodways and careful documentation of the diversity of coal mining towns broadens too-easy definitions of what qualifies as Appalachian food. Tony's mother, for example, illustrates that in a coal town, olive oil sopped up with crusty bread is every bit as "Appalachian" as soup beans sopped up with cornbread. Not only is Giardina ahead of the celebratory trend that promotes mountain food, but she also explodes common misunderstandings about the assumed "Anglo-Saxon stock" of the region.

Likewise, Kentucky writer Crystal Wilkinson, whose novel *Birds of Opulence* I discuss at length in chapter 4, usefully complicates tired stereotypes of an all-white Appalachia. Food references permeate her work but are perhaps nowhere as clear as in "Praise Song for the Kitchen Ghosts," an essay published in *Emergence Magazine* in 2019 that is slated to become a culinary memoir, including recipes, with a projected publication date of 2023. In this piece, Wilkinson stretches time and memory to reach back across generations of women in her family, all of whom were responsible for feeding their families. In that remembering, she highlights both the suffering and joy of black womanhood, whether during enslavement, in the years following emancipation, or in the contemporary moment. She tells us that her grandmother "cooked with both a fury and a quiet joy," a fury that presumably stems from generational oppression and trauma.[21] But moments of joy also permeate the text, and readers come to understand that through hours spent laboring in the fields and kitchen, Wilkinson's ancestors created a life both sustainable and delicious. Perhaps most importantly, in that remembering, she creates a space in which African-American Appalachian culinary identity and identity more generally may be celebrated.

As in Rondal's description of his hardworking parents in Giardina's *Storming Heaven*, Wilkinson highlights her grandparents' labors and rewards: "My grandparents lived primarily off the land. They owned sixty-four acres and had a modest income from the crops they raised. My grandfather prided himself on taking care of his family, his animals, and his land. My grandmother prided herself on making sure her family was fed." Her grandmother manages this feat while toiling as a domestic worker and completing a dizzying number of farm chores. Wilkinson notes, "But still there were always three meals on the table. Precise. Orderly. Delicious." Wilkinson follows in these footsteps, preparing elaborate meals for her own three children, even as she worked multiple jobs and pursued a college degree. The oral histories Karida Brown includes in *Gone Home: Race and Roots through Appalachia* tell a similar story of hard work and culinary rewards. Ernest Pettygrue, for example, tells Brown, "Gardens. I mean we just had yards and yards of gardens. . . . Wherever you see a spot that's clear and you want to make a garden, you just make a garden."[22] These representations make clear that not only were African-Americans present in Appalachia—and still are—but also that they were/are knowledgeable, hardworking food producers.

For Wilkinson, remembrance and the specific act of remembering and sharing recipes function as an act of communion with her ancestors. Wilkinson chronicles the phone conversations she has with relatives as they try to recreate certain dishes, including a gingerbread sauce her Aunt Lo remembers but no one else does. These memories do more than lay the groundwork for a delicious meal; they solidify a path to the past at the same time that they forge a space for the celebration of black identity in Appalachia. Wilkinson begins the essay, "People are always surprised that black people reside in the hills of Appalachia." Wilkinson's beautiful rendering of generations of women whose culinary talents have been passed on from one generation to the next emphasizes to readers that black people are in these hills and have been for a long time, a fact that only began to gain traction in academia with the publication of William Turner and Edward Cabbell's seminal 1985 book, *Blacks in Appalachia*. In our panel discussion at the Appalachian Studies Association conference mentioned in the last chapter, Wilkinson said, "My family has lived in these hills for over one-hundred-and-fifty years [. . .] and here we are in 2021 still trying to make our presence known."[23]

Wilkinson writes specifically about Aggy, one of her ancestors who was born into slavery in 1795 in Virginia and was later brought to Kentucky. Wilkinson wonders how Aggy fed her ten children using her allotted rations, and she tells us, "From Aggy (3rd great grandmother) to Lizzie (2rd great grandmother) to Lillie (great grandmother) to Christine (grandmother) to Dorsie (mother) to me—we are all the links in this chain." Moreover, that chain of women used dried apples to make fried pies and cooked up pots of shuck beans like many of the other women discussed in this book. Yet Wilkinson emphasizes that given their historical ties to enslavement, their experiences are also different, though many of the same foods may be shared.

Michael McFee, a white poet from Western North Carolina, likewise writes about food memories connected across generations in a poem called "Recipes."[24] The speaker makes no mention of a history of enslavement, but like in Wilkinson's essay, recipes are "handed down / from grandmother to mother to daughter." The speaker explains that these recipes may be found in "cookbooks or boxes" or even a drawer, calling them "Concentrated manuscripts." Near the end of the poem, the speaker declares, "They are receipts for some unaccountable hunger." Here McFee uses "receipt," the older word for recipe, encouraging readers to consider a play on words that opens a double meaning: in one reading, they are recipes for an unaccountable hunger, but in another they are proof that something once existed and has the potential to be recovered. Considered in this way, the receipts verify transactions that were made, between food served and ingredients recorded, between members of a family. The speaker emphasizes giving and receiving, speculating that the recipes are "prescriptions that might yet cure." Notably, these recipes are written down, whereas some of the ones Wilkinson describes are either transmitted orally between family members or pulled from her own memory.

McFee writes often about memory and its connections to food. In a poem called "Cornbread in Buttermilk," the speaker, presumably McFee, recalls the cornbread his father would crumble in a glass of buttermilk and eat with a long-handled spoon.[25] McFee remembers being repulsed by the concoction, calling it a "thick tart soup," recalling that when he sniffed the empty glass after his father had finished eating, he gagged. Such a description of what has now become an iconic food represented in Appalachia hardly seems celebratory, but in an essay about mountain food writer John Parris, McFee includes a recipe for "Cornbread and milk" and asks, "Why did [my father] eat it, whenever possible, with such relish? What times, happy or hard, was he remembering from his growing up on Arlington Street in Asheville without a father, or from his time in the orphanage in Sylva with his two brothers?"[26] In these questions, McFee urges readers to think about the important connections different foods have to one's sense of self. While the speaker may not cherish the dish, his father undoubtedly celebrates it.

In the contemporary moment, diners interested in mountain food traditions seem to prize the dish just as much as McFee's father. In her award-winning cookbook, *Victuals*, Ronni Lundy includes a recipe for "John Fleer's Buttermilk Cornbread Soup" (125). Fleer, a well-known Asheville-based chef, first made a culinary name for himself at Blackberry Farm in eastern Tennessee; as Lundy points out, his "mountain-flavored menu at Blackberry . . . was the first to win fine-dining recognition for the products and traditions of the southern Appalachians." In 2013 he opened Rhubarb in Asheville, where diners may enjoy in-season ramps, cornbread buttermilk soup, and other dishes showcasing local heritage ingredients. Five years later, Fleer opened Benne on

Eagle, a restaurant that pays homage to African-American and Appalachian cuisines. Celebration of these regional food traditions lies at the heart of both restaurants, and Lundy calls Fleer's soup "life-changing," advising readers that "It's also quite delicious served chilled" (125). Although Fleer's version is undeniably more elaborate than the bread and milk in a glass McFee's father consumed—Fleer's recipe calls for leeks, celery, garlic, and heavy cream—the inspiration is a shared one, as is the veneration of this once-humble food by McFee's father and Fleer.

Unlike in "Cornbread in Buttermilk," in a poem called "Roadside Table," the speaker does not criticize foods consumed but rather venerates them.[27] The speaker describes his family's ritual of packing their car with various foods to share during a picnic lunch held at a roadside table. The speaker acknowledges, "Tourists driving by us might have laughed / at this simple mountain clan," believing that they could not afford to eat in a restaurant. He goes on to emphasize that these tourists would "have been wrong," explaining instead that "it was pure holiday." Poems like this one comment on how culinary choices—and the communal acts that surround those choices— simultaneously acknowledge and disrupt lingering judgments about mountain people and the food that they eat.

McFee's speaker is keenly aware of how others view his family and their culinary traditions, a trend that becomes paramount in Robert Gipe's *Trampoline*, *Weedeater*, and *Pop*. Gipe's trilogy follows the Jewell family of Canard County, Kentucky, and their unrelenting litany of problems in a landscape ravaged by mountaintop removal. Considered together, the novels narrate the myriad problems of environmental destruction, drug addiction, dysfunctional family relationships, and a community's heavy reliance on coal. Like *Trampoline* and *Weedeater*, *Pop* is noticeably postmodern. Characters address readers directly, and the novel repeatedly draws attention to narrative construction: it is metafiction at its finest. Readers are encouraged to question the veracity of any given version of a story and to pay attention to whose version is heard and whose is not. These questions play out in several different scenarios, from the active role community members play in rewriting a movie script about Appalachia to the book's treatment of the region's foodways. At the same time *Pop* parodies current obsessions with Appalachian food—poking fun at foodies inclined to buy heirloom sorghum soda—it also celebrates previously denigrated mountain food traditions, defending their deliciousness and inviting readers to join characters at the metaphorical table.

Yet Gipe's celebration of these traditions is not without critique: the novel criticizes LGBTQIA+ phobia that some might consider "traditional" in Appalachia. *Pop* makes clear that any aspect of so-called tradition that breeds inequality must be rewritten. The table Gipe sets is one for all.

Questions about representation are paramount in *Pop*, especially when a movie crew selects Canard County as the site to film a new science fiction film. Dawn's Uncle Hubert hopes to capitalize on the situation by renting cabins to the crew, though his rustic design choices and décor do not appeal to the moviemakers. Daphne Deeskins, a journalist for an "upscale travel magazine" called *Sophisticated South*, tries to give Hubert advice about improving his amenities, telling him they would pay "for [themselves] if [he] did his marketing right."[28] But instead of heeding her advice, he thinks about the requests his regular customers have made: "Gojo dispensers for the kitchen and a pressure washer station for their four-wheelers" (58). Deeskins accompanies the crew to gather research for an article about "how the other half vacations, but how to do it stylishly," telling Hubert, "we are profiling your community as an all-terrain vehicle" (55). In this scenario, Gipe clearly parodies magazines like *Garden and Gun* that promise readers a glimpse into the lives of various groups of Southerners. Notably, Gipe does not present readers with Deeskins's article but rather Hubert's internal thoughts about it. Hubert's reaction highlights the absurdity of Deeskins's assignment, as well as her inability to see the cabins for what they are and to ask Hubert about his customer base and their preferences when traveling. Readers are left with the impression that Deeskins will write the article as she sees fit, ensuring a one-sided view of "the other half" that at best is patronizing and at worst, insulting.

When Dawn's aunt, June, tells her about the movie and its science fiction plotline in which "aliens are bringing in drugs that turn the mountain people into monsters," or in the words of director Quin Pennyroyal, "a new street drug . . . sold by space alien gangsters [that] literally turn[s] hillbillies into wild animals," June defends it, calling the idea "textured," "layered," and "very metaphorical" (69, 76, 69). Dawn responds, "People from off coming in and turning us into druggies. Sounds like reality. But dumber" (69). Dawn's sarcastic response highlights her awareness of how mainstream America views the opioid crisis in Appalachia. A May 16, 2021, article published in the *Guardian* reveals that pharmaceutical executives wrote offensive emails and rhymes to one another mocking the drug epidemic in Appalachia their companies were on trial for helping create. As journalist Chris McGreal reports, "One email in 2011 included a rhyme built around 'a poor mountaineer' named Jed who 'barely kept his habit fed.'"[29] Here representatives evoke the stereotypical television program, *The Beverly Hillbillies*, and in other messages refer to "pillbillies," an offensive play on the already problematic word "hillbillies." While Gipe does not explore the perspective of drug makers who produce the substances responsible for affecting so many lives in America and Appalachia in particular, he does spotlight character responses to denigrating portrayals like those showcased in McGreal's article. Dawn asks June, "Why their stories? . . . Why can't we tell our own stories?" (69). While pharmaceutical representatives may not hear Dawn's questions, readers do and are prompted to ponder the same question.

Hubert shares Dawn's opinion about the movie's plotline, and when filmmakers gather with community members, he makes his voice heard. In a conversation between moviemakers and local community members, poet Sam Haney asks the director, Quin, "Why must it be so simple?" (77). When Quin asks Sam what he means, Sam immediately responds, "Big Pharma would be selling that dope," and he continues, creating a much more elaborate plotline full of fantastical science fiction elements that still ring true to the lived realities of people in Canard County (77). Hubert remarks, "We kept talking. Nobody had ever asked us what a movie about us should be like" (79). In a brilliant postmodern fashion, the characters of Gipe's novel indeed keep talking, literally rewriting the script of outsider perceptions of Appalachia. Later in the novel, Hubert muses, "Down through our history, the stories people away from Canard told about Canard were about mine strikes and poverty programs and everybody being hooked on pills. That summer though, they was other kind of stories to tell" (137). One of the stories that helps rewrite the Appalachian script is about the region's food.

Gipe simultaneously parodies the current national obsession with mountain cuisine, sincerely celebrates those traditions, and gives readers insight into what it must feel like to observe a nation celebrating your culinary traditions at the same time it lambastes the consumption of "junk food" associated with Appalachia. In 2014 a group of "chefs, writers, activists, entrepreneurs, and economic development professionals" founded the Appalachian Food Summit (AFS). Since then, the group has held several multiday conferences celebrating Appalachian food traditions, as well as several other events that promote the foodways of the region while emphasizing its diverse history.

Gipe spoke at the Cornbread Convocation for the 2016 summit held in Berea, Kentucky, sharing a hilarious story with audience members about working in a pickle plant that he later published.[30] He even drew the "Soup Beans for the Appalachian Food Summit" logo for the T-shirts attendees received upon registering for the summit. As someone who attended that conference, Gipe's support for the organization was clear, which makes his fictional portrayal of it even more interesting.

Early in *Pop*, readers understand that Dawn's daughter, Nicolette, aspires to work as a chef. She feels inspired by her culinary past, and like members of the AFS, she wants to celebrate it. Like many contemporary chefs who celebrate mountain cuisine, Nicolette also feels comfortable experimenting with traditional recipes. In her culinary class at Kingsport High School, she uses Hubert's apple stack cake recipe as the inspiration for an award-winning lemon-curd poppyseed stack cake (117). Organizers of a dinner celebrating mountain foods in Berea also invite her to cook for them, and her description of the event is both comical and sincere. She explains, "The Berea thing [is] a dinner of fancy takes on traditional Appalachian food hosted by the Sisterhood of the Grub," whom she explains are "food experts from around the Appalachian region." She announces without fanfare that she will be receiving the "Self-Rising Star award." She goes on to explain, "There were cookbook writers and chefs there, all of them talking about how Appalachian food has been underappreciated and how now was the time to step into the light, onto the center of the world food stage." Nicolette's description accurately describes the Appalachian Food Summit held in Berea in 2016. While her quips about a flour pun award likely make readers grin, she is also aware that "this thing might lead to jobs for us, or at least work, and maybe in time make Canard County a place where people who knew the difference came to eat our cooking to see what the new face of Appalachian cookery looked like" (118). But Nicolette is also not the only character narrating the novel; through Dawn and Hubert's perspectives, readers gain a fuller understanding of what these long-overdue culinary celebrations might mean for residents in the region.

Gipe is also affiliated with the Southern Foodways Alliance (SFA), an organization based in Oxford, Mississippi, whose mission is similar to the Appalachian Food Summit's but is not limited to Appalachia, instead considering the South broadly. In 2018 he published an excerpt from *Pop* in *Gravy*, the SFA journal, in which Nicolette tells her mother about the dinner and makes a practice dish of macaroni and cheese using gorgonzola.[31] When Nicolette gives Dawn a bite, she spits it out, telling Nicolette "it tastes like ass" (118). Dawn's rejection of Nicolette's experimentation with a traditional recipe is meaningful, suggesting a larger rejection of the trend to venerate but also inherently change recipes associated with Appalachia. The fact that Gipe publishes this excerpt in the SFA's journal is especially noteworthy, as it indicates a humorous critique of this trend, one often forwarded by the SFA, but a critique all the same. Dawn's reaction understandably hurts Nicolette's feelings, and Dawn confesses that what bothers her is that "who you cook for is who you are," meaning Nicolette may be losing touch with her roots. In a demonstration of care for her daughter, Dawn asks how much the tickets to the dinner cost, indicates an interest in going, and even tells Nicolette to "leave [her] some of that macaroni" (119). In other words, she wants to support Nicolette; the food Nicolette created is not the issue but rather what it could represent.

In addition to her culinary talents, Nicolette also has a good business sense, realizing early on that she and others can capitalize on contemporary interest in mountain cuisine. She and her friends found a soda pop company called Feral Girl. Nicolette tells her friend, Pinky, "Let's make something mountain, something that tastes like here." As the girls consider different flavor options, Nicolette suggests sassafrass, mountain mint, and sorghum. Pinky immediately asks, "You aren't getting us into a bunch of ass-tasting pop are you? Cause I ain't putting a lot of work into a pop we know before we start is gonna taste like ass." Nicolette wryly responds, "People pay good money for ass-tasting stuff" (89). Here the novel makes commentary on several aspects of the trend to celebrate mountain food: Nicolette says that sorghum pop would be "authentic," which would presumably appeal to foodies in search of "real" culinary experiences. Her choice to make sorghum-flavored soda also deserves attention; as discussed in the previous chapter, sorghum was historically the sweetener used when sugar was not available. Hubert's friend, Tildy, even tells Nicolette, "In the olden days, honey, sorghum was all people had for sweetening. White sugar was hard to get. Sorghum you could grow yourself" (97). It signaled a lower socioeconomic status, whereas now, some view sorghum as superior, or at least exotic, and it is often more difficult for contemporary consumers to procure than sugar.

In a nod to sorghum's popularity, a 2021 *Garden & Gun* article features Charleston, South Carolina, distillers Ann Marshall and Scott Blackwell, who pair up with Tennessee's country ham master, Allan Benton, to create a smoke and ham-infused bourbon. But first, they "considered making an experimental smoked sorghum spirit" but then deemed the concept "unexciting."[32] The fact that they even consider sorghum as a contender signals its popularity in the trendy food scene. In other words, the script has flipped, and Nicolette knows it. Moreover, her decision to make soda with "authentic" flavors offers implicit commentary on stereotypes about Appalachian people consuming too much sugary soda, prompting the genesis of the term "Mountain Dew Mouth," as featured in a 2009 episode of *20/20*.[33] Instead of presenting readers with poor hillbillies guzzling Mountain Dew, Gipe gives us Nicolette, who plans to market authentic sorghum-flavored pop to people with enough resources to purchase tickets to dinners held in university towns. In this way, the idea of Appalachian-inspired pop bridges two culinary worlds that are often pitted against one another. Pop, a processed sugary drink often linked to poor people in the mountains, is connected to an upscale celebration of traditional mountain foods. Gipe blurs that line, suggesting that commerce between the two may be possible after all, but perhaps not without some consequences.

Processed foods appear in all of Gipe's novels, especially soda pop and oatmeal creme pies. In *Trampoline*, readers witness a prolonged story of addiction and its fallout. Although Dawn does not become addicted to drugs or alcohol, she exhibits signs of a food addiction, which only become more apparent in *Pop*. Early in the novel Nicolette introduces her mother to readers by explaining, "Mom was hiding out from life, weighed down by grief and stale honey buns," adding that she "drank a case of pop a day" (10, 21). Nicolette is horrified by her mother's grocery list, which includes Fruity Pebbles, Pop Tarts, Pepsi, and plenty of other items considered junk food, telling her, "If I'm going to the store, I ain't buying this junk." When Dawn asks her what she will buy instead, Nicolette responds, "Beans. Stuff for cornbread. Greens." Nicolette lists foods traditionally associated with Appalachia, believing them to be healthier fare for her mother, yet in the store she buys Dawn much of what she requests. These competing grocery lists represent an ideological divide between Dawn and Nicolette, as well as between the desire to celebrate traditional foods without disparaging Appalachian residents who do not always eat those foods. The novel emphasizes that Dawn does not appreciate Nicolette's judgments, noting that "ever since she'd been watching them food shows and going to these Appalachian food festivals and cooking competitions … [she] thought she was the hillbilly Julia Child" (15). Dawn's comment illustrates that while celebratory, such media attention can introduce questions about identity that have the potential to affect family relationships.

Although Dawn does not regularly cook meals featuring foods associated with the region, other characters do. The novel emphasizes that plenty of mountain food traditions exist and continue in everyday life, in addition to those celebrated at formal gatherings. Hubert, for example, shows Nicolette "how to clean fish, how to make soup beans and cornbread, [and] let [her] come with him to a hog killing" (20). Cornbread plays an important role in the novel, as does Nicolette's experience boiling down sorghum with Hubert's relatives, Homer and Della. One of Hubert's mother's friends in North Carolina, Janine Busby, wants to learn as much about these traditions as she can. Busby works as a journalist, writing articles for fictional publications like *Talepacker: The Online Travel Magazine for the Rest of Us*, another humorous jab at publications featuring regional attractions. She looks forward to learning how to make apple stack cake from Tildy.

Apple stack cake has become perhaps the most iconic food associated with Appalachia. It graces the homepage of the Appalachian Food Summit website and is arguably the most important food symbol in *Pop*. While people in the mountains did make the labor-intensive cake, it was not a dessert that families enjoyed on a regular basis. Perhaps anticipating readers who do not know the many steps involved in making such a cake, Hubert speaks directly to readers: "I don't know if you've ever had an apple stack cake the way mountain people make them. They're a lot of work, especially if you grow the apples and make your own sorghum" (56). He narrates the entire process, concluding, "there's hundreds of hours in one cake" (57). Instead of romanticizing the delicious taste of a homemade apple stack cake, Hubert's explanation draws attention to the work involved in making one. Thus, celebrating the cake is not just about celebrating its taste but also about uplifting the labor and creativity that went into making it.

Moreover, Gipe's novel makes important commentary about cultural ownership and appropriation. Near the end, Hubert decides to throw a party to celebrate Old Christmas. He tells readers he had been thinking about "who [he] was, about where [he] was, and what was worth saving" (288). He decides the party will feature an apple stack cake, and he asks attendees to each bring a layer, so it would be "different people making layers of the same cake" (289). The cake turns out beautifully, but Dawn throws it off the hill and

Nicolette later reconstructs it. Dawn explains: "I went in there and seen that cake so perfect and I thought to myself, 'I don't want to see that cake on Instagram.' I just want us to eat it and then us remember it. I don't want to see it online all cropped and filtered and looking like an advertisement for something. I just want it to be cake. A cake we ate together. I just want it to be the love we had for one another" (325). In this instance, Gipe invites readers to consider the impact their celebration of foods traditionally associated with Appalachia may have on residents who were already celebrating those foods, long before it was trendy to do so. Dawn emphasizes that she does not want to see a representation of the cake on social media, nor does she want viewers to consume that image. Rather than elevate it to a symbol of tradition made consumable to all with Internet access, Dawn just wants to share the dessert with her family.

Even so, the novel suggests that the coexistence of these different forms of celebration may be possible. Throughout the novel, Nicolette has visions of people she met as a child with her great-grandfather Houston. June tells Nicolette she was his "little Appalachian savant" and that he saw her as the bearer of regional traditions (292). Nicolette likewise saves a pack of index cards with recipes written on them from Hubert's mother and is distraught when she thinks they are gone. Near the end of the novel, she has a prolonged vision in which old and new are combined: "Women hung leather britches off their porches. Fancy people ate skillets of white asparagus at Asheville tables" (272). In this instance, techniques meant to survive a winter in the mountains meet fancy dining in Western North Carolina's "Foodtopia." There is also room at the table for convenience foods. Dawn lists the dishes served at Hubert's Old Christmas feast, which include greens, soup beans, cornbread, and chow chow, but also weenies. Dawn tells us, "It looked like the prize display on *Wheel of Fortune* if all the prizes was food" (328). The novel does not suggest that such coexistence is easy but rather emphasizes the importance of people narrating their own stories, writing their own menus, and deciding when a cake is just a cake. In the end, Nicolette decides against becoming a chef, explaining to Dawn that "it don't feel that good" (325). Her explanation invites readers to consider why innovating traditional recipes might be uncomfortable for her, which likewise invites readers to consider both positive and negative implications of current food trends that celebrate the region.

Whereas writers including Arnow, Ritchie, and Dykeman venerated mountain foods before it was mainstream to do so, and Giardina, Wilkinson, and McFee diversify and complicate popular conceptions of mountain food in their celebrations, Gipe reminds us that when such recognition becomes widespread, the effects for people eating those foods all along are worth recognizing.

From Coarse to Haute

A Gentle Reminder

IN THE SPRING SEMESTER OF 2005, I ENROLLED IN A FOLKLORE seminar with Dr. Carolyn Ware at Louisiana State University. It was the first time elements of Appalachian culture were presented to me in an academic setting, and I remember how proud I felt to be talking about such things in graduate school. For my end-of-semester project I interviewed my father, Bert Abrams, and his friend, Fred King, about the cultural significance of ramps in Western North Carolina. None of my classmates had ever heard of ramps, though finding some at Whole Foods for $19.99 a pound led me to believe that at least some (wealthy) Baton Rouge residents were familiar with them. After finishing my degree in 2008 and moving back home to accept a position at UNC Asheville, I began noticing that Appalachian food was becoming "a thing." There was the 2008 "Field to Table Festival: A Taste of Appalachia" held at the Biltmore Estate in Asheville, the frequent mention of ramps on national cooking shows, and then the publication of books like Sean Brock's *Heritage* (2014) and Ronni Lundy's *Victuals* (2016), both of which celebrate mountain cuisine.[1] As mentioned in the introduction, in 2016 journalist Jane Black predicted mountain cooking would be "the next big thing in American regional cooking."[2] It seems her prediction came true, as evidenced by her September 2019 article in the *New York Times* entitled "Long Misunderstood, Appalachian Food Finds the Spotlight."[3] In it, she features chefs and restaurants, including Sean Brock, John Fleer, Ashleigh Shanti, Hanan Shabazz, and more. She also features the 2019 Chow Chow Festival in Asheville, North Carolina, a multiday event that organizers hoped would "serve as a public coming-out party for modern Appalachian cuisine." At the time of publication, Black reported that Brock had plans to open two new restaurants in Nashville, Audrey and Red Bird, both of which would pay homage to his Appalachian roots, with Red Bird "aim[ing] to be a kind of Chez Panisse for Appalachian cooking." Only a few months later, reports of a mysterious and deadly virus began circulating, and by the spring of 2020, the COVID-19 pandemic made indoor dining seem like a relic of the past. As I write this conclusion, Audrey is open with COVID precautions in place.[4] Likewise, Appalachian chef Travis Milton's restaurant featuring Appalachian dishes, Taste, is also open.[5] Nationally speaking, Appalachian cuisine was gaining a lot of momentum prepandemic, but it is hard to know how a radically different culinary landscape will affect that trend. Programs like the Smoky Mountains episode of *Gordon Ramsay: Uncharted*, filmed at the height of the pandemic in the fall of 2020, indicate a continued interest from national audiences.

As this book emphasizes, perceptions of Appalachian food have changed in profound ways since the late 1800s. Cuisine once deemed coarse is now haute. While this recognition is long overdue, we should also proceed with caution. In 2015, foodways scholar Elizabeth Engelhardt wrote, "If we do it right, Appalachian food studies can correct the excesses of southern food fetishism; open up fertile ground for a complicated story of race, class, gender, region and food; and tell a heck of a good story at the same time."[6] To avoid the kind of fetishism Engelhardt references, we should keep a few things in mind.

First, the tendency to decide what "counts" as Appalachian food can—and often does—exclude the food histories of many people who live in the region. The foods most commonly associated with Appalachia—think soup beans, cornbread, moonshine, leather britches, and apple stack cake—often imply whiteness, even when the origins of those foods (as with corn) indicate otherwise. Whenever possible, we should pay homage to the varied histories of mountain cuisine. As Engelhardt asserts, "Appalachian foodways projects ought not to romanticize the shuck beans and fried dried apple pies to the exclusion of the rest of the table."[7] Likewise, we would do well to remember that food served at high-end restaurants both in the late 1800s and today are part of the region's food story, as are the incorporation of convenience items. Nicolette's lemon-curd poppyseed stack cake might be the perfect conclusion to a meal of soup beans, cornbread, and weenies. As my grandmother's cookbook taught me, mountain cooks may be just as prone to clip a recipe

Fig. 10. The left side features my grandmother's handwritten recipe
for a blackberry pudding meant to top a cake, while the right side includes a
recipe for banana upside-down cake. Photo © Tim Barnwell.

for date nut fondant or Baby Ruth cookies as they are to save one for chow
chow. Figure 10 demonstrates my point clearly: on one page, my grandmother
included a handwritten recipe for blackberry pudding, an ideal way to use
sweet summer berries that ripened on her farm every summer. On the facing
page she saved a recipe for banana upside-down cake, a coincidental but no
less perfect last word on whether mountain cooks use "exotic" fruits in their
recipes (they do).

Second, elevating Appalachian heritage foods can result in exclusionary
practices, including high menu prices, preparation techniques perhaps unfamiliar to some mountain residents, and dining spaces that may be equally uncomfortable. Robert Gipe's portrayal of Dawn Jewell's reaction to her daughter's gorgonzola macaroni and cheese seems an apt example of the internal
conflict that culinary innovation can produce when it collides with beloved
food traditions.

Perhaps most importantly, we must remember that the increasing national
popularity of food historically associated with Appalachia does not automatically elevate public perception of mountain residents. In the same way that

mountain people were associated with "coarse" food in the late nineteenth and early twentieth centuries, a similar present-day paradigm exists equating processed, "junk" food with people in Appalachia. Kelly Bembry Midura's *Bitter Southerner* essay described in this book's introduction provides one problematic example. As Kentucky writer Chris Offutt wrote in 2015, "The term 'trash food' is not about food, it's coded language for social class."[8] Though national understandings of mountain cuisine are no doubt changing, public perceptions of mountain people remain troublingly stagnant.

But lest we fret, fiction writers like Robert Gipe present readers with rich, complex characters whose food choices represent much more than caloric intake. Moreover, work like his helps us understand that the study of Appalachian foodways is not an all-or-nothing proposition. Dawn Jewell's fondness for Pop-Tarts, soda, and oatmeal creme pies, for example, coexists with her penchant for soup beans, cornbread, and apple stack cake. In the same way that one word—Appalachia—embodies regional diversities that often go unrecognized, the idea of "Appalachian foodways" defies simplistic definitions and exclusionary understandings.

NOTES

Introduction

1. Elias, *Food on the Page*, 4.

2. Black, "The Next Big Thing in American Regional Cooking: Humble Appalachia"; Lundy, *Victuals: An Appalachian Journey, with Recipes*.

3. Midura, "A Story about a Mountain."

4. Offutt, "Trash Food," 126.

5. Offutt, 126.

6. Allison, "A Lesbian Appetite," 162–163.

7. A few key texts include: Shapiro, *Appalachia on Our Mind*; Batteau, *The Invention of Appalachia*; Pudup, Billings, and Waller, *Appalachia in the Making*; Williamson, *Hillbillyland*; Harkins, *Hillbilly*.

8. Passidomo, "Southern Foodways in the Classroom and Beyond," 12–13.

9. Davis and Powell, *Writing in the Kitchen*, 6.

10. Vester, *A Taste of Power*, 1–2.

11. Ferris, "The Edible South," 1.

12. In discussions of Southern (as opposed to mountain) food, this trend is definitely shifting. The influx of Latino foods in the South provides a wellspring of cultural intersections. In one example of many, Tom Hanchett and Eric Honenes del Pinal write about the phenomenon in Charlotte, North Carolina, where "hot tamales share space with biscuits under heat lamps" at a gas station off of I-85 (16). Certainly this trend is also taking place in Appalachia, but representations of the region do not seem to have caught up with the reality of culinary intersectionality. Katy Clune's work on Laos culture and foods in Morganton, North Carolina, is one welcome exception. For more, see Hanchett and Hoenes del Pinal, "Charlotte in Five Tamales"; Clune, "Tasting Laos in the North Carolina Mountains."

13. Balestier, "The Poetry of Pepperoni Rolls," 71.

14. For one clear example, see Semple, "The Anglo-Saxons of the Kentucky Mountains: A Study in Anthropogeography."

15. Tipton-Martin, *The Jemima Code: Two Centuries of African American Cookbooks*, 13.

16. Witt, "From Fiction to Foodways: Working at the Intersections of African American Literary and Culinary Studies"; Tipton-Martin, *The Jemima Code*; Burton et al., "The Legacy of Malinda Russell, the First African-American Cookbook Author."

17. Russell, Malinda, *A Domestic Cook Book.*

18. Lundy, *Victuals*, 151.

19. Lewis, "The Case of the Wild Onions: The Impact of Ramps on Cherokee Rights."

20. Lundy, *Victuals*, 192.

21. Vester, *A Taste of Power*, 8.

22. Levenstein, *Revolution at the Table*, 178.

23. W. B. McEwen and Caroline Nichols McEwen Collection, D. H. Ramsey Library, Special Collections, University of North Carolina at Asheville 28804. Hereafter cited as McEwen Collection, UNC Asheville.

24. McEwen Collection, UNC Asheville.

25. Western North Carolina has a long history of tourism and luxury resorts that catered to travelers, from hog drovers to elite travelers from the North and elsewhere. To learn more about that history, see Starnes, *Creating the Land of the Sky: Tourism and Society in Western North Carolina.*

26. Olcott explains that beef costing twelve cents a pound was extravagant when it could be purchased elsewhere for seven and a half cents a pound.

27. Olcott, *The Greenbrier Heritage*, 42.

28. Unless otherwise noted, all Greenbrier menus cited were provided by Dr. Robert Conte, the hotel's historian.

29. Unless otherwise noted, all Homestead menus cited were provided by Lynn Swann, the hotel's director of marketing and communications.

30. Unless otherwise noted, all Grove Park Inn menus cited were provided by Rebekkah Blenkitni, the hotel's public relations and special events coordinator.

31. Litchfield Family Household Ledger, Ms2013-008, Special Collections, Virginia Tech, Blacksburg. Hereafter cited as Litchfield Ledger, Virginia Tech.

32. Bell peppers were sometimes called mangoes during this time period, but the Litchfield recipe was most likely for pickled cantaloupe: many thanks to April McGregor, expert of all things pickled and preserved, and food historian David Shields for helping me unravel the "oiled mango" mystery.

33. Litchfield Ledger, Virginia Tech.

34. Bettie D. Cramer Manuscript Book, Ms2013-062, Special Collections, Virginia Tech, Blacksburg. Hereafter cited as Cramer Manuscript, Virginia Tech.

35. Bourdieu, *Distinction.*

36. Finn, *Discriminating Taste.*

Chapter 1. Fiction Made Real

1. Shapiro, *Appalachia on Our Mind*, 18. Future citations to this work in this chapter appear parenthetically in the text.

2. A few of these studies include: Pudup, Billings, and Waller, eds., *Appalachia in the Making: The Mountain South in the Nineteenth Century*; Billings, Norman, and Ledford, eds., *Back Talk from Appalachia: Confronting Stereotypes*; Williamson, *Hillbillyland: What the Movies Did to the Mountains and What the Mountains Did to the Movies*; McCarroll, *Unwhite: Appalachia, Race, and Film*.

3. Dirks, *Food in the Gilded Age*, 2.

4. Dirks, *Food in the Gilded Age*, 3–4.

5. Vester, *A Taste of Power*, 2.

6. Vester, *A Taste of Power*, 2.

7. Grammer, "Southwestern Humor," 370.

8. Grammer, "Southwestern Humor," 382.

9. Pratt, *Archives of American Time*, 126.

10. George Washington Harris, *Sut Lovingood. Yarns Spun by a "Nat'ral Born Durn'd Fool." Warped and Wove for Public Wear*. 261. Future citations to this work in this chapter appear parenthetically in the text.

11. I presume that the author was male, though this is not necessarily the case.

12. "Poor White Trash," 129. Future citations to this work in this chapter appear parenthetically in the text.

13. For more about the field of white trash studies, see Newitz and Wray, *White Trash*; Wray, *Not Quite White*; Isenberg, *White Trash*.

14. Black, "How Watermelons Became a Racist Trope."

15. Klotter, "The Black South and White Appalachia," 832.

16. Inscoe, *Appalachians and Race*.

17. Cooley, *To Live and Dine in Dixie: The Evolution of Food Culture in the Jim Crow South*, 20.

18. O'Donnell and Hollingsworth, *Seekers of Scenery*, 29. Future citations to this work in this chapter appear parenthetically in the text.

19. Allen, "Through Cumberland Gap on Horseback," 50. Future citations to this work in this chapter appear parenthetically in the text.

20. Gross and Snyder, *Philadelphia's 1876 Centennial Exhibition*. Many thanks to David Davis for sharing his work on bananas and the Global South with me.

21. Jenkins, *Bananas*, 12, 15. Future citations to this work in this chapter appear parenthetically in the text.

22. Charles Dudley Warner, *On Horseback*, 15. Future citations to this work in this chapter appear parenthetically in the text.

23. For more on tourism in Asheville, see Starnes, *Creating the Land of the Sky*.

24. For a more in-depth treatment of Warner's depictions of food, see Locklear, "A Matter of Taste: Reading Food and Class in Appalachian Literature," in *Writing in the Kitchen: Essays on Southern Literature and Foodways*.

25. Hilliard, *Hog Meat and Hoecake*, 38. Future citations to this work in this chapter appear parenthetically in the text.

26. Carter, "Now Is the Winter of Our Discontent," 200.

27. Carter, "Now Is the Winter of Our Discontent," 201.

28. Satterwhite, *Dear Appalachia*, 56.

29. Algeo, "Locals on Local Color: Imagining Identity in Appalachia," 52.

30. Fox, *The Trail of the Lonesome Pine*, 199–200.

31. Portor, "In Search of Local Color (Part One)," 282.

32. Portor, "In Search of Local Color (Part One)," 294.

33. Portor, "In Search of Local Color (Part Two)," 453.

34. Portor, "In Search of Local Color (Part Two)," 454.

35. Messenger, "An Appreciation: Big Things Done by One Little Woman."

36. Frost, "Our Contemporary Ancestors in the Southern Mountains."

37. Messenger, "An Appreciation: Big Things Done by One Little Woman."

38. Gielow, *Old Andy the Moonshiner*, 4.

39. Gielow, *Old Andy the Moonshiner*, 5, 8.

40. Gielow, *Uncle Sam*, 16.

41. Gielow, *Uncle Sam*, 59.

42. Gielow, *Uncle Sam*, 61.

43. Lee, "The Carolina, Clinchfield and Ohio Railroad and the Case (Study) for Appalachian Agricultural History," 20.

44. Quoted in Lee, "The Carolina, Clinchfield and Ohio Railroad," 22.

45. Ellison, "Introduction," in *Our Southern Highlanders: A Narrative of Adventure in the Southern Appalachians and a Study of Life Among Mountaineers*, xlii. Future citations to this work in this chapter appear parenthetically in the text.

46. https://www.wcu.edu/library/DigitalCollections/Kephart/onlineexhibit/Cooking/index.htm. Accessed May 18, 2022.

47. Kephart, *Camp Cookery*, 4.

48. Kephart, *Our Southern Highlanders*, 38–39. Future citations to this work in this chapter appear parenthetically in the text.

49. Ellison, *Our Southern Highlanders*, xl.

50. Levenstein, *Paradox of Plenty*; Veit, *Modern Food, Moral Food*; Dirks, *Food in the Gilded Age*; Finn, *Discriminating Taste*.

51. Becker, *Selling Tradition*, 63.

52. Finn, *Discriminating Taste*, 42–43.

53 O'Donnell and Hollingsworth, *Seekers of Scenery*, 19; Cuthbert and Poesch, *David Hunter Strother: "One of the Best Draughtsmen the Country Possesses,"* 31.

54. Hsiung, *Two Worlds in the Tennessee Mountains*, 163.

55. Strother, "A Winter in the South: First Paper," 433.

56. Strother, "A Winter in the South: First Paper," 434.

57. Strother, "A Winter in the South: Second Paper," 596.

58. Strother, "A Winter in the South: Second Paper," 596–597.

59. Strother, "A Winter in the South: Second Paper," 597.

60. Strother, "A Winter in the South: Second Paper," 606.

61. Strother, "A Winter in the South: Third Paper," 729.

62 Strother, "A Winter in the South: Third Paper," 740.

63. Hsiung, *Two Worlds in the Tennessee Mountains*, 167.

64. Strother, "A Winter in the South: Fourth Paper," 175.

65 Strother, "A Winter in the South: Fourth Paper," 175–176.

66. Strother, "A Winter in the South: Fifth Paper," 721.

67. Hsiung, *Two Worlds in the Tennessee Mountains*, 175.

68. Strother, "A Winter in the South: Fifth Paper," 721.

69. Strother, "A Winter in the South: Sixth Paper," 289.

70. Inscoe and McKinney, *The Heart of Confederate Appalachia*, 169–171.

71. "From the Carolina Planter," *Highland Messenger*, December 25, 1840. Many thanks to David Whisnant for sending this source to me. I surely would not have found it otherwise.

72. Sharon M. Harris, *Rebecca Harding Davis*, 29. Future citations to this work in this chapter appear parenthetically in the text.

73. Rose, "A Bibliography of Fiction and Non-Fiction by Rebecca Harding Davis," 67.

74. Davis, "The Yares of the Black Mountains," 35. Future citations to this work in this chapter appear parenthetically in the text.

75. Quoted in O'Donnell and Hollingsworth, *Seekers of Scenery*, 173; Sharon M. Harris, *Rebecca Harding Davis*, 207.

76. Davis, "By-Paths in the Mountains (I)," 167.

77. Davis, "By-Paths in the Mountains (I)," 168.

78. Davis, "By-Paths in the Mountains (II)," 355.

79. Davis, "By-Paths in the Mountains (II)," 356.

80. Davis, "By-Paths in the Mountains (III)," 545.

81. Davis, "By-Paths in the Mountains (II)," 367.

82. Davis, "By-Paths in the Mountains (II)," 369.

83. Davis, "By-Paths in the Mountains (III)," 545.

84. Davis, "The Mountain Hut," 271. The story is printed on one page, thus all quotes are from page 271.

85. Jones, "In the Highlands of North Carolina," 378, 379. Future citations to this work in this chapter appear parenthetically in the text.

86. Jones, "In the Backwoods of Carolina," 749.

87. Klingberg, "Glimpses of Life in the Appalachian Highlands," 373. Future citations to this work in this chapter appear parenthetically in the text.

88. Cox, *Traveling South*, 142.

89. Cox, *Traveling South*, 144.

90. Olmsted, "The Highlanders," 247. Future citations to this work in this chapter appear parenthetically in the text.

91. Davis, "Qualla," 585. Future citations to this work in this chapter appear parenthetically in the text.

92. Stewart, "'These Big-Boned, Semi-Barbarian People,'" 183.

93. Allen, "Mountain Passes of the Cumberland," 570.

94. Allen, "Mountain Passes of the Cumberland," 565.

95. Starnes, *Creating the Land of the Sky*, 4.

96. Nicklin, *Letters Descriptive of the Virginia Springs; the Roads Leading Thereto, and the Doings Thereat*, 25.

97. Lanier, "Sawney's Deer Lick."

98. Colton, *Mountain Scenery: The Scenery of the Mountains of Western North Carolina and South Carolina*, 15.

99. Dimmock, "A Trip to Mt. Mitchell in North Carolina," 142.

100. J. H., "Where to Go."

Chapter 2. Competing Culinary Discourses

1. Engelhardt, *A Mess of Greens*; Roe, *A Plague of Corn: The Social History of Pellagra*; Etheridge, *The Butterfly Caste*; Kraut, *Goldberger's War*.

2. The Conference of Southern Mountain Workers (CSMW), for example, was founded in 1913 and was an important group that promoted networking among progressives in Appalachia. CSMW helped train new workers in the field and promoted immersion in mountain life as an important teaching tool. The group also published *Mountain Life & Work* to educate the reading public about the region and its accompanying social problems. To learn more, see Penny Messinger, "Professionalizing 'Mountain Work' in Appalachia," in *Women in the Mountain South*, edited by Connie Park Rice and Marie Tedesco.

3. Harney, "A Strange Land and a Peculiar People."

4. Frost, "Our Contemporary Ancestors in the Southern Mountains." A number of scholars have explored how the concept of Appalachia formed in the national consciousness: Shapiro, *Appalachia on Our Mind: The Southern Mountains and Mountaineers in the American Consciousness, 1870–1920*; Batteau, *The Invention of Appalachia*; Pudup, Billings, and Waller, *Appalachia in the Making: The Mountain South in the Nineteenth Century*.

5. The American Missionary Association (AMA) by-laws stated that in order to help a population, it must be deemed exceptional. Literary scholar Chris Green cites 1883 as the year in which "mountain white" appeared in the *American Missionary*. For more about the AMA's role in promoting the image of a white Appalachia, see Green, *The Social Life of Poetry: Appalachia, Race, and Radical Modernism*.

6. Frost, "The Last Log School-House."

7. Frost, "The Southern Mountaineer: Our Kindred of the Boone and Lincoln Type."

8. Frost, "Our Contemporary Ancestors in the Southern Mountains," 311.

9. Frost, "Our Contemporary Ancestors in the Southern Mountains," 318.

10. Frost, "Our Contemporary Ancestors in the Southern Mountains," 319.

11. "To the Executors of the Estate of Horace Smith, Esq. of Springfield, Mass., in Behalf of the Trustees of Berea College," Series 4, Box 22, W. G. Frost Papers, Berea College Archives, BCA RG 03/3.03, Berea College Special Collections & Archives, Berea, KY. (BCSC hereafter).

12. Frost, "Our Contemporary Ancestors in the Southern Mountains," 319.

13. Frost, "The Southern Mountaineer," 305.

14. W. B. Forbush, "The Firelight Club: Some Unusual Characters," Series 1, Box 2, W. G. Frost Papers, BCSC.

15. For more, see Engelhardt, *A Mess of Greens*, 51–80; Ferris, *The Edible South*.

16. Vester, *A Taste of Power*, 22–32.

17. "The Two Secrets of Health," Series 4, Box 22, W.G. Frost Papers, BCSC.

18. "Berea Commencement," Series 1, Box 2, W. G. Frost Papers, BCBS.

19. Cady, "A Summer Outing in Kentucky," 56.

20. Williams, *Tales from Sacred Wind*, 133.

21. Message to the author, May 15, 2017. For more, see http://www.biodiversity library.org/item/201776#page/40/mode/1up. Accessed April 4, 2022.

22. Sumac lemonade uses berries from the ubiquitous sumac bush to make a tangy, acidic drink reminiscent of cranberry juice. Because of its acidic properties, sumac can be substituted for lemon in a number of recipes. Message to the author, May 26, 2017.

23. Edge, *The New Encyclopedia of Southern Culture*, vol. 7, 216–218; Shields, *Southern Provisions*, 305.

24. Shields, *Southern Provisions*, 309.

25. Cady, "A Summer Outing in Kentucky," 56.

26. Blackwell, "Eleanor Marsh Frost and the Gender Dimensions of Appalachian Reform Efforts," 230.

27. Eleanor Frost Diaries and Transcripts, Series 7, Box 36, W. G. Frost Papers, BCSC. The next seven direct quotes are from this source.

28. Eleanor Frost Diaries and Transcripts, Series 7, Box 31, W. G. Frost Papers, BCSC.

29. The original version is housed in the Southern Historical Collection at the University of North Carolina at Chapel Hill. In 2012 the University Press of Kentucky published *Appalachian Travels: The Diary of Olive Dame Campbell*, making it available to a wide audience for the first time.

30. Here and throughout the rest of the chapter, I use "Campbell" to refer to the authors of *The Southern Highlander and His Homeland*, since we cannot know whether John or Olive wrote any particular section.

31. Campbell, *The Southern Highlander and His Homeland*, 81, 82. Future citations to this work in this chapter appear parenthetically in the text.

32. John C. Campbell letter to John M. Glenn dated March 9, 1910, Series 5, Microfilmed Letters, 1909–1919, folder 229, 1909–1910, in the John C. Campbell and Olive D. Campbell Papers #3800, Southern Historical Collection, Wilson Library, University of North Carolina at Chapel Hill (SHC hereafter).

33. Campbell, Series 5, Microfilmed Letters, 1909–1919, Folder 229, 1909–1910. SHC.

34. Campbell, Series 5.

35. Campbell, Series 5.

36. Campbell, *The Southern Highlander and His Homeland*, 198.

37. Veit, *Modern Food, Moral Food*, 48.

38. Wilson, "Health Department," 178.

39. Wilson's explanation of who tolerates hog grease and who does not is steeped in notions of biological racism. He writes: "Fat bacon and pork are peculiarly appropriate for negroes on account of their habits of life, and their defective heat-generating powers; but for white women, and especially for Southern white women, in their present mode of living, no diet could be selected that would be more injurious," 178.

40. Olmsted, "The Highlanders," 247.

41. Campbell, *Appalachian Travels*, 66.

42. This approach could have allowed Olive to insert herself in the narrative without taking full ownership of it, or perhaps John decided to write about himself in third person, which makes more sense chronologically since he opened his first school while married to Grace, not Olive.

43. Campbell, "Social Betterment in the Southern Mountains," 130. Future citations to this work in this chapter appear parenthetically in the text.

44. The notion of education resulting in getting above one's raising is a common one in Appalachian studies. For more, see Locklear, *Negotiating a Perilous Empowerment: Appalachian Women's Literacies*; Sohn, *Whistlin' and Crowin' Women of Appalachia: Literacy Practices Since College*.

45. Engelhardt, *A Mess of Greens*.

46. John C. Campbell, draft of "Social Betterment in the Mountains," written "somewhere around 1908–1909," Series 2, Writings, 1895–1965, Folder 132, Articles 1907–1909, SHC.

47. Campbell, *Appalachian Travels*, 26. Future citations to this work in this chapter appear parenthetically in the text.

48. Levenstein, *Revolution at the Table*, 87.

49. Levenstein, *Revolution at the Table*, 93.

50. Engelhardt, *A Mess of Greens*, 75.

51. In *Hog Meat and Hoecake: Food Supply in the Old South, 1840–1860*, Sam Hilliard writes that in the South generally, "wheat was consumed over a wide area, but its role in the diet was a minor one. It was grown in the Hill South in substantial quantities but elsewhere was more of a garden crop than a major field cereal" (170). In Horace Kephart's 1913 book, *Our Southern Highlanders*, he writes, "Wheat is raised, to some extent, in the river bottoms, and on the plateaus of the interior," but "corn was the staple crop" (38).

52. The *Comet*, December 10, 1908, image 5.

53. The *Comet*, August 12, 1909, image 2.

54. Grace Buckingham letter to her mother dated February 24, 1896, Series 1, Correspondence, 1865–1962, Folder 5, 1895–1897, SHC.

55. Grace Buckingham, Cullman Academy, Joppa, Alabama, January 1896, Series 1, Correspondence, 1865–1962, Folder 5, 1895–1897, SHC.

56. Ferris, *The Edible South*, 143.

57. Grace Buckingham, Cullman Academy, Joppa, Alabama, January 1896, Series 1, Correspondence, 1865–1962, Folder 5, 1895–1897, SHC.

58. Grace Buckingham letter to her father dated January 24, 1896, Series 1, Correspondence, 1865–1962, Folder 5, 1895–1897, SHC.

59. Finnegan, *Making Photography Matter*, 92.

60. After researching mill conditions in Concord, North Carolina, in 1906 Holland Thompson published a book arguing that living in a mill town supplied workers with better, more nutritious food than life on the farm. Foodways scholar Elizabeth Engelhardt problematizes Thompson's claim with her chapter on mill work, pellagra, and gendered consumption in *A Mess of Greens*, noting that Thompson seemed blind to the many nutritional deficiencies around him.

Marcie Cohen Ferris discusses Thompson's work in the context of John C. Campbell, explaining that Campbell disagreed with Thompson's claims. Thomas Robinson Dawley's 1912 publication adds another dimension to the pro-mill rhetoric Thompson touted six years earlier. For more, see Thompson, *From the Cotton Field to the Cotton Mill*; Engelhardt, *A Mess of Greens*, 119–164; Ferris, *The Edible South*, 143–144.

61. Finnegan, *Making Photography Matter*, 89.

62. Finnegan, *Making Photography Matter*, 92.

63. "Defending Child Labor"; "The Child Labor Problem"; Foley, Review of "*The Child That Toileth Not*," 94.

64. Dimock, "Children of the Mills," 44.

65. Dimock, "Children of the Mills"; Finnegan, "'Liars May Photograph'"; Finnegan, *Making Photography Matter*.

66. Dawley, *The Child That Toileth Not*, 276–277. Future citations to this work in this chapter appear parenthetically in the text.

67. Finnegan, *Making Photography Matter*, 125.

68. Finnegan, *Making Photography Matter*, 124.

69. Dawley, "Our Mountain Problem and Its Solution," 150.

70. Dawley, "Our Mountain Problem and Its Solution," 151.

71. Dawley, "Our Mountain Problem and Its Solution," 151.

72. Montague, "The Use of Pork in the Family," 229.

73. Dawley, "Our Mountain Problem and Its Solution," 151.

74. Dawley, *The Child That Toileth Not*, 422.

75. Foley, review of "*The Child That Toileth Not*," 94.

Chapter 3. Writers Respond

1. Many thanks to Carrie Helms Tippen for the organizational idea of this opening and, once again, to Elizabeth Engelhardt, whose chapter on beaten biscuits in *A Mess of Greens* provided a helpful model.

2. Petty, *Standing Their Ground*, 75. Future citations to this work in this chapter appear parenthetically in the text.

3. Cooperative Extension Service Annual Reports UA 102.002, Box 16, Folder 10, Third Annual Report, Agricultural Extension Service, 1917. Special Collections Research Center, North Carolina State University Libraries, Raleigh, North Carolina. (NSCU hereafter)

4. Lee, "Southern Appalachia's Nineteenth-Century Bright Tobacco Boom," 178.

5. Algeo, "The Rise of Tobacco as a Southern Appalachian Staple," 46.

6. Van Vorst, *Amanda of the Mill: A Novel*, 88, 89. Future citations to this work in this chapter appear parenthetically in the text.

7. Engelhardt, *A Mess of Greens*, 133.

8. Vorse, *Strike!*; Anderson, *Beyond Desire*; Burke, *Call Home the Heart*; Lumpkin, *To Make My Bread*; Page, *Gathering Storm*; Rollins, *The Shadow Before*; Cash, *The Last Ballad*.

9. Lumpkin, *To Make My Bread*, xii. Future citations to this work in this chapter appear parenthetically in the text.

10. Jones, "In the Backwoods of Carolina," 749.

11. North Carolina Cooperative Extension Service, Office of the Director Records UA 102.001 Series 1.2; Box 2, Folder 6. NCSU.

12. Bowen, Brenton, and Elliott, *Pressure Cooker*.

13. Morrison, *Governor O. Max Gardner*, 75.

14. North Carolina Cooperative Extension Service, Office of the Director Records, UA 102.001, Series 1.2, Box 3, Folder 4, Live at Home Dinner O (Oliver) Max Gardner. NCSU.

15. Morrison, *Governor O. Max Gardner*, 78.

16. Burke, *Call Home the Heart*, 6, 8. Future citations to this work in this chapter appear parenthetically in the text.

17. Beetham, *A Magazine of Her Own?*, 158–159.

18. Elias, *Stir It Up*, 79.

19. Cooperative Extension Service Annual Reports UA 102.002 Box 17, Annual Report of Agricultural Extension Work in North Carolina, 1933. NCSU.

20. https://www.archivesfoundation.org/documents/smith-lever-act-1914/. Accessed April 4, 2022.

21. Cooperative Extension Service, Assistant Director's Office, Cooperative Extension Service History, UA 102.005 Box 1, Legal Size Box, Series 1, Box 1 (Legal Size), Folder 5. NCSU.

22. Cooperative Extension Service Annual Reports, UA 102.002, Box 16, Folder 11, Fourth Annual Report, Agricultural Extension Service, Year Ended June 30, 1918, 36. NCSU.

23. North Carolina Cooperative Extension Service, Office of the Director of Records, UA 102.001, Series 1.2, Box 2, Folder 3, 2–3. NCSU.

24. Dobbs, "Agricultural Adjustment Act."

25. Katie Algeo, "The Rise of Tobacco as a Southern Appalachian Staple," 46.

26. Catherine Algeo, *Tobacco Farming in the Age of the Surgeon General's Warning*, 41. Future citations to this work in this chapter appear parenthetically in the text.

27. North Carolina Cooperative Extension Service, Office of the Director Records UA 102.001 Series 1.2, Box 1, Folder 15. NCSU.

28. Cooperative Extension Service Annual Reports, UA 102.002, Box 17, Folder 4, "Rebuilding a Fair Land," Report of Agricultural Extension in North Carolina for the Year 1936. NCSU.

29. Ferris, *The Edible South*, 154.

Chapter 4. Feeling Poor and Ashamed

1. Naccarato and Lebesco, *Culinary Capital*, 1–2.

2. Bourdieu, *Distinction*.

3. Vester, *A Taste of Power*, 3.

4. Vester, *A Taste of Power*, 2, 1.

5. Green, "Mother Corn and the Dixie Pig," 116.

6. Southern Foodways Alliance, "Lumbee Indians of NC."

7. Hill, "It's a Greens Thing."

8. Willis, "Community School, Community Garden."

9. Hilliard, *Hog Meat and Hoecake*, 48–49.

10. Hilliard, *Hog Meat and Hoecake*, 157.

11. Jessica Harris, *High on the Hog*; Opie, *Hog and Hominy*.

12. Burke, *Call Home the Heart*, 97.

13. Lundy, *Sorghum's Savor*, 6–9. Future citations to this work in this chapter appear parenthetically in the text.

14. Hilliard, *Hog Meat and Hoecake*, 52.

15. Tippen, *Inventing Authenticity*; Stokes and Atkins-Sayre, *Consuming Identity*.

16. Vester, *A Taste of Power*, 1–2.

17. Williams, *Tales from Sacred Wind*. Future citations to this work in this chapter appear parenthetically in the text.

18. Bourdieu, *Distinction*, 79.

19. Engelhardt, *A Mess of Greens*.

20. Jones, "In the Backwoods of Carolina," 749.

21. Engelhardt, *A Mess of Greens*; Ferris, *The Edible South*.

22. Engelhardt, *A Mess of Greens*, 51–80.

23. Jurafsky, *The Language of Food*, 9.

24. Finn, *Discriminating Taste*, 11.

25. Crum, "Constructing a Marketable Writer," 430.

26. Still, *River Of Earth*, 51. Future citations to this work in this chapter appear parenthetically in the text.

27. Wilkinson, *The Birds of Opulence*, 90. Future citations to this work in this chapter appear parenthetically in the text.

28. Locklear, Wilkinson, and Lundy, "Gathering at the Table."

29. Decker, "Origin(s), Evolution, and Systematics of Cucurbita Pepo (Cucurbitaceae)," 4.

30. Fox-Genovese, *Within the Plantation Household*; Jacobs, *Incidents in the Life of a Slave Girl*.

31. Miller, *Newfound*, 98; An excerpt from this novel is also included in Lundy, *Cornbread Nation 3: Foods of the Mountain South*.

32. Hamby, *Memoirs of Grassy Creek*, 22. Future citations to this work in this chapter appear parenthetically in the text.

Chapter 5. The Main Best Eating in the World

1. Ramsay, "Quest for the Best."

2. Lunsford, "Asheville Culinary Pros Join Gordon Ramsay on National Geographic Show."

3. National Geographic, "Gordon Ramsay."

4. Oates, "Harriette Arnow's the Dollmaker," 15.

5. Olsen and Fishkin, *Silences*, xii.

6. Satterwhite, *Dear Appalachia*.

7. Brosi, "This Issue," 11.

8. Miller and Arnow, "A MELUS Interview," 93.

9. Miller and Arnow, "A MELUS Interview," 90.

10. Arnow, *The Dollmaker*, 78. Future citations to this work in this chapter appear parenthetically in the text.

11. Ritchie, *Singing Family of the Cumberlands*, 72. Future citations to this work in this chapter appear parenthetically in the text.

12. Lundy, *Victuals*, 123. Future citations to this work in this chapter appear parenthetically in the text.

13. Dykeman, *The Tall Woman*, 75. Future citations to this work in this chapter appear parenthetically in the text.

14. Farr, *Table Talk*, 162. Future citations to this work in this chapter appear parenthetically in the text.

15. Giardina, *Storming Heaven*, 27. Future citations to this work in this chapter appear parenthetically in the text.

16. Giardina, *The Unquiet Earth*, 5. Future citations to this work in this chapter appear parenthetically in the text.

17. Brown, *Gone Home*, 11.

18. Brown, *Gone Home*, 12–13.

19. Obermiller and Wagner, *African American Miners and Migrants*, 5.

20. Balestier, "The Poetry of Pepperoni Rolls," 71.

21. Wilkinson, "Praise Song for the Kitchen Ghosts."

22. Brown, *Gone Home*, 61.

23. Locklear, Wilkinson, and Lundy, "Gathering at the Table."

24. McFee, *Colander*, 80.

25 McFee, "Cornbread in Buttermilk," 12.

26. McFee, "Mountain Cooking," 134.

27. McFee, "Roadside Table," 34.

28. Gipe, *Pop*, 55, 57. Future citations to this work in this chapter appear parenthetically in the text.

29. McGreal, "Big Pharma Executives Mocked 'Pillbillies' in Emails, West Virginia Opioid Trial Hears."

30. Gipe, "Confessions of a Spear Packer."

31. Gipe, "Comfort Food."

32. Curtis, "A Perfect Mash-Up," 36.

33. Locklear, "Setting Tobacco, Banquet-Style," 38–39.

Conclusion

1. Brock and Edwards, *Heritage*; Lundy, *Victuals*.

2. Black, "The Next Big Thing in American Regional Cooking: Humble Appalachia."

3. Black, "Long Misunderstood, Appalachian Food Finds the Spotlight."

4. https://www.audreynashville.com/. Accessed April 4, 2022.

5. https://www.nicewonderfarm.com/taste-about. Accessed April 4, 2022.

6. Engelhardt, "Appalachian Chicken and Waffles," 76.

7. Engelhardt, "Appalachian Chicken and Waffles," 78.

8. Offutt, "Trash Food," 126.

Algeo, Katie (Catherine Marie). "Locals on Local Color: Imagining Identity in Appalachia." *Southern Cultures* 9, no. 4 (2003): 27–54.

———. "The Rise of Tobacco as a Southern Appalachian Staple: Madison County, North Carolina." *Southeastern Geographer* 37, no. 1 (1997): 46–60.

———. *Tobacco Farming in the Age of the Surgeon General's Warning: The Cultural Ecology and Structuration of Burley Tobacco Production in Madison County, North Carolina*. PhD diss., Louisiana State University, 1984.

Allen, James Lane. "Mountain Passes of the Cumberland." *Harper's New Monthly Magazine*, September 1890.

———. "Through Cumberland Gap on Horseback." *Harper's New Monthly Magazine*, June 1886.

Allison, Dorothy. "A Lesbian Appetite." In *Trash*, Plume ed., 161–178. New York: Penguin Group, 2002.

Anderson, Sherwood. *Beyond Desire*. New York: Horace Liverwight, 1932.

Appalachian Food Summit. "Appalachian Food Summit." https://www.appalachian food.com. Accessed July 2, 2021.

Arnow, Harriette Simpson. *The Dollmaker*. New York: Perennial, 2003. First published 1954 by Macmillan (New York).

Balestier, Courtney. "The Poetry of Pepperoni Rolls." *Appalachian Heritage* 45, no. 1 (Winter 2017): 69–75.

Batteau, Allen. *The Invention of Appalachia*. Tucson: University of Arizona Press, 1990.

Becker, Jane S. *Selling Tradition: Appalachia and the Construction of an American Folk, 1930–1940*. Chapel Hill: University of North Carolina Press, 1998.

Beetham, Margaret. *A Magazine of Her Own? Domesticity and Desire in the Woman's Magazine, 1800–1914*. London, New York: Routledge, 1996.

Billings, Dwight B., Gurney Norman, and Katherine Ledford, eds. *Back Talk from Appalachia: Confronting Stereotypes*. Lexington: University Press of Kentucky, 2000.

Black, Jane. "Long Misunderstood, Appalachian Food Finds the Spotlight." *New York Times*, September 9, 2019.

———. "The Next Big Thing in American Regional Cooking: Humble Appalachia." *Washington Post*, March 29, 2016.

Black, William R. "How Watermelons Became a Racist Trope." *Atlantic*, December 8, 2014. http://www.theatlantic.com/national/archive/2014/12/how-watermelons-became-a-racist-trope/383529/. Accessed May 18, 2022.

Blackwell, Deborah L. "Eleanor Marsh Frost and the Gender Dimensions of Appalachian Reform Efforts." *Register of the Kentucky Historical Society* 94, no. 3 (Summer 1996): 225–246.

Bourdieu, Pierre. *Distinction: A Social Critique of the Judgement of Taste.* Cambridge, MA: Harvard University Press, 1984.

Bowen, Sarah, Joslyn Brenton, and Sinikka Elliott. *Pressure Cooker: Why Home Cooking Won't Solve Our Problems and What We Can Do about It.* New York: Oxford University Press, 2019.

Brock, Sean, and Peter Frank Edwards. *Heritage.* New York: Artisan, 2014.

Brosi, George. "This Issue." *Appalachian Heritage* 40, no. 2 (Spring 2012): 11.

Brown, Karida. *Gone Home: Race and Roots through Appalachia.* Chapel Hill: University of North Carolina Press, 2018.

Burke, Fielding (pseudonym for Olive Tilford Dargan). *Call Home the Heart: A Novel of the Thirties.* 1st Feminist Press ed. Novels of the Thirties Series. Old Westbury, NY: Feminist Press, 1983. First published 1932 by Longmans, Green (New York).

Burton, Monica, Osayi Endolyn, and Toni Tipton-Martin. "The Legacy of Malinda Russell, the First African-American Cookbook Author." *Eater* (February 23, 2021). https://www.eater.com/22262716/malinda-russell-author-a-domestic-cookbook. Accessed April 5, 2022.

Cady, J. Cleveland. "A Summer Outing in Kentucky." *Outlook*, January 11, 1896.

Campbell, John C. "Series 5. Microfilmed Letters, 1909–1919. Folder 229, 1909–1910," n.d.

———. "Social Betterment in the Southern Mountains." *Proceedings of the National Conference of Charities and Correction*, 1909, 130–137.

———. *The Southern Highlander and His Homeland.* Lexington: University Press of Kentucky, 1969. First published 1921 by the Russell Sage Foundation (New York).

Campbell, John C., and Olive D. Campbell Papers. #3800. Southern Historical Collection, Wilson Library, University of North Carolina at Chapel Hill.

Campbell, Olive Dame. *Appalachian Travels: The Diary of Olive Dame Campbell.* Edited by Elizabeth M. Williams. Lexington: University Press of Kentucky, 2012.

Carter, Mary Nelson. "Now Is the Winter of Our Discontent." In *North Carolina*

    Sketches: Phases of Life Where the Galax Grows, 197–208. Chicago: A. C. McClurg, 1900.

Cash, Wiley. *The Last Ballad*. New York: William Morrow, 2017.

"The Child Labor Problem." *Washington Post*, February 11, 1913.

Clune, Katy. "Tasting Laos in the North Carolina Mountains." *Gravy* 57 (Fall 2015): 39–45.

Colton, Henry E. *Mountain Scenery: The Scenery of the Mountains of Western North Carolina and South Carolina*. Raleigh, NC: W. L. Pomerboy, 1859.

The *Comet*. August 12, 1909, Image 2, August 12, 1909. Newspaper distributed from Johnson City, Tennessee, 1884–1916.

The *Comet*. December 10, 1908, Image 5, December 10, 1908. Newspaper distributed from Johnson City, Tennessee, 1884–1916.

Cooley, Angela Jill. *To Live and Dine in Dixie: The Evolution of Urban Food Culture in the Jim Crow South*. Athens: University of Georgia Press, 2015.

Cooperative Extension Service. Annual Reports. UA 102.002, Special Collections Research Center, North Carolina State University Libraries, Raleigh.

———. "Cooperative Extension Service History." UA 102.005, Special Collections Research Center, North Carolina State University Libraries, Raleigh.

Cox, John D. *Traveling South: Travel Narratives and the Construction of American Identity*. Athens: University of Georgia Press, 2005.

Cramer, Bettie D. "Bettie D. Cramer Manuscript Book." Ms2013-062, Special Collections, Virginia Tech, Blacksburg.

Crum, Claude Lafie. "Constructing a Marketable Writer: James Still's Fictional Persona." *Appalachian Journal* 32, no. 4 (2005): 430–439.

Curtis, Wayne. "A Perfect Mash-Up." *Garden & Gun*, August/September 2021.

Cuthbert, John A., and Jessie Poesch, eds. *David Hunter Strother: "One of the Best Draughtsmen the Country Possesses."* Morgantown: West Virginia University Press, 1997.

Dargan, Olive Tilford. See Burke, Fielding.

Davis, David A., and Tara Powell, eds. *Writing in the Kitchen: Essays on Southern Literature and Foodways*. Jackson: University Press of Mississippi, 2014.

Davis, Rebecca Harding. "By-Paths in the Mountains (I)." *Harper's New Monthly Magazine*, July 1880.

———. "By-Paths in the Mountains (II)." *Harper's New Monthly Magazine*, August 1880.

———. "By-Paths in the Mountains (III)." *Harper's New Monthly Magazine*, September 1880.

———. "The Mountain Hut." *Youth's Companion*, July 2, 1885.

———. "Qualla." *Lippincott's Magazine*, November 1875.

———. "The Yares of the Black Mountains." *Lippincott's Magazine*, July 1875.

Dawley, Thomas Robinson. *The Child That Toileth Not: The Story of a Government Investigation That Was Suppressed*. New York: Gracia, 1912.

———. "Our Mountain Problem and Its Solution." In *Proceedings of the Fourteenth Annual Convention of the American Cotton Manufacturers Association*, 149–155. Charlotte, NC: Queen City, 1910.

Decker, Deena S. "Origin(s), Evolution, and Systematics of Cucurbita Pepo (Cucurbitaceae)." *Economic Botany* 42, no. 1 (1988): 4–15.

"Defending Child Labor." *New York Times*, January 26, 1913.

Dimmock, George. "A Trip to Mt. Mitchell in North Carolina." *Appalachia*, June 1877.

Dimock, George. "Children of the Mills: Re-Reading Lewis Hine's Child-Labour Photographs." *Oxford Art Journal* 16, no. 2 (1993): 37–54.

Dirks, Robert. *Food in the Gilded Age: What Ordinary Americans Ate*. Rowman & Littlefield Studies in Food and Gastronomy. Lanham, MD: Rowman & Littlefield, 2016.

Dobbs, Chris. "Agricultural Adjustment Act." In *New Georgia Encyclopedia*, 2018. https://www.georgiaencyclopedia.org/articles/business-economy/agricultural -adjustment-act. Accessed April 6, 2022.

Dykeman, Wilma. *The Tall Woman*. Newport, TN: Wakestone Books, 1982. First published 1962 by Holt, Rinehart, and Winston (New York).

Edge, John T., ed. *The New Encyclopedia of Southern Culture*, vol. 7: *Foodways*. Chapel Hill: University of North Carolina Press, 2007.

Ehrenreich, Barbara. *Nickel and Dimed: On (Not) Getting by in America*. New York: Henry Holt, 2001.

Elias, Megan J. *Food on the Page*. Philadelphia: University of Pennsylvania Press, 2017.

———. *Stir It Up: Home Economics in American Culture*. Philadelphia, Oxford: University of Pennsylvania Press, 2008.

Eller, Ronald D. *Miners, Millhands, and Mountaineers: Industrialization of the Appalachian South, 1880–1930*. Twentieth-Century America Series. Knoxville: University of Tennessee Press, 1982.

Ellison, George. "Introduction." In *Our Southern Highlanders: A Narrative of Adventure in the Southern Appalachians and a Study of Life Among Mountaineers*, by Horace Kephart, viiii–xlviii. Knoxville: University of Tennessee Press, 1976.

Engelhardt, Elizabeth S. D. "Appalachian Chicken and Waffles: Countering Southern Food Fetishism." *Southern Cultures* 21, no. 1 (2015): 73–83.

———. *A Mess of Greens: Southern Gender and Southern Food*. Athens: University of Georgia Press, 2011.

Etheridge, Elizabeth W. *The Butterfly Caste: A Social History of Pellagra in the South*. Contributions in American History, No. 17. Westport, CT: Greenwood, 1972.

Farr, Sidney Saylor, ed. *Table Talk: Appalachian Meals and Memories*. Pittsburgh: University of Pittsburgh Press, 1995.

Ferris, Marcie Cohen. "The Edible South." *Southern Cultures: The Edible South* 15, no. 4 (Winter 2009): 3–27.

———. *The Edible South: The Power of Food and the Making of an American Region*. Chapel Hill: University of North Carolina Press, 2014.

Finn, S. Margot. *Discriminating Taste: How Class Anxiety Created the American Food Revolution*. New Brunswick, NJ: Rutgers University Press, 2017.

Finnegan, Cara A. "'Liars May Photograph': Image Vernaculars and Progressive Era Child Labor Rhetoric." *Poroi* 5, no. 2 (November 1, 2008): 94–139.

———. *Making Photography Matter: A Viewer's History from the Civil War to the Great Depression*. Urbana: University of Illinois Press, 2015.

Foley, Roy William. *"The Child That Toileth Not,"* by Thomas Robinson Dawley. Review in *American Journal of Sociology* 19, no. 1 (1913): 94.

Fox, John, Jr. *The Trail of the Lonesome Pine*. New York: C. Scribner's Sons, 1908.

Fox-Genovese, Elizabeth. *Within the Plantation Household: Black and White Women of the Old South*. Chapel Hill: University of North Carolina Press, 1988.

Franks, Julia. *Over the Plain Houses*. Spartanburg, SC: Hub City Press, 2016.

"From the Carolina Planter." *Highland Messenger*, December 25, 1840.

Frost, William Goodell. "The Last Log School-House." *Commercial Gazette*, December 14, 1895.

———. "Our Contemporary Ancestors in the Southern Mountains." *Atlantic Monthly* 83, no. 497 (March 1899): 311–320.

———. "The Southern Mountaineer: Our Kindred of the Boone and Lincoln Type." *American Monthly Review of Reviews* 21, no. 3 (March 1900): 303–311.

Frost, W. G., Papers. Berea College Archives, BCA RG 03/3.03, Berea College Special Collections & Archives, Berea, Kentucky.

Giardina, Denise. *Storming Heaven: A Novel*. New York: Ballantine, 1999. First published 1987 by W. W. Norton & Company (New York).

———. *The Unquiet Earth*. New York: Ivy Books, 1992.

Gielow, Martha S. (Martha Sawyer). *Old Andy the Moonshiner*. Washington, DC: W. F. Roberts, 1909.

———. *Uncle Sam*. New York, Chicago: Fleming H. Revell, 1913.

Gipe, Robert. "Comfort Food." *Gravy*, no. 69 (Fall, 2018): 60–67.

———. "Confessions of a Spear Packer." In *The Food We Eat, the Stories We Tell*, edited by Elizabeth D. Engelhardt and Lora E. Smith, 126–131. Athens: Ohio University Press, 2019.

———. *Pop: An Illustrated Novel*. Athens: Ohio University Press, 2021.

———. *Trampoline: An Illustrated Novel*. Athens: Ohio University Press, 2015.

———. *Weedeater: An Illustrated Novel*. Athens: Ohio University Press, 2018.

Grammer, John M. "Southwestern Humor." In *A Companion to the Literature and Culture of the American South*, edited by Richard Gray and Owen Robinson, 370–387. Oxford: Blackwell, 2004.

Green, Chris. *The Social Life of Poetry: Appalachia, Race, and Radical Modernism*. New York: Palgrave Macmillan, 2009.

Green, Rayna. "Mother Corn and the Dixie Pig: Native Food in the Native South." *Southern Cultures* 14, no. 4 (Winter 2008): 114–126.

Gross, Linda P, and Theresa R Snyder. *Philadelphia's 1876 Centennial Exhibition*. Charleston, SC: Arcadia, 2005.

Hamby, Zetta Barker. *Memoirs of Grassy Creek: Growing Up in the Mountains on the Virginia-North Carolina Line*. Jefferson, NC: McFarland, 1997.

Hanchett, Tom, and Eric Hoenes del Pinal. "Charlotte in Five Tamales." *Gravy* 62 (Winter 2016): 15–21.

Harkins, Anthony. *Hillbilly: A Cultural History of an American Icon*. New York: Oxford University Press, 2004.

Harney, Will Wallace. "A Strange Land and a Peculiar People." *Lippincott's Magazine* 12, no. 31 (October 1873): 429–438.

Harris, George Washington. *Sut Lovingood: Yarns Spun by a "Nat'ral Born Durn'd Fool." Warped and Wove for Public Wear*. New York: Dick & Fitzgerald, 1867.

Harris, Jessica B. *High on the Hog: A Culinary Journey from Africa to America*. Reprint edition. New York: Bloomsbury USA, 2012.

Harris, Sharon M. *Rebecca Harding Davis: A Life among Writers*. Morgantown: West Virginia University Press, 2018.

"Hell's Kitchen: Young Guns." https://www.fox.com/hells-kitchen/. Accessed June 11, 2021.

Hill, Cynthia. "It's a Greens Thing." *Somewhere South*, PBS broadcast, April 24, 2020.

Hilliard, Sam Bowers. *Hog Meat and Hoecake: Food Supply in the Old South, 1840–1860*. Carbondale: Southern Illinois University Press, 1972.

Hsiung, David C. *Two Worlds in the Tennessee Mountains: Exploring the Origins of Appalachian Stereotypes*. Lexington: University Press of Kentucky, 1997.

Inscoe, John C., ed. *Appalachians and Race: The Mountain South from Slavery to Segregation*. Lexington: University Press of Kentucky, 2005.

Inscoe, John C., and Gordon B. McKinney. *The Heart of Confederate Appalachia: Western North Carolina in the Civil War.* Chapel Hill: University of North Carolina Press, 2000.

Isenberg, Nancy. *White Trash: The 400-Year Untold History of Class in America.* New York: Viking, 2016.

J. H. "Where to Go." *Good Housekeeping,* June 1911.

Jacobs, Harriet A. *Incidents in the Life of a Slave Girl: Written by Herself.* Edited by Lydia Maria Child and Jean Fagan Yellin. Cambridge, MA: Harvard University Press, 1987. First published 1861 by the author (Boston).

Jenkins, Virginia Scott. *Bananas: An American History.* Washington, DC: Smithsonian Institution Press, 2000.

Jones, Louise Coffin. "In the Backwoods of Carolina." *Lippincott's Magazine,* December 1879.

———. "In the Highlands of North Carolina." *Lippincott's Magazine,* October 1883.

Jurafsky, Dan. *The Language of Food: A Linguist Reads the Menu.* New York: W. W. Norton, 2015.

Kephart, Horace. *Camp Cookery.* New York: Macmillan, 1926.

———. *Our Southern Highlanders.* New York: Outing, 1913.

Klingberg, Elizabeth Wysor. "Glimpses of Life in the Appalachian Highlands." *Southern Atlantic Quarterly* 14 (October 1915): 371–378.

Klotter, James C. "The Black South and White Appalachia." *Journal of American History* 66, no. 4 (1980): 832–849.

Kraut, Alan M. *Goldberger's War: The Life and Work of a Public Health Crusader.* New York: Hill and Wang, 2003.

Lanier, Charles D. "Sawney's Deer Lick." *Scribner's Magazine,* January 1895.

Lee, Tom. "The Carolina, Clinchfield and Ohio Railroad and the Case (Study) for Appalachian Agricultural History." Annual Meeting of the Society of Appalachian Historians. Knoxville, Tennessee, 2016.

———. "Southern Appalachia's Nineteenth-Century Bright Tobacco Boom: Industrialization, Urbanization, and the Culture of Tobacco." *Agricultural History* 88, no. 2 (Spring 2014): 175–206.

Levenstein, Harvey A. *Paradox of Plenty: A Social History of Eating in Modern America.* New York: Oxford University Press, 1993.

———. *Revolution at the Table: The Transformation of the American Diet.* New York: Oxford University Press, 1988.

Lewis, Courtney. "The Case of the Wild Onions: The Impact of Ramps on Cherokee Rights." *Southern Cultures* 18, no. 2 (Summer 2012): 104–117.

Litchfield Family Household Ledger. Ms2013-008, Special Collections, Virginia Tech, Blacksburg.

Locklear, Erica Abrams. "A Matter of Taste: Reading Food and Class in Appalachian Literature." In *Writing in the Kitchen: Essays on Southern Literature and Foodways*, edited by David A. Davis and Tara Powell, 124–142. Oxford, MS: University of Mississippi Press, 2014.

———. *Negotiating a Perilous Empowerment: Appalachian Women's Literacies*. Athens: Ohio University Press, 2011.

———. "Setting Tobacco, Banquet-Style." In *The Food We Eat, the Stories We Tell*, edited by Elizabeth S. D. Engelhardt and Lora E. Smith, 24–45. Athens: Ohio University Press, 2019.

Locklear, Erica Abrams, Crystal Wilkinson, and Ronni Lundy. "Gathering at the Table: Crystal Wilkinson and Ronni Lundy Discuss Culinary Representation, Shame, and Redemption." Presented at the virtual Appalachian Studies Association Conference, March 12, 2021.

Lumpkin, Grace. *To Make My Bread*. Urbana and Chicago: University of Illinois Press, 1995. First published 1932 by Macaulay (New York).

Lundy, Ronni, ed. *Cornbread Nation 3: Foods of the Mountain South*. Chapel Hill: University of North Carolina Press, 2005.

———. *Sorghum's Savor*. Gainesville: University Press of Florida, 2015.

———. *Victuals: An Appalachian Journey, with Recipes*. New York: Clarkson Potter, 2016.

Lunsford, Mackensy. "Asheville Culinary Pros Join Gordon Ramsay on National Geographic Show." *Asheville Citizen-Times*, June 1, 2021, sec. News.

McCarroll, Meredith. *Unwhite: Appalachia, Race, and Film*. Athens: University of Georgia Press, 2018.

McEwen, W. B., and Caroline Nichols McEwen Collection. D. H. Ramsey Library, Special Collections, University of North Carolina at Asheville 28804.

McFee, Michael. *Colander: Poems*. Pittsburgh: Carnegie Mellon University Press, 1996.

———. "Cornbread in Buttermilk." *Edible Piedmont*, Winter 2009, 12.

———. "Mountain Cooking." In *The Carolina Table: North Carolina Writers on Food*, edited by Randall Kenan, 129–135. Hillsborough, NC: Eno, 2016.

———. "Roadside Table." *Edible Piedmont*, Summer 2010, 34.

McGreal, Chris. "Big Pharma Executives Mocked 'Pillbillies' in Emails, West Virginia Opioid Trial Hears." *Guardian*, May 16, 2021. http://www.theguardian .com/us-news/2021/may/16/amerisourcebergen-pillbillies-emails-west-virginia -opioid-trial-. Accessed April 5, 2022.

Messenger, Lillian Rozell. "An Appreciation: Big Things Done by One Little Woman." *Southern Industrial Education Association*, 1914. Library of Congress.

Messenger, Penny. "Professionalizing 'Mountain Work' in Appalachia." In *Women in the Mountain South*, edited by Connie Park Rice and Marie Tedesco, 217–243. Athens: Ohio University Press, 2015.

Midura, Kelly Bembry. "A Story about a Mountain." *The Bitter Southerner*. http://bittersoutherner.com/a-story-about-a-mountain/. Accessed May 23, 2017.

Miller, Danny, and Harriette Simpson Arnow. "A MELUS Interview: Harriette Arnow." *MELUS* 9, no. 2 (1982): 83–97.

Miller, Jim Wayne. *Newfound: A Novel*. New York: Orchard Books, 1989.

Montague, Clinton. "The Use of Pork in the Family." *Good Housekeeping*, 1890.

Morrison, Joseph L. *Governor O. Max Gardner: A Power in North Carolina and New Deal Washington*. Chapel Hill: University of North Carolina Press, 1971.

Naccarato, Peter, and Kathleen Lebesco. *Culinary Capital*. London, New York: Berg, 2012.

National Geographic. "Gordon Ramsay: Uncharted." https://www.nationalgeographic.com/pages/topic/gordon-ramsay-uncharted. Accessed June 11, 2021.

Newitz, Annalee, and Matt Wray, eds. *White Trash*. New York: Routledge, 1996.

Nicklin, Philip Holbrook. *Letters Descriptive of the Virginia Springs; the Roads Leading Thereto, and the Doings Thereat*. Philadelphia: H. S. Tanner, 1835.

North Carolina Cooperative Extension Service, Office of the Director Records. UA 102.001, Special Collections Research Center, North Carolina State University Libraries, Raleigh.

Oates, Joyce Carol. "Harriette Arnow's the Dollmaker." In *Rediscoveries*, edited by David Madden, 57–66. New York: Crown, 1971.

Obermiller, Philip J., and Thomas E. Wagner. *African American Miners and Migrants: The Eastern Kentucky Social Club*. Champaign: University of Illinois Press, 2004.

O'Donnell, Kevin E., and Helen Hollingsworth, eds. *Seekers of Scenery: Travel Writing from Southern Appalachia, 1840–1900*. Knoxville: University of Tennessee Press, 2004.

Offutt, Chris. "Trash Food." *Oxford American* 88 (Spring 2015): 124–128.

Olcott, William. *The Greenbrier Heritage*. Philadelphia: Arndt, Preston, Chapin, Lamb & Keen, 1967.

Olmsted, Frederick Law. "The Highlanders." In *A Journey in the Back Country*, 221–282. London: Sampson Low, Son & Co., 1860.

Olsen, Tillie, and Shelley Fisher Fishkin. *Silences*. Twenty-Fifth anniversary ed. New York: Feminist Press at City University of New York, 2003. First published 1978 by Delacorte Press/Seymour Lawrence (New York).

Opie, Frederick Douglass. *Hog and Hominy: Soul Food from Africa to America*. New York: Columbia University Press, 2010.

Page, Dorothy Myra. *Gathering Storm: A Story of the Black Belt*. New York: International, 1932.

Passidomo, Catarina. "Southern Foodways in the Classroom and Beyond." *Southern Quarterly* 56, no. 1 (Fall 2018): 12–28.

Petty, Adrienne Monteith. *Standing Their Ground: Small Farmers in North Carolina since the Civil War*. New York: Oxford University Press, 2013.

"Poor White Trash." *Eclectic Magazine of Foreign Literature, Science, and Art*, July 1882.

Portor, Laura Spencer. "In Search of Local Color (Part One)." *Harper's Magazine*, August 1922.

———. "In Search of Local Color (Part Two)." *Harper's Magazine*, September 1922.

Pratt, Lloyd. *Archives of American Time: Literature and Modernity in the Nineteenth Century*. Philadelphia: University of Pennsylvania Press, 2010.

Pudup, Mary Beth, Dwight B. Billings, and Altina L. Waller. *Appalachia in the Making: The Mountain South in the Nineteenth Century*. Chapel Hill: University of North Carolina Press, 1995.

"Quest for the Best." May 19, 2021. https://www.nationalgeographic.com/pages /article/gordon-ramsay-uncharted-quest-for-the-best. Accessed April 5, 2022.

Ritchie, Jean. *Singing Family of the Cumberlands*. New York: Oak, 1963. First published 1955 by Oxford University Press (Oxford).

Roe, Daphne A. *A Plague of Corn: The Social History of Pellagra*. Ithaca, NY: Cornell University Press, 1973.

Rollins, William, Jr. *The Shadow Before*. New York: Robert M. McBride, 1934.

Rose, Jane Atteridge. "A Bibliography of Fiction and Non-Fiction by Rebecca Harding Davis." *American Literary Realism, 1870–1910* 22, no. 3 (1990): 67–86.

Russell, Malinda. *A Domestic Cook Book: Containing a Careful Selection of Useful Receipts for the Kitchen*. Paw Paw, MI, 1866.

Satterwhite, Emily. *Dear Appalachia: Readers, Identity, and Popular Fiction since 1878*. Lexington: University Press of Kentucky, 2011.

Semple, Ellen Churchill. "The Anglo-Saxons of the Kentucky Mountains: A Study in Anthropogeography." In *Appalachian Images in Folk and Popular Culture*, edited by W. K. McNeil, 146–174. Knoxville: University of Tennessee Press, 1995.

Shapiro, Henry D. *Appalachia on Our Mind: The Southern Mountains and Mountaineers in the American Consciousness, 1870–1920*. Chapel Hill: University of North Carolina Press, 1978.

Shields, David S. *Southern Provisions: The Creation & Revival of a Cuisine*. Chicago, London: University of Chicago Press, 2015.

Sohn, Katherine Kelleher. *Whistlin' and Crowin' Women of Appalachia: Literacy Practices Since College.* Carbondale: Southern Illinois University Press, 2006.

Southern Foodways Alliance. "Lumbee Indians of NC: Work and Cook and Eat." September 2, 2014. https://www.southernfoodways.org/oral-history/work-and-cook-and-eat-lumbee-indians-of-north-carolina/. Accessed April 6, 2022.

Starnes, Richard D. *Creating the Land of the Sky: Tourism and Society in Western North Carolina.* The Modern South. Tuscaloosa: University of Alabama Press, 2005.

Stewart, Bruce E. "'These Big-Boned, Semi-Barbarian People': Moonshining and the Myth of Violent Appalachia, 1870–1900." In *Blood in the Hills: A History of Violence in Appalachia*, edited by Bruce E. Stewart, 180–206. University Press of Kentucky, 2012.

Still, James. *River of Earth.* Lexington: University Press of Kentucky, 1978. First published 1940 by Viking (New York).

Stokes, Ashli Quesinberry, and Wendy Atkins-Sayre. *Consuming Identity: The Role of Food in Redefining the South.* Jackson: University Press of Mississippi, 2016.

Strother, David Hunter. "A Winter in the South: Fifth Paper." *Harper's New Monthly Magazine*, May 1858.

———. "A Winter in the South: First Paper." *Harper's New Monthly Magazine*, September 1857.

———. "A Winter in the South: Fourth Paper." *Harper's New Monthly Magazine*, January 1858.

———. "A Winter in the South: Second Paper." *Harper's New Monthly Magazine*, October 1857.

———. "A Winter in the South: Sixth Paper." *Harper's New Monthly Magazine*, August 1858.

———. "A Winter in the South: Third Paper." *Harper's New Monthly Magazine*, November 1857.

Thompson, Holland. *From the Cotton Field to the Cotton Mill: A Study of the Industrial Transition in North Carolina.* 1971 reprint. Freeport, NY: Books for Libraries Press. First published 1906 by Macmillan (New York).

Tippen, Carrie Helms. *Inventing Authenticity: How Cookbook Writers Redefine Southern Identity.* Food and Foodways. Fayetteville: University of Arkansas Press, 2018.

Tipton-Martin, Toni. *The Jemima Code: Two Centuries of African American Cookbooks.* Austin: University of Texas Press, 2015.

Turner, William H., and Edward J. Cabbell, eds. *Blacks in Appalachia.* Lexington: University Press of Kentucky, 1985.

Van Vorst, Marie. *Amanda of the Mill: A Novel*. New York: Dodd, Mead, 1904.

Veit, Helen Zoe. *Modern Food, Moral Food: Self-Control, Science, and the Rise of Modern American Eating in the Early Twentieth Century*. Chapel Hill: University of North Carolina Press, 2013.

Vester, Katharina. *A Taste of Power: Food and American Identities*. California Studies in Food and Culture 59. Oakland: University of California Press, 2015.

Vorse, Mary Heaton. *Strike!* New York: Horace Liverwight, 1930.

Warner, Charles Dudley. *On Horseback: Tour in Virginia, North Carolina, and Tennessee, with Notes of Travel in Mexico and California*. Boston: Houghton, Mifflin, 1888.

Wilkinson, Crystal. *The Birds of Opulence*. Lexington: University Press of Kentucky, 2016.

———. "Praise Song for the Kitchen Ghosts." *Emergence Magazine*, September 10, 2019. https://emergencemagazine.org/essay/praise-song-for-the-kitchen-ghosts/. Accessed April 6, 2022.

Williams, Cratis D. *Tales from Sacred Wind: Coming of Age in Appalachia*. Edited by David Cratis Williams and Patricia D. Beaver. Contributions to Southern Appalachian Studies 8. Jefferson, NC: McFarland, 2003.

Williamson, J. W. *Hillbillyland: What the Movies Did to the Mountains and What the Mountains Did to the Movies*. Chapel Hill: University of North Carolina Press, 1995.

Willis, Arcade. "Community School, Community Garden: Agricultural Education at Snowbird Day School." *Journal of Cherokee Studies* 35 (Summer 2020): 68–76.

Wilson, Jno. Stainback, M.D. "Health Department." *Godey's Lady's Book and Magazine* 60, February 1860.

Witt, Doris. "From Fiction to Foodways: Working at the Intersections of African American Literary and Culinary Studies." In *African American Foodways: Explorations of History and Culture*, edited by Anne L. Bower, 101–125. Champaign: University of Illinois Press, 2007.

Wray, Matt. *Not Quite White: White Trash and the Boundaries of Whiteness*. Durham, NC: Duke University Press, 2006.

CPSIA information can be obtained
at www.ICGtesting.com
Printed in the USA
LVHW091758230323
742396LV00004B/482